Errata

The following is a correction for the table on page 192.

TABLE B-1
A Summary of Index Features

IGI on Microfiche	OPR Index on Microfiche	IGI on CD-ROM	Scottish Church Records on CD-ROM
Arranged by county, then alphabetically using some standardized spellings; chronologically when names are the same.	Arranged by county, then alphabetically, but the alphabetical listing is by actual spelling, with M' and Mc treated as Mac.	Part of British Isles listings, but Scotland, or one (or several) Scottish county(ies) can be specified; alphabetical and chrono. as for IGI on fiche.	Can search entire country or specify a particular county or counties; alphabetical as for OPR Index.
Baptisms and marriages are together.	Baptisms and marriages are separate.	Baptisms and marriages are in separate searches, but moving from one to the other is easy.	Baptisms and marriages are in separate searches, but moving from one to the other is easy.
Not as complete as the OPR Index for Church of Scotland; includes many nonconformist entries, 20 years from civil registration indexes, and individual submissions.	Church of Scotland baptisms and marriages, some from kirk sessions and some for nonconformists bap. or married in the Church of Scotland; Addenda of 31,000 listings are separate.	Not as complete as Scottish Church Records for Church of Scotland; includes many nonconformist entries, 20 years from civil registration indexes, and individual submissions.	Church of Scotland baptisms and marriages, some from kirk sessions; no nonconformist entries, unless congregation rejoined the Church of Scotland; OPR Addenda are included.
	Baptism and marriage entries are listed by surname and given name in separate sets of fiche; Addenda do not have a given-name sort.	Parent Search lists together the names of individuals whose parents' names appear the same way.	Parent Search lists together the names of individuals whose parents' names appear the same way.
		Can filter a search to show entries limited by dates, geographic area, or by linkage to another name (or part of a name) in a marriage.	Can filter a search to show entries limited by dates, geographic area, or by linkage to another name (or part of a name) in a marriage.

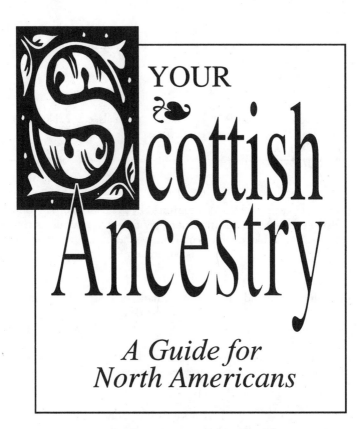

YOUR
Scottish
Ancestry

A Guide for North Americans

BY SHERRY IRVINE

Ancestry.

Irvine, Sherry.
     Your Scottish ancestry : a guide for North Americans / by Sherry
Irvine.
       p. cm.
     Includes bibliographical references and index.
     ISBN 0-916489-65-5
     1. Scotland—Genealogy—Handbooks, manuals, etc. 2. North America—
Genealogy—Handbooks, manuals, etc. I. Title.
     CS463.I78 1996
     929' . 1'0720411—dc21   96-39342

©1997 Ancestry Incorporated
Published by Ancestry Incorporated
P.O. Box 476
Salt Lake City, Utah 84110-0476

First printing 1996
10 9 8 7 6 5 4 3

Printed in the United States of America

In memory of my mother, Mary Joan Patricia (Nuttall) Howland,
who passed away 17 November 1994 while I was in Edinburgh.

Contents

Foreword

here was a lad was born in Kyle, [central Ayr]
But whatna day o'whatna style,
I doubt it's hardly worth the while,
To be sae nice wi' Robin.

Robin was a rovin' boy—
Rantin' rovin', rantin' rovin'—
Robin was a rovin' boy—
Rantin' rovin' Robin!

Our monarch's hindmost year but ane
Was five-and-twenty days begun,
'Twas then a blast o' Jan'war' win'
Blew hansel in on Robin. [a first gift]

In these opening stanzas of his autobiographical song—which admirers of the National Bard all over the world sing with fervor—Burns has indicated just when he was born: in effect, 25 January 1759 (the last year of George II's reign). He also draws attention to a factor which genealogists may at times have to consider: the "style" or method of reckoning dates—in this case because of the differences between the Julian ("Old Style") and Gregorian ("New Style") calendars.

Burns was keenly interested in genealogy: "I have not the most distant pretensions to assume that character which the pye-coated guardians of escutcheons call a gentleman." Yet while in Edinburgh he went to the Herald's Office. Looking through "that granary of honors, I there found almost every name in the kingdom; but as for me

My ancient, but ignoble blood

Has crept through scoundrels ever since the flood."

Be that as it may, tradition places his family tree in Kincardineshire.

All Scots, whether strict Presbyterians or dissenters like Burns, take with great seriousness the Lord's parable about the sower and his seed; where the seed has no root, it withers away, but that which falls upon good ground yields fruit, some a hundredfold. Hence the Scots' passion for burrowing into historical records to discover their roots—for they are a notoriously tenacious lot, and have no intention of ever withering away!

My own family is a case in point. My father, born in the highest village in the Grampians, sought out our lineage, derived from both Highland and Lowland stock. As a boy he had listened with great delight to his grandmother's accounts of how members of the Keppoch sept of the great Clan Donald had moved in previous centuries into regions which now include parts of Banffshire, and had intermarried with other clansfolk, notably Stewarts and Grants. For several generations back, these accounts could be verified and translated into a family genealogy replete with specific dates. But my father, a perfervid Scot and fired by the knowledge that the blood of the royal Stewarts flowed in his veins, then pressed his research into the murky mists of Scottish antiquity. This took him well into the stormy and unprincipled side of the Stewart monarchy, notably to one of Robert the Bruce's great grandsons, Alexander Stewart, earl of Buchan. This ancestor, whose father, Robert II, had sired at least eight bastard sons, had been given the rule of the turbulent Highlands. In John Prebble's words, "This ruffianly paranoiac, rightly called the Wolf of Badenoch, made a shambles of the glens during his viceroyalty, and when reproved by the Bishop of Moray for deserting his wife, plundered Elgin and burnt its hospices, churches, and cathedral. In energy at least, he was a Bruce." Obviously, Burns could not claim to have a monopoly of the "ignoble blood" of "scoundrels" in his veins (even though, technically, ours was in one instance "noble").

So much for our Highland lineage. But the Lowland input also had its share of derring-do calculated to raise the eyebrows and ire of god-fearing folk. In 1396, Robert III arranged to bring the warring Gaels within the national jurisdiction. To settle a feud between Clan Chattan and Clan Kay, each was asked to send thirty warriors to fight to the death in judicial combat. This contest took place on the North Inch of Perth, a flat meadow by the Tay River, and was watched by the royal court and a large group of townspeople. Prior to the combat, however, Clan Chattan found itself shy a fighter, and its leader sought out an armorer in the town called the Gow Crom. Gaelic for "crooked smith," the sobriquet referred to the smith's deformed leg, but the fact that he was persuaded to become a mercenary for the Clan gives the term a special nuance. On the field of battle, the Gow Crom dispatched several of the Kay, who at the end of the grisly struggle had all been slaughtered except one warrior who escaped by swimming the Tay.

This epic battle was immortalized by Scott in *The Fair Maid of Perth*, whose heroine, the daughter of the chief burgess, married the Gow Crom. But the townspeople never were reconciled to the mercenary's deeds on the North Inch, and the young couple subsequently migrated into the Highlands where other members of our family farmed.

My mother's forebears seem to have been much more respectable and law-abiding. My maternal grandfather provided our only known Sassenach blood. He was born in Yorkshire in the small village of Hawarth in the West Riding–home of the Brontës and the bleak locale of Emily's *Wuthering Heights*. My mother recalled that her father was baptized by the three authors' father, Patrick Prunty or Brontë, an Irishman and perpetual vicar of Hawarth from 1820 until his death in 1860. My grandfather's family subsequently settled in Keithley, and in turn he moved to Aberdeen, where he engaged in the woolen industry. For our part, we are attempting to track down more details about his early life in Hawarth and a possible association with the famous Brontës there.

Persons who claim to remember past lives always seem to recall only distinguished historical ancestors, such as Julius Caesar or Cleopatra. Why not? We are all members of a single global family whose roots go back some three million years–and probability theory can assure us that our DNA does, in fact, carry elements of the gene pools of both Caesar and the Egyptian queen.

So if our immediate genealogy seems bereft of famous—or even infamous—names, does it matter? Every one of us shares equally the entire behavioral spectrum of what it means to be human—and to be able to delight in that condition.

In this book, itself a pleasure to read, Sherry Irvine provides the essential steps to undertake one's genealogical journey into the storied past. In setting forth the fundamentals of that enterprise, the author assists the neophyte in organizing materials, developing necessary research skills, avoiding pitfalls, and, far from least important, building knowledge of the sources for the quest. She has emphasized that we are not engaged in a "dry bones" exercise, but a bold adventure into our own gene pool, the lives of our "flesh and blood" forebears. And as part of this adventure, she stresses the importance of becoming as familiar as possible with the times and events which helped to shape our ancestors' lives. That is what my father did in his genealogical quest—and his heirs, in turn, are the richer for understanding their intertwined family roots.

Alastair MacDonald Taylor
M.A. (USC), D.Phil. (Oxon)
Professor Emeritus, Queens' University,
Kingston, Canada
Co-author of Civilization Past and Present,
a college text on world history in its eighth edition.

Introduction

an there really be a need for another book on Scottish genealogical research? The answer is yes. I can repeat here what I stated in the introduction to my first book (*Your English Ancestry: A Guide for North Americans*), " . . . none of the books I have read focuses on a logical research routine for family historians based in North America." There are several excellent books which provide information on the content of the records, the years they cover, the geographic area they relate to, where they are housed in Scotland, and what tools exist for access. There are differing perspectives and emphases, glossaries of terms, lists of parishes, and case studies. All this is very useful, but fails to meet the need for a guide which will help a researcher anywhere in North America explore the best way to approach Scottish family history research.

Resources to help amateur genealogists are continually expanding. The amount of material that is now accessible is staggering. It can be found via computer, such as online library catalogs and bulletin board exchanges, through membership in a genealogical club, or through the family history centers of The Church of Jesus Christ of Latter-day Saints (LDS church), which are located across North America. For many people, the most difficult step has been the first one—realizing that researching family history is not an intimidating chore to be postponed indefinitely, awaiting some hoped-for canyon of time.

Successful research requires an understanding of the knowledge you are working from (how much you know now and what you want to know), the resources you are working with (what records are available and how they may be useful), and where you will find the information (in what form and how it can be collected). This book will help you make those assessments. It is a distillation of information about resources in North America and Scotland, combined with summaries and suggestions for thinking through just how you will get at them. The choice of records is based on several criteria. Generally speaking, I have selected records that have been created since the late seventeenth century and that fall into one or more of the following categories:

- Records in the collections of the LDS Family History Library (FHL).
- Printed records that may be in public, university, or genealogical society libraries.
- Records that have been gathered in some central location in the United Kingdom.
- Records that have been indexed.
- Records that are important in completing a search.

Thanks are due to many, but first and foremost to my family, who were always supportive, and always accommodating when I asked them to pretend I wasn't home. Then there are the many people who have told me how helpful they found my book on English research; without that positive feedback it would have been difficult to start another project. My hectic schedule in Edinburgh was possible because Sara and George Anderson were so hospitable, and in Glasgow I gained much because Susan Miller and Anne Escott cheerfully answered endless questions. Through references in the text you will see that I am indebted to those who have written about Scottish research before me, in particular David Moody and Cecil Sinclair. The cooperation of the LDS Family History Library has been appreciated, notably the advice of Paul Smart and the assistance of David Dilts with some of the illustrations.

Finally, to Anne Lemmon, former managing editor at Ancestry, a very special thank you for encouragement and feedback—whenever I called.

Sherry Irvine
Victoria, British Columbia
October 1996

1 • Prudent Preliminaries

A young Scotsman of your ability let loose upon the world with £300, what could he not do? It's almost appalling to think of; especially if he went among the English. (J.M. Barrie, *What Every Woman Knows*)

 scan through the volumes of national biography for the United States, Canada, and many other nations reveals a high proportion of entries for men and women whose origins were in Scotland. Many of them started with a good deal less than £300. If some measure of determination, thrift, and ambition is lurking in the character of all of you of Scottish descent, then you have the essential qualifications for genealogical research. Add a thirst for knowledge and a dose of common sense and you will do even better.

About Scotland

Scottish genealogical research has some unique characteristics. Until the Act of Union in 1707, Scotland had its own parliament and its own legal system. The latter remains distinctly different to this day, and, over the centuries, has produced many records which have no counterpart in England or Wales. It is particularly important that researchers of Scottish family history give some time and attention to identifying and understanding these differences. Equally important is some knowledge of Scottish history, taking note of patterns of migration to North America.

Scotland is located on the northern edge of Europe. Geography has placed the country in a harsher climate and away from the economic pulse, factors which have contributed to its status as a nation of emigrants. For centuries, the adventurous, the talented, the risk-takers, and the impoverished have sought new opportunities in the centers of activity and commerce in England, Europe, and all other parts of the world. North America has been a favorite destination.

Scottish Emigration

Before 1770, the Thirteen Colonies were the destination of choice. Some settlers found their way to the Canadian eastern colonies in what is now Nova Scotia, New Brunswick, and Prince Edward Island, but the largest numbers went to the colonies further south. The five regions with the highest Scottish population in the 1790 census were Virginia and West Virginia, Kentucky and Tennessee, North Carolina, South Carolina, and Georgia.

The Scots left their homeland for religious, political, and economic reasons. Covenanters were transported or left the turbulent religious situation of the seventeenth century. The Jacobite uprisings of 1715 and 1745 contributed both refugees and those sentenced to servitude in America, and the Highland Clearances fit into the economic category as a cause of emigration. Another fairly significant number of Scottish settlers came from the disbanded soldiers left behind at the end of the French and Indian War (the Seven Years' War), 1756-1763. Before 1815 the migrants were more likely to be Highlanders, but after 1815 the pattern changed and the majority were from the Lowlands.

Other conclusions can be drawn by looking at some numbers. Between 1820 and 1900, roughly 365,000 Scots emigrated to the United States and 250,000 to Canada. When considered in the context of the populations of the two countries, the post 1815 Scottish element in Canada is huge relative to the total population. Not so in the United States. In other words, proportionately, Canadians are more likely to be engaged in nineteenth century Scottish research.

If the origins of your Scottish ancestors are unclear, you may gain some insights by learning more about the patterns of migration. However, by far the best way to start is to discover who actually crossed the Atlantic, when, and where he or she originally settled. Knowing this location is particularly important because it may lead you to infer which area of Scotland was home to the family. In other words, when beginning your research do everything possible on this side of the ocean first.

There is another very good reason for building extensive knowledge of the family after its arrival in America. The best way to describe this reason is family reconstruction. Many of you will face the problem of very few different surnames in the area of origin in Scotland. It will help to sort out all the MacKinnons or MacDonalds if you carry a batch of given names into your Scottish research. If you are fortunate, you may also have a wife's or mother's maiden name. In Scotland, a woman retained her maiden name throughout her lifetime. Although she may have used a husband's surname while married, she was recorded in parish registers and many other records by her maiden name, and she might have reverted to this name if predeceased by her husband. Knowing a woman's maiden name may be the key to beginning successful research in Scotland. On the other hand, there may be confusion if you have not identified a woman's name correctly as her maiden or married name.

At this early stage, it will do no harm to question the validity of your assumptions about Scottish origins. When settlers were arriving from Scotland in the eighteenth century there was also a great influx of Scots-Irish from Ulster. They left Ireland because of high rent, famine, and the decline in the linen industry. The Scottish-sounding name in your background may not be a direct import from Scotland. The family may have spent many generations in Ulster.

More than a simple lack of knowledge may hide the truth. My maternal grandmother's maiden name was Blackhall. The family sprang from Aberdeenshire and was very proud of it. In fact, this was the only beginning I, or my mother, ever heard about (her mother died when she was six). It was not until I researched the family that I discovered that it was transplanted from Aberdeenshire to County Down in Northern Ireland nearly two hundred years before emigrating to New York State, and from thence two generations later to Canada. In nineteenth-century Toronto, it was more acceptable to be Scottish; thus, the Irish interlude faded from the family tradition.

A further caution is warranted for those of you who find a name in a list of the so-called septs of a particular clan. *Sept*, from the Irish language, has a connotation similar to *clan*, and is a subject of some debate. The lists have been the creations of the manufacturers and sellers of mementos and tartan-traps created by nineteenth- and twentieth-century romantics and opportunists more interested, then and now, in a sale than the truth. Some families and clans have recognized the connections, but the better term is *associated families*. There are other lists which link names with suggested tartans to be worn, but they are nothing more than that; they should never be taken as indicating a connection to a clan. To find out more bout surnames—in particular, their origin and use in the Highlands—and about clans, their history, tartans, and associated families, refer to the books listed in the bibliography.

Pitfalls

Once you are past the issues of being certain about origins and whether or not a clan association is meaningful, names can still hold traps for the unwary. The most frequently mentioned difficulty among my students stems from too many individuals of the same surname. This can occur at any geographical level—the country as a whole, the county, or the parish. If there are too many individuals of one surname, checking for naming patterns among the families in the parish might help. This pattern was not followed rigidly but was common enough to warrant consideration. The eldest son was named after his paternal grandfather, the next boy after the maternal grandfather, and third after the father. A parallel pattern was followed for girls, who were named after their grandmothers.

Sometimes you will continue to be stymied because several families of the same surname were remarkably unimaginative when selecting given names. In this case, you can only hope that the parish registers and other records may slip in additional identifiers such as address or location or occupation.

If common names are not enough, interchangeable names are another trap. Jean might be Janet or Jane, Daniel might be Donald, and James, Hamish. More interesting naming problems, especially associated with the north and remote areas of Scotland, are found in *Tracing Your Scottish Ancestry* (Cory, 1997) and in the introduction to *Surnames of Scotland* (Black, 1973).

There are several other possible name problems to watch for. First, remind yourself that outright errors by officials, transcribers, and indexers are not unknown. These errors come in many forms because something was written as it sounded, copied in haste, or missed completely. The use of patronymics may cause confusion (the surname changes in each generation based upon the given name of the father, i.e., Duncan MacDonald, the son of Donal Robertson). Spelling variations are another problem, sometimes several in ones person's lifetime. Variations in surnames can be surprisingly different, to the extent that the connection isn't obvious. The variation may be in a completely different part of an index, perhaps outside the list of standardized spellings used in some finding aids. Some variations come readily to mind, such as those arising from the addition or deletion of a silent letter, the doubling of a vowel or consonant, or confusion between two letters resembling each other. *Surnames of Scotland* (Black, 1973) lists many variations, especially the less obvious. Two examples illustrate the difficulties. Without looking it up, you might not know that MacMurchie is a form of Murdoch, nor would you think of checking for Slater under Sclater. Other themes to watch for are changes between M', Mc, and Mac (which, in some records, are indexed separately), a change in the order of names, and differences due to a phonetic representation of what was heard. Scan lists carefully if you must look for several variations, and be prepared to search more than one part of an alphabetical index.

Place names also create possible pitfalls. The same place name is often found in more than one location. Is your ancestor from Craigton? There were four, two of them in Forfarshire (Angus). Not only that, but Craigton estate in Dumbartonshire sits in the parish of New Kilpatrick, which happens to straddle the county line and is also partly in Stirlingshire. Seven Newtons are listed in the *Ordnance Gazetteer of Scotland*,[1] and twenty-two other places have Newton as the first part of their names. Another possible problem is altered spellings and complete name changes. Far from home, an ancestor may not have used the name of his actual place of origin, but instead used that of a nearby town. Villages have been swallowed up by the spread of cities and may no longer be shown on maps. The name you are dealing with may be an estate name rather than an actual place name. Resolving place name problems is discussed in chapter 2.

Coping with old handwriting is usually a matter of practice. If you are tracing one or more families back through several generations in one register, you will probably be able to follow and interpret the various styles of handwriting. Difficulties are more likely to arise with documents and registers which predate 1750. Some useful guides are listed in the bibliography. If you come across what appears to be an unfamiliar combination of letters, consult glossaries of Scottish terms. The Scottish Association of Family History Societies publishes *A Scottish Genealogist's Glossary* (Burness, 1990), *In Search of Scottish Ancestry* (Hamilton-Edwards, 1983) includes a glossary, and there is a list of abbreviations and terms in the back of *Tracing Your Scottish Ancestry* (Cory, 1997).

Problems with dates arise more often from misinformation or incorrect estimates than from the calendar itself. Scotland adopted 1 January as New Year's Day at the beginning of 1600. This eliminates the problem, present in English research, of what year to date events which occurred between 1 January and 25 March (Lady Day, which was considered the first day of the new year in England until 1752). There is less certainty about what happened to the eleven days which disappeared from the calendar south of the border in 1752. Evidence provided in an article in the *Scottish Genealogist* ("Gregorian Calendar," Gillespie, 1988) would suggest that Scotland realigned its days at the same time and also removed 3 to 13 September inclusive. The necessity for change arose from a slight miscalculation in the Julian Calendar, instituted by Julius Caesar in 45 B.C. By the late sixteenth century, an eleven minute error per year had created a ten-day discrepancy between the lunar and calendar years. The church had terrible problems calculating feast days. Pope Gregory removed ten days from the month of March and at the same time decreed that the year 1582 would begin on 1 January. The Gregorian Calendar was adopted at the same time by Catholic Europe, but it was not accepted by Protestant countries until much later.

Conclusion

Be sure that you begin from a sound basis of evidence, that Scottish records are the next logical step in research, and that you have found all the information that it is possible to find in American or Canadian repositories. Retain this thoroughness and some skepticism as you research Scottish sources.

The chapters in this book are arranged by record type, beginning with the most recent. For many of you, civil registration and census returns do not fit the parameters of your search; however, before you dismiss them entirely and skip a chapter or two, consider that they may have value. When did your ancestors leave Scotland? Might a parent, sibling, child, niece or nephew, have stayed behind and been captured in these records? Could the indexes for these records provide some clues as to name distribution? There are bonuses of information in statutory records of birth, marriage, and death, especially in the initial year of 1855. Census returns can be used to link generations and to provide information on families and conditions in a place of origin, even if the census occurred some years after your ancestor departed.

Note
1. Groome, 1883-85, Vol. V, p. 111.

2 • Well Begun Is Half Done

ou will learn as you go. This chapter outlines the skills you should develop and the background knowledge you should acquire, all of which will go a long way toward making the research more interesting and less frustrating. Don't worry about asking silly questions—once—and never mind your mistakes; each and every one contains a lesson that will contribute to your expertise. This chapter is divided into two sections, one about the skills you should develop and the other on the knowledge and experience you should acquire.

Develop Skills
Library Skills
What do you do when you visit a library for the first time? Regard each visit to a different library in somewhat the same manner that a sales representative views each new introduction as a possible client. This is an opportunity for profit. Imposing libraries in strange places are not intimidating when you know what to do.

The catalog is the search tool, so first develop a familiarity with public and university library classification systems. Public libraries use the

Dewey Decimal system; university libraries use the Library of Congress system. Areas of particular interest to genealogists under each of these arrangements are highlighted in tables 2-1 and 2-2. The Family History Library Catalog® (FHLC) is unique in its organization. The FHLC is the guide to the contents of the Family History Library (FHL) in Salt Lake City, where the collection of the Family History Department of The Church of Jesus Christ of Latter-day Saints (LDS or Mormons) is housed. As there is little doubt that you will use the resources of one of the many LDS family history centers in North America, a good understanding of this catalog is also essential. Appendix A describes the FHLC in detail.

Genealogy is not confined neatly to a single classification in one particular area of a library. Three or four generations of one family might turn up a dozen or more occupations, several religious denominations, more than one country of residence, wealthy individuals, poor ones, the famous, or the criminal. Finding facts or background material on these individuals and the related subjects will take a researcher into many different areas of the library, far beyond the confines of the 929s or the CSs. Some rudimentary knowledge of catalog structure will transform random wanderings through the stacks into strategic browsing sessions.

Dewey is a number-based system. It suffers from a lack of main divisions, which results in some very long, complex decimal numbers. The 929.** classification for genealogy, names, heraldry and related subjects gets particularly complicated. Browsing would be difficult if the titles did not appear on the spines! The Library of Congress system is a combination of letters and numbers; hence, it allows for many more headings and subheadings. In both systems, general categories are listed at the beginning of each section. For example, the start of the 900s in Dewey is dictionaries of dates; the start of D within Library of Congress organization is general world history.

Equally as useful as knowledge of the classification systems is an understanding of subject headings. Many are obvious, such as a country name or a topic like immigration. However, some of these subject headings may be so general that hundreds or even thousands of entries might fit, and a qualifying subheading must be found to reduce the catalog search to manageable proportions. There are huge tomes describing headings and their subcategories. If you have trouble deciding which subject to look under, or if all your efforts have failed to produce an entry, there are two options. The obvious one is to seek the assistance of a librarian. On your own, you can try working backward from a known title in the subject area to its catalog entry where the heading and subheading would appear. Then use these categories to continue the catalog search.

TABLE 2-1
Selective Guide to the
Dewey Decimal Classification System

000	GENERALITIES
	010 bibliographies and catalogs
	030 general encyclopedic works
100	PHILOSOPHY AND RELATED DISCIPLINES
200	RELIGION
	270 church history, geography
	274.1 Scottish church history
	280 Christian denominations and sects
	285.271 Presbyterian religion in Scotland
300	SOCIAL SCIENCES
	325 emigration/immigration
	325.241 from Scotland
	330 economics
	340 law
	356 army
	359 navy
	370 education
	380 commerce and trade
	390 customs and folklore
400	LANGUAGE
500	PURE SCIENCES
600	TECHNOLOGY (APPLIED SCIENCES)
	610 medical sciences
	620 engineering
	630 agriculture
	690 buildings
700	FINE ARTS AND RECREATION
	720 architecture
	740 drawing
	750 painting
	770 photography
800	LITERATURE
900	GENERAL GEOGRAPHY AND HISTORY
	910 general geography, travel (includes atlases)
	914 geography and travel, Great Britain
	920 biography
	929 genealogy
	940 history of Europe
	941.1 history of Scotland

TABLE 2-2
Selective Guide to the
Library of Congress Classification System

A	GENERAL WORKS
B	PHILOSOPHY-RELIGION
	BL-BX religion
C	AUXILIARY SCIENCES OF HISTORY
	CD holdings of archives and libraries
	CS genealogy, names, peerage
D	HISTORY-GENERAL AND OLD WORLD
	DA Great Britain
E-F	HISTORY OF AMERICA
G	GEOGRAPHY, ANTHROPOLOGY, FOLKLORE
H	SOCIAL SCIENCES
	HC production and economic conditions
	HD agriculture
	HE transportation and communication
	HN social history and conditions
J	POLITICAL SCIENCE
K	LAW
L	EDUCATION
M	MUSIC
N	FINE ARTS
	NA architecture
P	LANGUAGE AND LITERATURE
Q	SCIENCE
R	MEDICINE
S	AGRICULTURE
T	TECHNOLOGY
U	MILITARY SCIENCE
V	NAVAL SCIENCE
Z	BIBLIOGRAPHY AND LIBRARY SCIENCE

Most libraries of any size now have their catalogs online, accessible from computer terminals. The library staff may present tutorials. It also may be possible to view the catalog on microfiche. For some institutions, the computerization of the catalog is a long-term project, so the catalog drawers remain, usually for items acquired before a particular cut-off date. Dial-up access is available in many places, or you can search catalogs through the Internet. Computer searches are possible on the customary author or title basis, but keyword searches are possible when you know only part of a title or part of a name. Handy though the online catalogs may be, you too may sometimes regret the demise of the banks of wooden drawers and the option of flipping through the cards. Going backward or forward screen by screen just doesn't seem the same.

Archives Skills

Archives are different from libraries. Libraries seek to distribute books and information; archives are primarily in the business of preservation, and dissemination of information is of secondary importance. Library books are located on open shelves. Browsing in archives is restricted or even disallowed. Books, manuscripts and artifacts are located in closed shelves, classified by record type rather than by name. Items must be requested on an order slip. Whereas books given to a library are spread about according to subject or author, a box of family papers donated to the local archives, although it covers many subjects, is kept together. This retention of original order is the reason materials must be classified by type in manuscript and record groups with finding aids to describe their contents. It is therefore much more important to have a clear sense of research objectives before visiting archives. If you cannot identify the record you want to view, at least be able to state clearly the facts you are seeking. Some advance knowledge of a repository's holdings will also contribute to the success of a visit or a written inquiry.

Some repositories are finding ways to provide freer access and save on staff time, through the use of film, fiche, or computer finding aids and indexes. Some frequently used records may be available on a self-serve basis. On the other hand, facilities may be limited. Inquire in advance of a visit whether desk space or film readers must be reserved and whether any materials are located in remote storage; if so, several days' advance notice may be required to make them available.

Objectives and Strategy

Some of you will have thought out what you are trying to achieve and may even have written specific objectives. Objectives facilitate the search and are reasonably easy to determine. Make sure that your pedigree charts are filled out as completely as possible. Where the information on the charts ends is where the objectives begin. This concept is shown clearly in figure 2-1. At the simplest level, one objective is to select a line to work on first. Next, identify an individual and the new facts that are required. Finally, consider the documents to be consulted. Thinking things through in this manner takes you from the general (which family?) to the particular (what records?).

The pedigree chart is an excellent guide for planning your strategy. It clearly shows where you run out of fact on the direct line, and this point can be highlighted by marking the details which have been proven. The chart, by its structure, also encourages the formulation of research plans, which should always take you from known information to the unknown. As obvious as this may sound, many people are tempted to begin research on some colorful figure reputed to exist in the family's history, and move forward toward the present. The surest way to prove any line of ancestry is to begin with recent family and work back. The search is focused, the easy part comes first, and a logical chronology is followed.

Each research plan is based on stipulating who is being researched, over what time period, over what geographical area, and in what records. Where little is known, estimate. The information known about Mary Rennie (see figure 2-1) is approximate, so allowances must be made for searching outside the years of death and birth shown on the chart. The information on James and William Russell is specific and has come from statutory records and church registers. This provides more surely defined boundaries for the research into the next generation. The records selected for the plan should meet several criteria:

- The record exists for all or part of the time span covered by the search.
- The record exists for all or part of the geographic area covered by the search.
- The record has been indexed, grouped, or summarized in some way to facilitate research.
- The facts required for access to the record are straightforward.
- New information gained from the record is expected to be useful.
- Access is neither a serious problem nor a great expense.

As your knowledge and experience grow, these thought processes will become almost automatic. One additional piece of advice—whenever something fails to turn up, carefully review your file on the family and the sources for the time and place; then take another look at your research plan. It may surprise you how a different approach or a forgotten fact may suddenly become apparent.

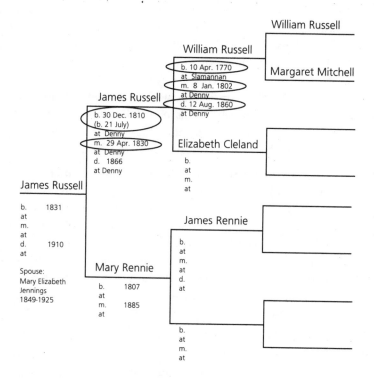

1. Select the line to research; here there are three possibilities:
   a. Fill in and extend the Russells.
   b. Fill in and extend the Rennies.
   c. Fill in and extend the Clelands.
2. Select the individual to work from.
3. List the facts required; if, for example, Rennie is selected, there is no choice but to begin with Mary, seeking the dates and places of her birth and death and the full names of both parents.

Items circled have been located in statutory or parish records.

Figure 2-1. The Pedigree of James Russell of Stirlingshire and Ontario.

Research Skills

The more familiar you are with a library, the sooner you can find materials. The better you understand the organization of the record groups in the archives, the more efficiently you can work. Other good habits are also worth practicing. Always check for finding aids. Consulting finding aids first will help, regardless of where or how a record is accessed. The finding aid may be a national index maintained by a government department, or it may be a strictly defined index kept by a private individual. There are many lists of lists (i.e., bibliographies of finding aids) which tell you about these tools, and they are indicated throughout this book. Purchase the ones that you will use most frequently. Consider buying a finding aid for your own use and later donating it to the local society so others can benefit.

Develop note-taking patterns that suit you and that speed up your work. If you use abbreviations and point form notations, be consistent so you are not baffled by what you wrote weeks before. Do not expand abbreviations seen in old records unless you are absolutely sure of what they stand for, and note that the document used the abbreviation. An inaccurate expansion could lead you in the wrong direction. Note any gaps in a record to prevent erroneous conclusions. If you cannot read what you are trying to note, copy it as closely as possible, or make a photocopy, and record your uncertainty.

Record the bibliographic details for the sources you consult, including those which produce no result; otherwise, the search may have to be repeated if you forget. Teachers, librarians, archivists, and professional genealogists continually ask the question, "where did you get this?" You should always have the answer. Advice is easier to provide when the provenance of the information is known. Just as important as the origin of a fact is the degree of authority which should be ascribed to the source. Probate records, military records, and statutory records are good examples of primary sources. The information is contemporary and probably accurate. Secondary sources cannot be regarded with the same assurance. They may be based on memory, on point of view, or on documentary evidence, all subject to selectivity and personal interpretation. Autobiographies, biographies, history books, and newspaper accounts are examples of secondary sources.

Computers are changing the way we perform research, and, eagerly or reluctantly, you will acquire some computer skills. For some people, the change is comfortable and fundamental. All the data goes into a genealogy program; the card index or the three-ring binders disappear. Helpful records available on CD-ROM are purchased (the number and variety grows continually). More and more people use computers to discover new friends and new sources or to share information through electronic communications. Dial-up access to libraries, bulletin board chat, and the Internet create all kinds of opportunities. For everyone, computers are tools to be used to access books, certain records, and finding aids in a growing number of libraries and record offices.

Organization

Organization is a personal thing, whether it is a supremely logical filing system or creative chaos understandable only by the perpetrator. A pedigree chart, like the one shown in figure 2-1, neatly separates ancestors into families and families into generations. This is a good basis for any system, whether built around index cards, or three-ring binders or computers. Regardless of your chosen instrument of storage, be sure your system accomplishes the following:

- Incorporates a system of ready reference. It must be easy to determine quickly what facts are known and what sources have been consulted. This is the basis for further planning. One way to do this is to keep a short summary of known facts and a log of all sources consulted for each ancestor.

- Contains a record of all work done. Make a full bibliographic notation for all sources consulted, whether or not they revealed any helpful information. Note when and where the work was done and the thoroughness of the search. A missing fact may be due to your rushed efforts, rather than because it wasn't there. You will also avoid duplication of effort. Maintain a separate record of useful general sources (local histories, gazetteers etc.) to consult as you research new family lines. A computer database is an ideal way to do this as you can search it by keyword.

- Has room for expansion. The system must be able to accommodate the insertion of new material in the right place.

- Is standardized. Standardization applies to paper size and abbreviations. Try to avoid having to recopy notes from odd chits of paper, envelopes, etc., by carrying a stock of standard paper with you. Some of you carry your notebook computer along, or your data manager (if it has good notepad space and can be uploaded into your home computer). Consistency in abbreviations ensures that you or someone else will know what was intended.

- Is followed consistently. Adding material on a regular basis is not a time consuming chore, but catching up a long time after can be a daunting task not only because of the backlog, but because the work is no longer fresh in your mind.

Seeking Assistance

Begin by recognizing your own style and preferences, and your own strengths and limitations. If you are a joiner, attend classes and get involved in a local society. Classes may be offered at different levels by a college or a society, nearby or through correspondence. Be sure that your objectives for taking the program match the course outline. A class is an excellent way to build a knowledge base, and if it is held locally, you will meet like-minded people and learn about local resources. The local society's library collection is likely to be built around the most pressing needs of the membership, and the society probably receives many journals on an exchange basis.

The staff of libraries and archives, at home or away, can provide some assistance. More and more institutions, however, are charging for these services. In any case, staff time is limited so be sure that your question clearly states the information you seek. When writing, inquire about genealogical guides or finding aids for sale. You can phrase future inquiries or directions to a professional researcher more precisely when the information outlining the records is at hand.

Family history societies in Scotland are an excellent source of assistance. As a new member, you can add the names you are researching to the list of members' interests. Your additions will be printed in the journal and checked against those already entered. The society probably maintains a bookstall with mail-order items available, and may also issue its own publications relative to the records of the region in which it is located. Contributing an article to the journal is an effective way to tell others about your research and may result in a profitable exchange of information with some other members.

Professional assistance will be necessary from time to time, either for some specialized skill, such as reading Latin, because you cannot travel to view a record yourself, or because you require assistance in planning the approach to a difficult problem. Find an affordable researcher in terms of rates, amount of advance payment required, and maximum expenditure permitted before reporting. Membership in a society in Scotland is one way to identify possible researchers; another way is to write to the Association of Scottish Genealogists and Record Agents whose members must ascribe to a code of ethics and meet a certain level of expertise.

Help from others comes on a more casual basis. Family historians are always eager to share stories and research tips. Attending a conference, talking after club meetings, chatting via the computer—these are ways to exchange information. Whatever you do, and fun though it may be, remember that all this talk can take time away from actual research.

Build Knowledge and Experience
Libraries and Archives

How well do you know your local public library? Even if it is small, do you know whether it has interlibrary loan service, a microfiche reader, or a microfilm reader? These three items mean that materials can be brought in from any institution which is part of the interlibrary loan system. You can obtain some records on microfilm, and many societies now publish finding aids or sources such as directories on fiche. How close is the nearest library of a substantial size? Can you visit it from time to time? Is it worth your while to pay the yearly fee for nonresidents to obtain borrowing privileges? If you practice the library skills outlined in the previous section, you may be astonished at what you may discover among the books which can be found in the reference collection, the periodicals, and the unclassified materials in vertical files. Is there a university or college library nearby? Is history, in particular Scottish history, represented in its collections? Museums usually have reference collections associated with their respective themes. If places in your vicinity have Scottish connections, find out about the library holdings of historical museums.

How far is it to the nearest LDS family history center? Family history centers vary in size, but all of them have a copy of the Family History Library Catalog (FHLC), Scottish Church Records©, and the International Genealogical Index™ (IGI; see appendix B). Items available in the family history centers on an indefinite loan basis are those most heavily used by local patrons. You may be able to contribute to building this stock by borrowing certain types of records for an extended period. Family history centers often convert long-term loans of popular items to permanent stock. Take time to discover all the patron services, such as copying, publications for sale, introductory videos or classes, and computer tutorials.

The public and university libraries of major North American cities are likely to be the best hunting grounds for the drop-in traveler. Vancouver and Seattle are two excellent examples of cities with large public libraries. Seattle's has an extensive genealogical collection. Vancouver's new downtown library, which opened in May 1995, is a stunning piece of architecture, and a very patron-friendly facility. Some smaller centers may provide surprises because of special collections. In Canada, there is a very fine collection of Scottish material at the McLaughlin Library at the University of Guelph, Ontario. If you are planning a trip, find out in advance about the libraries near your destination. Your local library is a good place to begin inquiries about repositories at a distance. Also, more and more libraries and archives can be accessed via the Internet, and if you do not have this capability at home, your community library may have public terminals. With a floor plan (usually free at the information counter), and some basic catalog knowledge, you can always enjoy a visit to an unfamiliar library.

Broadening your knowledge of the collections at libraries and archives located at a distance from home serves several purposes. You will increase your awareness of available records. You will usually discover any records that have been published, indexed or otherwise made more readily accessible. You may resolve a thorny research problem because information about the holdings of a library or archives reveals the existence of a record not otherwise known. A great deal of information is available about libraries and archives in Scotland and their collections. Several helpful publications, general and particular, are listed here (see also the bibliography).

Tracing Your Scottish Ancestors (Sinclair, 1997). Required reading.

Exploring Scottish History (Cox, 1999). Essential for anyone researching seriously in two or more counties.

Data Sheet No. 6, Summaries of Archival Holdings (Scottish Records Association, 1994). The detailed listings of unusual sources are astonishing.

Tracing Scottish Ancestors (Bigwood, 1998). A useful, and compact, general guide.

Strathclyde Sources (Miller, 1995). First class regional guide.

North East Roots (Diack, 1996). Another excellent regional guide.

Family History Sources in Kirkcaldy Central Library (Campbell, 1994). A good sample of what local libraries may produce.

Has it been done before? Or is someone else working on the same line of research now? There are ways to find out. Each time you start work on a different surname, make several routine checks.

Two lists are available at LDS family history centers. These are the Surname portion of the FHLC and the Ancestral File™ . The former lists alphabetically by surname family histories in the library, whether printed books or typescripts. The catalog entry is generally detailed enough for you to conclude whether a title would be of interest. The Ancestral File is part of Family Search®, available on CD-ROM (it is also available on fiche), and gives the specific research interests of those who have made submissions, rather like a huge computer version of a genealogical society surname index.

Most societies maintain a members' interest file or database. On joining, new members submit their special interest for inclusion and receive a list of any matches. From time to time, the society may publish the list of surnames and associated dates and places. Another form of surname index is the *Genealogical Research Directory* (GRD) (Johnson & Sainty, 1998). Contributors submit entries, usually surnames, but sometimes topics, along with geographic area and approximate date. You do not have to submit in order to consult; however, the fee for submission includes the price of a copy of the GRD. At least take the time to look for your names in a recent edition. The book is in alphabetical order by name being researched and refers you to the name and address of the individual who made the submission. Other databanks of research interests are maintained by societies, commercial enterprises, and private individuals. Determine the size of the name bank, its circulation, cost, and the reputation of the organizer before participating.

You may be aware of a connection to a prominent Scot, in which case look up the name in the *Dictionary of National Biography*, and in the series of volumes *The Scottish Nation; the surnames, families literature, honours and biographical history of the people of Scotland* (Anderson, 1863). This series is quite widely available in larger general-reference libraries and at the FHL. If the family had some social standing you might check for the name in either work. It only takes a moment and may produce a reference. However, this advice comes with a warning. Do not jump to hasty conclusions without proof of a connection; it may send you on a wasted search. File anything of interest in case it subsequently proves to be useful. To find out whether printed works on the family exist (again you must be sure it is your family) consult *Scottish Family Histories Held in Scottish Libraries* (Ferguson, 1986) and *Scottish Family History: a Guide to Works of Reference on the History and Genealogy of Scottish Families* (Stuart, rep. 1994). These volumes are available in many North American libraries. About fifty works on Scottish names are listed in *Scottish Personal Names and Place Names* (Torrance, 1992).

If you have the time and the opportunity to browse through less common sources, look for volumes of *Scottish Notes and Queries*. The questions and answers in each issue frequently contain genealogical information, and indexes have been produced periodically. *Scottish Texts and Calendars: An Analytical Guide to Serial Publications* (D. & W.B. Stevenson, 1987) contains informative notations on the contents of the publications of private historical societies. Over the years, these societies have issued printed volumes of primary and secondary sources. It is worth thumbing through back issues of the *Scottish Historical Review* and the *Scottish Genealogist*. These publications can be found at the Society of Genealogists in London. If you are there and unable to make the journey north, visit the Society's library. It has all the periodicals previously mentioned, and it has its own unique document collection housed in row upon row of sturdy file boxes containing the miscellaneous contributions of members and nonmembers over the years. It is arranged alphabetically. Finding something is purely good luck, but the collection does include the McLeod papers—the very extensive files of a genealogist working primarily in Scottish families.

The Records

This is one situation where familiarity does not breed contempt. Better knowledge of the records will contribute to better results and suggest alternative sources when an ancestor continues to elude detection. Never pass up a chance to scan a different bibliography or a guide to the contents of a record office (many are noted in the bibliography). Venture beyond the most common sources; if a book or record type catches your attention, investigate. There is nothing to lose except a little time. The experience will be useful, and there is always the possibility of finding new information. No one will ever produce a complete list of sources for Scottish genealogy; materials remain uncataloged, and unique searches require source material no one has yet thought to consider. So, you can never stop learning about the records.

For researchers in North America, it is really important to know and distinguish between what exists, what is in the FHL, what is in print or on film (or fiche or CD-ROM), what is in Scottish repositories, and what has been indexed or calendared (a calendar is a descriptive list, essentially a précis of the documents in a class of records). The FHLC Locality section tells you what records are in a collection by category for a particular place, be it parish, burgh, or county; however, by reading through the listed items, you cannot tell whether these LDS holdings are all or part of what exists, and if none is listed, you cannot tell whether any survive at all. With ready access to an LDS family history center, a basic collection of source guides for making comparisons would be *Tracing Your Scottish Ancestors* (Sinclair, 1997), *Exploring Scottish History* (Cox, 1999), and any available guide or source list from the local library and regional archives. Helpful as a guide to resources and the FHL collection is *Scotland Research Outline* (1997). If it is inconvenient to visit a family history center, check the web site (see page 208) for the research outline and the FHLC. The outline, and the catalog on fiche, can also be purchased.

Additional dividends may be derived from an awareness of how the custodian of the original records describes them. Each classification or record group in the National Archives of Scotland (NAS)[1] has its own descriptive listing of the contents in summary form. The types of headings and descriptions to expect are shown in chapter 5, figure 5-5. You will hear of or see a classification guide variously described as a repertory, an inventory, or a calendar. Even if you never visit the NAS, the guides can help because you learn about the material and you can better understand the extent of the holdings of the FHL. You could send an inquiry to the NAS, but if you can assess the situation for yourself, why not do so? Some repertories and inventories are referred to in this book, including where they are available through an LDS family history center. If you want to look for the listings in the FHLC, look under SCOTLAND–RECORD TYPE, or use the author/title section (see appendix A).

Guides to the contents of regional or local record offices and libraries serve a similar purpose and make it possible to compare what is accessible with what exists in total. Making yourself aware of this comparison should deter you from abandoning a search too soon. Content guides and finding aids will also assist in the planning of a research trip to Scotland. Some archives, notably the NAS, are moving increasing amounts of material to other sites with a resultant wait of at least twenty-four hours for production of some material. The NAS will be undergoing major refurbishment for about three years beginning in the fall of 1995 which will also cause delays in access. If you are coming from a distance, call ahead to check on access in general and for any record classes of particular interest. The more you know about the records, the more effective your planning and inquiries will be.

Historical Context

This is where I get side-tracked! Genealogy and family history in the truest senses of the words are not synonymous. Family history implies an interest in what was influencing the lives of long-dead ancestors, even if they had no way of knowing it themselves. It also implies building a picture of daily lives and immediate surroundings.

For Scotland, reference to dictionaries of dates and annuals of significant events will be disappointing. Scotland gets lumped in with Britain, which tends to mean not much is reported. *Harrap's Book of British Dates* (Castleden, 1991) mentions major political events such as the Union of 1707, and the dates of publication of the novels of Sir Walter Scott, but not much else. Nevertheless, this and similar volumes will at least provide perspective on what was going on in the rest of the world at any particular time.

Figure 2-2 is a retrograph. The life spans of several individuals (they could all be members of one family, or each from a different family) are drawn against a list of national/international events and a list of regional/local events. The only requirement is that at least a decade of someone's life falls within the selected 100 years. Choose the events for the twenty boxes on the basis of your knowledge of the chosen individuals. Of course, the regional/local events should be for the area where the listed individuals lived. This diagrammatic summary can become a talking point with relatives or other researchers, or it can be a window on history that leads you to investigate something more thoroughly.

100 Year Family History Retrograph
for RUSSELLS AND RENNIES OF DENNY

Events of major importance in each decade →	Walter Scott b. in Edinburgh 1771	James Watt invents double-acting rotary steam engine 1782	Firth-Clyde canal opens 1790	Power loom arrives in Scotland 1807	Victory at Waterloo 1815	William Burke hanged for smothering 15 people 1829	Factory Act limits hours of work for children 1833	The Disruption 1843	Civil Registration begins 1855	Second Reform Bill further extends the vote 1867
Name / Decade:	1770-80	1780-90	1790-1800	1800-10	1810-20	1820-30	1830-40	1840-50	1850-60	1860-70
James Russell										
James Russell										
William Russell										
William Russell										
Mary Rennie										
James Rennie										
Decade:	1770-80	1780-90	1790-1800	1800-10	1810-20	1820-30	1830-40	1840-50	1850-60	1860-70
Events of local significance in each decade →	development of carpet industry, continued (continuing) tartan production in the region	1787 Thrashing mill first used in the region	1800 Population of Denny is 1967	new bridge completed	1813 Denny church built	1820 Stirling Journal began publication	1838 parish population has grown to 3,843	1842 Queen Victoria visited Stirling	1859 branch of Caledonian Railway reached Denny	1870 Wallace Monument built

Note: Dotted-line extensions to life-span lines indicate that exact years of birth and death are not known.

Figure 2-2. 100-Year Family History Retrograph for the Russells and Rennies of Denny.

The first step then is to read some Scottish history. Start at your public library to ascertain what is available. Poke about in used bookshops where you may find older histories or school and college texts. If you want to expand your knowledge of some aspect of Scottish history, the bibliographies found within general histories will suggest further reading. For books on a local region, once again, used book stores are worth scouting. Out-of-date travel guides come cheaply and can be informative. You can obtain suggestions for current titles from the regional family history society and by writing to the local libraries, which may sell something themselves.

A picture of an ancestor's surroundings can be created partly through the research you perform. Census returns are very helpful provided you read beyond the listings for the immediate family and look at the neighbors and the neighborhood. Additional information can be found in the preliminary descriptions in directories, in gazetteers, and in the first two *Statistical Accounts of Scotland* (1799 and 1845)—the third one too, if a mid-twentieth century view is desired. The first *Account* was under the direction of Sir John Sinclair. Each minister in each parish was asked to provide a verbal illustration discussing such topics as numbers of births, marriages and deaths, emigration, agriculture and industry, characteristics of the local population. Some reports were brief, but many included the personal opinions of the author on matters as diverse as drunkenness, irregular marriages, the ague, and the prejudices of the lower orders regarding inoculation against smallpox. Sinclair's own analysis of the reports which came back makes fascinating reading and could be useful. It might be important for your research, for example, to know that the inclement summer of 1782 was followed by severe and calamitous cold at harvest time. In Cabrach in Aberdeenshire, heavy snow flattened the crops on September 14th, and this was not an isolated report.[2] References to the *Statistical Accounts* appear throughout this book.

For information on the dress, food, clothing, and housing of your ancestors look for a social history or for books of people in particular locations or occupations. Good ideas can be found in the extensive bibliographies in *Scottish Local History* (Moody, 1986) and *Scottish Family History* (Moody, 1988). Shire Publications has several titles of interest in these areas including *Discovering Scottish Architecture* (West, 1985), *Shawls* (Swain, 1990), and *Scottish Agricultural Implements* (Powell, 1988).

Books on description and travel occupy a grey area which straddles history and geography. They have a very strong appeal and, if written before 1939, for all but the large urban centers, they are describing scenes not much changed from a century before. Your prospecting may unearth such unusual treasures as the privately printed *Around the Ancient City* (Ryan, 1933), which extols the beauty and history of the area around Brechin. The books nearly always include a map and photographs or drawings.

Geographical Context

Maps are one of the delights of family history research. There have been some fine mapmakers and their story is told in a fascinating book issued by the Scottish Library Association, *The Scot and His Maps* (Wilkes, 1991). Spatial perspective, topographic detail, man-made features of the landscape, boundaries, and names—maps depict and explain all these things. It is very important information.

Maps can also be created around an economic, social, or political theme. They can be found in atlases, books on historical geography, and histories. You might decide to make your own. You can use a map to plot the distribution of a surname or color code shifts in population, or mark points of departure for ships taking emigrants to North America. Whatever interests you or whatever will graphically represent a vague idea and perhaps turn it into a valid hypothesis is worth depicting. Some examples of sources for data to create your own maps are the *Statistical Accounts of Scotland*, the population summaries of the census returns, or any of the church record indexes described in chapter 5.

Pay attention to boundaries. Always identify the correct parish, and the county. In some counties it is useful to know that they were also divided into districts. If you are looking for probate prior to 1823, then a special jurisdiction, the commissariot, must be identified. The Aberdeen and North East Scotland Family History Society produces an inexpensive series of county plans with parish boundaries and the date of earliest entry in the parish register. The revised edition of the *Phillimore Atlas and Index of Parish Registers* (Humphery-Smith, 1995) includes maps showing parish and commissariot divisions.

Several counties have undergone name changes. The most usual form is that used between 1890 and the reorganization of local government in 1974, when the old counties disappeared and were replaced by regions. Archives have been established on the basis of these regions. In 1996 Scotland has again undergone local government reorganization, and some pre-1974 names are back. There should not be any immediate, serious impact on archival collections, although the names of some archives may change and some decentralization of records may occur (i.e., some materials may be moved to smaller local repositories). As for county names, six had a name change at some point in time:

- West Lothian was Linlithgowshire
- Mid-Lothian was Edinburghshire
- East Lothian was Haddingtonshire
- Angus was Forfarshire
- Elgin was Morayshire
- Shetland was Zetland

Figure 2-3 shows the boundaries of the counties prior to 1974; the numbers on the map correspond to the counties listed below.

1. Shetland Isles (SHI)
2. Orkney Isles (OKI)
3. Caithness-shire (CAI)
4. Sutherland (SUT)
5. Ross & Cromary (ROC)
6. Inverness-shire (INV)
7. Nairnshire (NAI)
8. Morayshire (MOR)
9. Banffshire (BAN)
10. Aberdeenshire (ABD)
11. Kincardineshire (KCD)
12. Argyllshire (ARL)
13. Perthshire (PER)
14. Angus (ANS)
15. Dunbartonshire (DNB)
16. Stirlingshire (STI)
17. Clackmannanshire (CLK)
18. Kinross-shire (KRS)
19. Fifeshire (FIF)
20. Renfrewshire (RFW)
21. Lanarkshire (LKS)
22. West Lothian (WLN)
23. Midlothian (MLN)
24. East Lothian (ELN)
25. Buteshire (BUT)
26. Ayrshire (AYR)
27. Peebleshire (PEE)
28. Berwickshire (BEW)
29. Wigtownshire (WIG)
30. Kirkcudbrightshire (KKD)
31. Dumfriesshire (DFS)
32. Selkirkshire (SEL)
33. Roxburghshire (ROX)

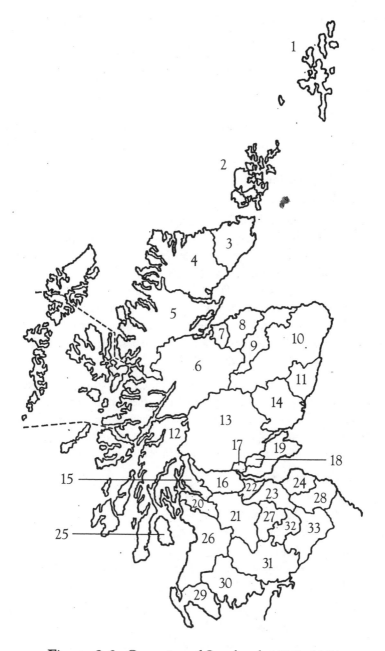

Figure 2-3. Counties of Scotland, 1890–1974.

Figure 2-4 indicates the location of the Highland Line. The distinction between the Highlands and the Lowlands involves significant cultural and linguistic differences, but there also is an identifiable geological demarcation between the two. The Highland Line in the illustration runs east across Angus and then north. Geologists call it the "Highland Boundary Fault" marking the visible difference between older, harder Highland rock and the younger, softer, sedimentary deposits of the Lowlands. Whether discussing geological or cultural differences (which do not divide so sharply), the important point to remember is that the division is not a straight east-to-west one, and that the entire east coast is in the Lowlands.

Make it a matter of habit to locate a new place of interest on maps of different types and scales. On a map of the country, where is it? On a map of a county, which parish is it in? On a detailed regional map, what is the lie of the land and what nearby features can be noted? The best maps of Scotland have been issued by the Ordnance Survey. Reprints of the 1890 series can be purchased (1 inch = 1 mile), and modern Ordnance Survey maps have three commonly used scales, all with topographic features. The larger the scale, the smaller the geographic area on the page and the more detail (i.e., 1:2500 is very detailed for a small area, and 1:200,000 is much less detailed for a large area).

Even when you practice good habits, locating some places can be a challenge for reasons other than those discussed in chapter 1. The place may simply be too small to be shown on most maps, or it may have completely disappeared. Whenever this problem arises, work your way through the following suggestions before admitting defeat:

1. Check an atlas with a gazetteer and a scale of one inch = four miles (1:200,000).

2. Look up the name in *The Ordnance Gazetteer of Scotland* (Groome, 1883-85).

3. Check an area map with a scale of 1.25 inch = one mile (1:50,000), or better (maps at 1:25,000, 2.5 inch = one mile are available).

4. Check a map contemporary to the time of the ancestor.

5. In urban areas check a street plan, both present day and historical, contemporary to the time of the ancestor.

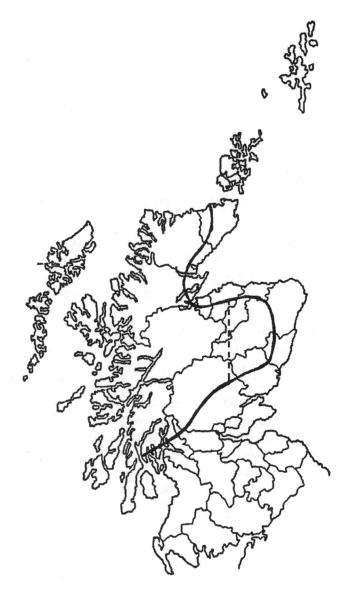

Figure 2-4. The Highland Line. Depicted here by the solid line is the approximate place of the Highland Boundary Fault. Linguistically, differences were farther to the west about 200 years ago—in the vicinity of the dashed line.

6. Look up the place in the *Directory to Gentlemen's Seats, Villages, etc. in Scotland* (Findlay, 1843) and/or in *A Directory of Land Ownership in Scotland circa 1770* (Timperley, 1976), and/or in the place-name index volumes of the Sasine Abridgements which begin with 1780 and are available through LDS family history centers. All these sources contain small place names or estate names which may not appear anywhere else. Remember that your ancestor did not have to own an estate to call it his or her home.

7. Where the county or vicinity is known and none of the sources above have provided an answer, write to the local archives or library.

Help might also be found in one of the hundreds of books on Scottish place names identified in *Scottish Personal and Place Names–a bibliography* (Torrance, 1992). However, the availability in North America of the listed works is unknown. An interlibrary loan request might prove successful.

Building a Reference Library

For most of us, book-buying is dictated in part by budget constraints. If cost is a concern, buy books which will serve a useful purpose and be referenced often enough to make ownership more sensible than occasional consultation at a library. If you are working in only one county, it does not make sense to buy a guide to sources in every county of Scotland. Select something regional or county specific. If your ancestors left Scotland prior to 1840, do not buy a book which focuses mainly on civil registration and census returns. The entries in the bibliography include comments, with these points in mind, on content or usefulness.

A good, basic reference collection should include the following:

- An outline history of Scotland.
- A pre-1974 atlas of Britain, scale four miles to the inch.
- At least one how-to book which matches your search needs.
- A book or pamphlet which outlines the contents of archives and libraries in the area(s) of interest.
- A map of the region at a more detailed scale of 1:50,000.
- A map of the parish boundaries in the area of interest.

- A regional or local history.
- The key finding aids and bibliographies which you will refer to again and again.
- Your own bibliography of books, finding aids, and articles which you have found useful, including those you own and those you don't; this bibliography can be on index cards sorted into regional sections, and then by author or subject, or it can be in a computer database (keyword access would be a bonus).

Note

1. The Scottish Record Office, at the beinning of 1999, changed its name to the National Archives of Scotland (NAS).

2. Sinclair, *Analysis*, 1826, p. 41.

Summary—Research Essentials

1. Visit local libraries to become familiar with the cataloging systems and all other services, such as interlibrary loan or periodical indexes on CD-ROM.

2. Establish a filing system (paper or electronic) which incorporates ready reference, correct bibliographic details, and a standardized format.

3. Take time to formulate research objectives, and review them as you progress.

4. Join at least one family history society, preferably two—one close to home and the most appropriate one in Scotland.

5. Check—has it been done before?

6. Do not neglect a background study of the records or the historical and geographical contexts of your research.

3 • Civil Registration

onsider yourself fortunate if you have ancestors or close collateral relations recorded in the Scottish civil registers of birth, marriage, and death. Scottish civil registration is much more informative than its counterpart to the south. Record keeping may have started nearly twenty years later than in England and Wales, but the information about parents on each and every type of certificate more that makes up for the tardy start.

If a search for a record of birth, marriage, or death is the start of your research, consult several maps before you begin. You will need some familiarity with the applicable part of Scotland, in particular the county name, the names of neighboring towns, or the neighborhoods of a major city. Map work is even more important if you must choose between several civil registration entries for the same name clustered close together in time and place.

From your pedigree chart or your family tree, determine the events for which you need to acquire civil records. Keep in mind that registration began 1 January 1855. Are you fortunate enough to have specific details? Will it be necessary to search over a period of several years? Can the search be limited geographically? In other words, do you need only to watch for entries which fall within a particular county or district? Lack of information may dictate that you collect all of the entries for one particular name (and obvious variations of the name) over a number of years and a fairly wide geographic area. Such considerations will influence the search method you select.

Details

Since the beginning of civil registration in 1855, the form of the indexes and the registers has changed (see tables 3-1, 3-2, and 3-3). Male and female listings have always been separated, sometimes within the same volume and sometimes in different ones. Indexes were handwritten for ten years; then, from 1866 they were printed until computerized indexes were introduced. Arrangement is first by year, then alphabetically by surname, Christian name(s), and then sequentially if names are identical. Entries will be found in the year in which the event was registered—check the following year for events that occurred in November or December. Other variations within the different indexes will be discussed in turn.

A page of a birth index will show the name, the parish or district of birth, and the entry number of each event. From 1929 on, the maiden surname of the mother appears in the index.

Marriage indexes similarly indicate the name, the parish or district of the marriage, and the entry number of each event. If you know the maiden name of the bride, look up the entry under both parties—the match in reference numbers is assurance that you have identified the correct entry. For nine years, from 1855 to 1863, a woman's married surname appeared in brackets. If a woman was married more than once and if the registrar was informed (which was usually the case), all her surnames were indexed with her other names in brackets. This fact can be a real bonus if there has been no evidence that a woman was married more than once or when you are trying to distinguish your ancestor of a common name from many others. In 1864, the other names in brackets no longer appear, but for 1864 and 1865, the indexes show a maiden surname for a woman married previously, and she is indexed under both names. No further changes occur until 1929, when the surname of the spouse is shown.

In the death indexes, the basic name, place, and entry number information is supplemented from 1866 with the addition of the person's age at death. For women, also from 1866, entries are indexed by maiden name and by married name or names, if the woman married more than once. A widow might be indexed only under her maiden name, if she reverted to that name after the death of her husband.

In all cases, computer indexes, which visitors to the General Register Office (GRO) in Edinburgh will consult, also indicate the registration district number. Microfilm copies of the original indexes do not. One other small point, which you will probably notice for yourself, is always to search for names beginning Mc or Mac in both forms, in particular because the original index volumes list them separately.

Some parts of Scottish civil registration indexes have been incorporated into the International Genealogical Index (IGI) which will speed up the search process considerably. These parts are marriages and births from 1855 to 1875, coinciding with the consecutive run of years of register copies in the Family History Library (FHL). Also, a new series of death indexes is being produced in New Zealand. The McKirdy index is emerging on a county basis; the years to be covered are 1855 to 1875. This index includes the name of the deceased, age, occupation, spouse (when indicated) or parents, parish, entry number, year, and LDS film number (see the bibliography).

TABLE 3-1
Details of Statutory Records—1855

Birth	Marriage	Death
• name	• names	• name
• date and time	• date	• date and time
• place	• place	• place
• sex	• form (i.e., rites)	• sex
• father's name, age, occupation and birthplace	• ages and birthplaces	• age
	• occupations	• occupation
• mother's name, maiden name, age, and birthplace	• present residence	• where born
	• usual residence	• name of spouse plus occupation for husband
• date and place of parents' marriage	• condition	• any other marriages
	• signature or mark	• name and ages of issue in order of birth
• no. and sex of other issue, living and dead	• relationship if related	
	• any former marriage if applicable	• father's name and occupation
• was informant present?	• no. of other issue, living or dead	• name and maiden name of mother
• was place lodgings?	• names of parents	
• name of informant	• occupation of father	• cause of death and name of medical attendant
• residence of same if not place of birth	• maiden name of mother	
	• witnesses	• place of burial
		• signature of informant, relationship, and address if different

TABLE 3-2
Details of Statutory Records—1856-60

Birth
- name
- date and time
- place
- sex
- name of father
- occupation of father
- name of mother and maiden name
- signature and quality of informant and residence if different

Marriage
- names
- date
- place
- form (i.e., rites)
- ages
- addresses
- conditions
- occupations
- name and occupation of fathers
- name and maiden name of mothers
- witnesses

Death
- name
- date and time
- place (and home address if different)
- age and sex of deceased
- occupation
- condition
- name and occupation of father
- name and maiden name of mother
- cause of death and name of medical attendant
- burial place
- signature of informant, relationship and address if different

TABLE 3-3
Details of Statutory Records—1861 and After

Birth
- name
- date and time
- place
- sex
- name of father
- occupation of father
- name of mother and maiden name
- date and place of parents' marriage
- signature and quality of informant and residence if different

Marriage
- names
- date
- place
- form (i.e., rites)
- ages
- addresses
- conditions
- occupations
- names and occupations of fathers
- names and maiden names of mothers
- witnesses

Death
- name
- date and time
- place and home address if different
- age and sex of deceased
- occupation
- name of spouse (plus occupation of husband)
- parents' names and occupations
- cause of death and name of medical attendant
- signature of informant, relationship, and address if different

Making the Search

For someone living in the United States or Canada, there are several choices as to how to access the indexes and entries of civil registration. It is possible to obtain records of civil registration up until 1875 entirely through the resources of the LDS library system. It is also possible to combine a search in LDS copies of the indexes with a postal or fax request for the extract or with assistance from someone in Scotland. The Family History Library in Salt Lake City has copies of the original index volumes on microfilm for the years 1855 to 1955 (births) or 1956 (marriages and deaths). The Library also holds copies of the actual registers, on film, from the beginning, up to, and including 1875, and for the census years of 1881 and 1891. This means that for the years not included in the collection of filmed birth, marriage, or death books, you will have to combine your index search with a direct request to Scotland. This topic is discussed further later in this chapter.

Beginning then with the resources of an LDS family history center, you would immediately determine two things—the required index film numbers and local holdings. Don't forget that some marriages and births are included in the IGI. Examine the listings of the Family History Library Catalog (FHLC), under SCOTLAND–CIVIL REGISTRATION, to note the film number for the index volumes required. Then look to see what is currently held on indefinite loan. It may be possible to carry out your entire index search without resorting to an order of films.

Once you have completed the index search, and if the years in question fall within the register collection of the FHL (1855-75, 1881, 1891), return to the Locality listings. What you need is the parish number, which is either with the index film listings you have just been looking at or with the individual place listings. This parish number is key to selecting the correct register book film. Parish numbers may also be found in *The Parishes, Registers and Registrars of Scotland* (SAFHS, 1993), *The Key to the Parochial Registers of Scotland* (Bloxham & Metcalfe, 1979) and *Tracing Your Scottish Ancestry* (Cory, 1997). Before placing a film order, once again check the list of short- and long-term loans at the center, just in case the film has been brought in by another researcher.

There are several other options for obtaining the registration entry:

- Obtain the registration code number at the local center and then get help at the FHL in Salt Lake City.
- Obtain the registration code number at the local family history center and then get help in Scotland.
- Write or fax the GRO.
- Write the local registrar.
- Obtain the assistance of an agent in Edinburgh or Salt Lake City.

In Salt Lake City, the search process is similar. It is facilitated by the fact that the index and registration book films for a twenty-two year period can be consulted together. Your nearest LDS family history center at home already has a fairly extensive portion of the indexes in its IGI and may have many additional index films; therefore, you may be able to find the references yourself, and, where the results fall within the twenty-two years, order a copy of the entry from the main library. If you perform an index search during a research trip to Salt Lake City, you can order registration records which are not included in the LDS collection on the British floor at the office beside the copy room.

Once you have located the index entry, or if you know the details of an event, name, place, and date within a year or two, it is possible to send your request to the General Register Office by mail or by fax (there is a saving if two or more are ordered at the same time). You can also write directly to the local registrar. Addresses are given in *The Parishes, Registers and Registrars of Scotland* (SAFHS, 1993). When you are reasonably sure of your facts, some form of direct inquiry may be the most efficient method to use. Do remember that local officials are primarily concerned with meeting the needs of the present and may require some time to respond.

You can, of course, turn the whole process over to someone else—a professional researcher or a relative who is willing and able to help. This researcher might be located in your own area, in Salt Lake City, or in Scotland. When a friend or relative volunteers to do the work, the choice is obvious but, when considering professional help, seriously consider assistance in Edinburgh before other options. An account of the process of acquiring vital records at the GRO makes the reason clear.

At New Register House, the location of the GRO, each researcher is assigned a desk equipped with a computer terminal, a microfiche reader, a light, and a supply of order slips. The chair is comfortable too. All the indexes to civil registration are now online. The system is menu-driven and user-friendly. In a matter of minutes, names are entered, entries are reviewed on screen, and order slips are filled out. Three orders at a time are taken to the room where the microfiche copies of the registers are stored. They are separated into births, marriages, and deaths, and are clearly marked as to dates. Part of the order slip is left in the drawer to mark the spot from which a fiche is pulled. Fiches are returned to the desk, viewed, and then placed in the fiche return tray. The staff refiles them in the drawers. You can copy entries onto plain paper, onto forms available for purchase (see figures 3-1 and 3-2), or order a photocopy. Official copies cost more and are sent by mail (figure 3-3).

Speed then is a factor. Someone in Edinburgh can work very quickly with this system. Not only that, but the same computer can be used for searches in the index to Church of Scotland registers of baptisms and marriages. There is no need to switch CD-ROM disks in and out, and, once again, copies of the registers are located just down the hall. Although your first impression may be otherwise, the cost may be more reasonable too. Initial reaction to the daily use charge is probably shock (£17.00 for one day in 1999). This could, nevertheless, be economical because a researcher would accomplish more in a given amount of time. In addition, there is no need to apply for individual certificates. For a well prepared researcher who is able to extract many entries in one day, the cost per entry could be much less than the same number of certificates ordered elsewhere. For example, at the General Register Office in London, the index search is free, but the unavoidable certificates cost £6.00 apiece. You have an attractive option when you add to that the fact that in Scotland a researcher has the information immediately. If you communicate with an agent by phone, fax, or e-mail, results will come promptly at a reasonable price.

Keep up-to-date with changes in regional archives and research services. In 1995, a new facility opened in Glasgow, the Strathclyde Genealogy Centre, which not only has the statutory records and census returns for the country, and the Old Parochial Registers for the Strathclyde region, but also shared access to the National Index Link in Edinburgh, in other words the computer indexes referred to above. Details regarding number of terminals, hours, and public transportation may be found in *Strathclyde Sources* (Miller, 1995). Not long after, a similar computer link service became available through the facilities of the City of Dundee. Both locations charge daily use fees. Up-to-date information can be found through the GENUKI web site by connecting to the information on the counties of Angus and Lanark.

For anyone contemplating a trip to Edinburgh, you will find many other useful materials elsewhere in New Register House. All the sheets of the series of Ordnance Survey maps, 1890, are bound, flat, in huge volumes in the map room. As previously mentioned, the indexes to Church

Certinf.pm4

REGISTRAR GENERAL FOR SCOTLAND

BIRTH CERTIFICATE INFORMATION

Name of Parish/District: Newington, City of Edinburgh   Parish/District Number: 685'   Entry Number: 468

Surname	Leslie	Maiden Surname of Mother (m.s.)	Heggie
Names(s)	Elizabeth		
Date of Birth	April 15th 1869	Mother's Occupation	
Sex	F	If Deceased Y/N	N
Place of Birth	29 Wright House Burntsfield Link Edinburgh	Date and Place of Parents' Marriage	January 11th 1868 Clough, Down, Ireland
Usual Residence (If Different from above)		Name of Informant	John Leslie
		Relationship to Child	Father
Name and Surname of Father	John Leslie	Residence of above (If Different)	
Father's Occupation	Gentleman's Gardener	Date and Place of Registration	May 4th 1869 Edinburgh
If Deceased Y/N	N	Registrar	N. Alexander
Name and Surname of Mother	Susan Leslie	RCE/Any other Information	

Crown copyright design reproduced with permission of Her Majesty's Stationery Office (HMSO) and General Register Office (GRO).

Figure 3-1. Birth Certificate Information Form.

GRO RECORDS ENTERPRISE

Cert inf.pm4

MARRIAGE CERTIFICATE INFORMATION

Name of Parish/District.................... Parish/District Number .... Entry Number ....

Date of Marriage	....	Age	Occupation
Place of Marriage	....	Marital Status	
According to the Forms and Rites of	....	Father's Name & Surname	
		If Deceased Y/N	Occupation
Name and Surname of Groom	....	Mother's Name & Surname/ Maiden Name	
Usual Residence	....	If Deceased Y/N	
Age .... Occupation		Witnesses	
Marital Status		Addresses	
Father's Name & Surname	....	Date and Place of Registration/ Registrar	
	Occupation		
If Deceased Y/N	....		
Mother's Name & Surname/ Maiden Name	....	Any Other Information	
If Deceased Y/N	....		
Name and Surname of Bride Usual Residence	....	R.C.E.	

Crown copyright design reproduced with permission of HMSO and GRO.

Figure 3-2. Marriage Certificate Information Form.

1861 – 1965

Extract of an entry in a REGISTER of DEATHS

Registration of Births, Deaths and Marriages (Scotland) Act 1965

No.	1 Name and surname, rank or profession and whether single, married or widowed	2 When and where died	3 Sex	4 Age	5 Name, surname, and rank or profession of father, Name and maiden surname of mother	6 Cause of death, duration of disease, and medical attendant by whom certified	7 Signature and qualification of informant, and residence, if out of the house in which the death occurred	8 When and where registered and signature of registrar
129	Jean DUNSMUIR Grocer Widow of William Dunsmuir Colliery Manager	1865 November Ninth 11h 0m p.m. Shettleston Lanark	F	63 Years	James Gray Coal Miner Deceased Jane Gray m.s. Allan Deceased	Hypertrophy Six Months As certified by Wm Young L.F.P.S.G.	*Signed* James Dunsmuir Son Residing in Shettleston Present	1865 November 11th At Shettleston *Signed* Andrew Garrand *Registrar*

The above particulars are extracted from a Register of Deaths for the .... District .... of .... Shettleston

in the .... County .... of .... Lanark

Given under the Seal of the General Register Office, New Register House, Edinburgh, on 14th January 1988

Crown copyright design reproduced with permission of HMSO and GRO.

Figure 3-3. Extract From Register of Deaths.

of Scotland baptisms and marriages, and all the registers as well, are available on microfilm. Located in the Dome Search Room are the various *Statistical Accounts* of Scotland, many directories, and family histories. Some readers may remember this from the old days as the location of the red-, green-, and black-spined index volumes. Here you can also consult the indexes to the registers of the General Register Office for England and Wales, which is useful when families have connections in both countries.

Where cost is a factor and you enjoy the work, combination searches are the best value. You can complete the index search in the LDS family history center and then forward the request to Edinburgh, the local registrar, or Salt Lake City, depending on the date and circumstances. As you move backward before 1875, you can also complete the search yourself.

Thinking It Through

Remind yourself of the date, 1 January 1855 whenever you consider the tactics to be utilized in a search, and make a note of those persons who were born, married, or died since that date. All register entries, where the facts were known, include the names of the mother and father. Do not think only in terms of the direct line, for the record of a brother, sister, aunt, or uncle could be equally illuminating. The death entry of an elderly maiden aunt in the late 1850s could provide key details to launch a search in parish registers for your direct line. You might extract similarly useful data from the marriage records of siblings of an emigrant.

The best feature of Scottish vital records is the inclusion of parent's marriage details (i.e., date and place) in a birth record. It is quite possible that a birth recorded in the first fifteen years or so of civil registration includes marriage information that predates the introduction of statutory records and perhaps even the first nominal census of 1841. This leap across time is extremely valuable, more so if the surname is common or if the marriage occurred in a secessionist church (see chapter 6). There is a hitch. For the five years from 1856 to 1860, this marriage information was omitted. If your ancestor was born within that period, you must seek a sibling's birth record for the marriage details. If you are among the unlucky few who do not find any births outside those years, you must rely on a search in the marriage indexes.

It is possible to opt for a search which is broad in scope yet not time consuming to complete. Needless to say, where microfilm readers are manual, speed may be dependent on the endurance of your right arm. You can contemplate long searches based on vague information, provided you can identify, within a handful of names, the entries in which you are interested. The search might center upon an unusual name over many years, or around a more common name in a populated area for only two or three years. Gambling on entries is not much of a risk when the only cost is a little more time.

Set your search parameters with some flexibility, and maintain a certain level of skepticism. The name spelling is not fixed. The dates are always open to question, and places named have been known to differ among records. Sometimes you will see "deceased" after a parent's name on a marriage record, but its absence does not guarantee that the person was alive at the time of the event. Think hard about what could be done to a name by the registrar or the person involved. Pronunciation may be the cause of a radically different appearance in the register. Poor handwriting created problems, and names are often misindexed because of reversals, transpositions, and omission of one name. Add a surname-style middle name and an entry could conceivably find its way into three places. Where information is scarce, begin by assuming that people could marry at a very young age, or become parents at an unusually advanced age, or live to be ninety plus. As for places, keep the map handy, and be prepared to find the name of a town you know from family notes to be several miles from the obscure village that was the true birthplace.

When you obtain the register details, pay attention to all of them. What do they tell you? Do they match information in other records such as census returns? If this is the first record obtained, where else should you look for corroboration? Who was the informant for a death? Errors are actually more common on death certificates, either because the informant was not a close relative or because the details became vague over time. Do the names of witnesses to a marriage mean anything? Even if they don't, jot them down for future reference. Finally, assess the facts in the new information and how they will advance your research.

Watch closely for the possibility of finding a family member, any family member, within the very informative entries for 1855. The birth record adds the ages and birthplaces of the parents and other issue, either living or dead. The marriage record includes present and usual addresses, any previous marriages, and any issue. The death record adds where the deceased was born, details of all marriages, and the names and ages of issue, in order. These additional facts can bridge years, help in the identification of a family, and facilitate the transition to parish registers.

The date an event was registered, and the type (i.e., birth, marriage, or death) will tell you if you can continue the search in the records of civil registration. Always note how closely an event falls to a census year. Moving back and forth from vital records to censuses is good strategy as the details complement one another and confirm family structures. This process may prove difficult if a family moved frequently and had a common name, in which case you must consider what other finding aids or records might assist you. Possibilities include census indexes (1881 and a growing list for other years), electoral rolls, and directories.

Whenever a record of birth, marriage, or death fails to turn up, consider in turn the standard cautions. Are the basic facts accurate? Have you checked both Mc and Mac? How might the name have been altered? (It is unlikely that an illiterate informant would have taken any interest in what the registrar wrote). Did the event take place in Scotland? Might the family have moved between birth and registration? Once ages appear in the death indexes (from 1866 on), have you allowed for the fact that the information may have come from an unreliable source?

Two features of Scots law may be a factor in a missing entry. An illegitimate child was legitimized by the later marriage of the parents, so consider a search under the maiden name of the mother. Also, divorce has always been possible in Scotland, so a missing death record may not be missing at all. You may simply be looking under the wrong married name. Be sure to search under the woman's maiden name.

Repeating the search is an option, with some alterations in the way you watch for possibilities. Alternatively, you may decide to seek additional information from some other record. If your estimated dates fall within striking distance of the 1881 census index, read about it in the next chapter. It does help to narrow choices where several people have the same last name. At the other end of the time frame, in the 1850s, can you find some member of the family in the Register of Neglected Entries? Made in retrospect after the start of civil registration, these entries, mostly births, should have actually appeared in parish registers at the time of the event but never did. They are on a single film which may be one of those on permanent loan at the nearest family history center.

Conclusion

For those who have more recent connections, civil registration is a great place to begin Scottish research. It is easy to consult and produces just what every genealogist wants—information about the previous generation. Combined with a search in census returns—work in one feeds off the other—and *vice versa*, you can make considerable progress and establish a sound basis of fact about your Scottish ancestral lines.

Summary—Civil Registration

1. Select the name, date, and place guidelines for the search. If you are sure of the facts, and that they are more recent than 1875, deal directly with the GRO or the local registrar. The addresses are in *Parishes, Registers and Registrars of Scotland* (1993). If the parameters fall within the period for which the FHL holds both the indexes and register copies (1855-75, 1881, 1891); then you may choose to search both the indexes and the registers yourself.

2. Find the location on a map and note names of neighboring parishes or districts.

3. If your search is for a death record or falls entirely or partly outside the marriage and birth entries incorporated into the IGI, determine whether the nearest family history center holds copies of the index films required for your search. If it does not, decide whether to order more films or to enlist assistance to complete the search (this decision will be influenced by such factors as the variations in name spellings you must search through).

4. Since April 1998, anyone with an Internet connection is able to search indexes to civil registration for the years 1855-97 using the GRO's special Web site (see appendix E). Available fields are surname, forename, event type, year, age, and registration district. When an entry is found it can be ordered immediately using a credit card.

5. When you seek help, weigh the pros and cons of an Edinburgh search (everything in one place), or a Salt Lake City search (all the indexes and some register volumes are available, and an application can be made to Scotland).

6. When you have acquired results, note every new fact, compare dates against census years and the start of civil registration, and determine the next step. Also, consider whether locating civil records for other family members would be useful (e.g., a possible 1855 event or the need to find a birth outside the years 1856 to 60).

4 • Bridging Decades and Centuries

cottish research is unusual in that there is a very sharp break where civil records end and centrally collected church records begin. Many records straddle the critical year of 1855. Census returns, voters' lists, directories, and newspapers all can enhance the knowledge gained in civil records and provide a link to earlier church records. These sources can also provide useful clues about people who left Scotland before civil registration began, but who had identifiable relatives who did not leave.

Pay attention to dates to assess what resources you can consult. Nominal census returns were taken every ten years and are available from 1841 to 1891. Note that the census returns for 1841 and 1851 predate the start of civil registration in Scotland, which can make them exceedingly important. Electoral rolls begin in 1832, but for many areas the start date is considerably later. The existence of directories and newspapers varies from place to place, but generally they exist from earlier dates in larger towns and cities.

When, What, and Where

The combination of household groupings, relationships, birthplaces and occupations found in all but the earliest nominal census returns means that they are wonderful resources and problem solvers. Six censuses are available for study, 1841 through 1891. For earlier returns, only statistical reports were to be submitted to the authorities. Some enumerators recorded names, but most of these lists were destroyed or lost. More information on surviving fragments is provided later in this chapter.

Censuses form a very remarkable record. There are gaps and misleading entries because our ancestors did not always tell the truth, and the enumerators were not infallible. Nevertheless, the census was taken in the same manner everywhere and stored centrally afterward, so it survives as a nearly complete, well-organized and accessible record of the nineteenth century. Census records less than one hundred years old are accessible only to lawyers dealing with inheritance problems.

The content of the 1841 census is sufficiently different from the others to warrant a separate description. The columns show the location (i.e., village name, street name), the names of everyone in the household, their occupations, approximate ages, and whether or not they were born in the county. The ages recorded were supposed to be the actual ages of anyone fifteen years old and under; for everyone else, the actual age was rounded down to the nearest five years. There was lots of room for error within these instructions. Some enumerators rounded up. Anyone who fibbed a little (e.g., was actually fifty-two but said he or she was forty-nine) ended up way off the mark. The rather vague birthplace question resulted in cryptic responses noted as Y (yes, born in the county), N (no, born in another county), E (born in England/Wales), I (born in Ireland), or F (born in foreign parts). Think about these possibilities as you check the place location against the location of the county boundary or the border with England. An answer could mean a few miles away, at the other end of Scotland, or at the other end of the kingdom. Another serious drawback of this census is that it does not reveal relationships. This means, for example, that a man, woman, and child living together could be a family or a brother and sister caring for a young relative. Similarly, a houseful of people with several surnames could be landlord and lodgers or members of one family. There is some compensation in the fact that where more than one household resided in one dwelling, the enumerator distinguished between them by using a double slash (//) between dwellings and a single slash (/) between family units.

The value of the 1841 enumeration lies in two factors. This is the first census for which nominal lists were retained for the entire country, and it predates civil registration by fourteen years. Relationships and birthplaces may be obscure, but the household groups still can assist with family reconstruction.

To a greater extent similar benefits can be found in the 1851 census, also nominal and also predating civil registration, but with the addition of relationships and accurate ages and birthplaces (figure 4-1). It, and succeeding returns, are therefore considerably more useful. The enumerator requested the actual present age of each individual and did not round off the response. Neither was the birthplace reduced to a minimally useful single letter, although the answer recorded may be less precise the further away it was from the place of enumeration. For those born locally, the parish and county should be indicated; otherwise, only the county name or the other part of Britain, such as Ireland, might appear. An important addition is the relationship of each person to the head of the household, so you can now distinguish between the family members and the lodgers and servants (some terms, e.g., in-law, were not always used in the clearly defined sense that is understood today). Marital status is also given, and in those instances where gender is not obvious from a name, the ages are noted in separate columns for males and females. As with the 1841 census you will find the address, sometimes with the street number, and the occupations of those in the household. Some additional pieces of information change in the various censuses. These supplementary bits and pieces, together with dates of enumeration, are summarized in table 4-1.

As you consider the research that you will undertake in census records, remember to investigate the possibility that fragments of pre-1841 returns survive for your places of interest. In some instances, the local enumerator (usually the schoolmaster) went beyond his instructions and zealously recorded all names, places of residence and occupations. To check whether any of these fragments survive for a selected area, consult one or more of three finding aids: *Local Census Listings 1522-1930* (Gibson and Medlycott, 1997), the first two appendices to *Pre-1841 Censuses and Population Listing in the British Isles* (Chapman, 1992), and "Pre-1855 Communion Rolls and Other Listings in Kirk Sessions Records" (Bigwood, 1988). Approximately fifty communities from eighteen counties have some surviving parts of the 1801-1831 returns.

GENERAL REGISTER OFFICE FOR SCOTLAND
RECORDS ENTERPRISE

CENSUS INFORMATION

District Name: Denny
District No: 473b

Year: 1851

Enumeration Book No: ___

Schedule: ___

Road, street etc. and no. or name of house	Name and surname of each person	Relation to head of family	Condition as to marriage	Age	Rank, profession or occupation	Where born (Parish & County)	Any other information
Broad Yett	Mary Russell	Head	Wid	55	Annuitant	Denny Stir.	
	James Russell	Son	Unm	38	Farmer of 30 acres	" "	
	Christina Russell	Dau.	"	31	—	" "	
	David Bennie	Serv.	"	15	Farm labourer	Clackmannan	
	Christian Libbald	Serv.	"	46	House Servant	Polmont. Stir.	

1841 - Ages mostly rounded down to nearest 5 years

Mar : Married
Unm : Unmarried
Wid : Widow

Figure 4-1. Census Information Form.

Note: An annuitant is one who receives an annuity or some form of pension income. Note that for the servant born out of the county, the parish is not given. Census forms like this one can be purchased at New Register House. Crown copyright design reproduced with permission of Her Majesty's Stationery Office (HMSO) and General Register Office (GRO).

TABLE 4-1
Census Dates, Additions, and Deletions

Date of Enumeration	Changes
7 June 1841	
31 March 1851	Accurate ages given Marital status added Details of birthplace included Relationship to head of household added Whether blind, deaf, or dumb added
8 April 1861	Whether blind, deaf, or dumb removed No. of children 5-15 attending school added No. of rooms with 1 or more windows added More detail in the parish description added
3 April 1871	Whether blind, deaf, or dumb restored Whether imbecile or idiot or lunatic added Whether unemployed added Age range of children in school (or educated at home) altered to 6-18
4 April 1881	Scholar now recorded in the occupation column Even more parish details added
5 April 1891	Notes Gaelic and English speakers Employment status is shown (employer, employee, self-employed)

Table 4-2 lists counties with no surviving fragments. Compare any entry of interest to the appropriate heading in the Locality section of the Family History Library Catalog (FHLC) under SCOTLAND, COUNTY, PLACE—CENSUS. To discover what exists in local custody, write or e-mail the nearest library or archives to inquire about any pre-1841 returns.

TABLE 4-2
Counties for Which No Pre-1841
Official Census Fragments Survive

Argyll*	West Lothian (Linlithgow)*
Bute*	Nairn
Caithness	Peebles
Clackmannan	Ross*
Cromarty	Selkirk*
Dumbarton*	Shetland*
Kinross	Stirling*
East Lothian (Haddington)	Wigtown*

*Indicates that other local returns (e.g., Communicant Rolls) survive.

This summary is based on listings in Gibson/Medlycott (1994), Chapman (1992), and Bigwood (1988).

The abstracts—or summaries—of the part of the statistics gathered from parish registers in the initial 1801 census can be viewed on microfilm. The abstracts make for interesting reading because they give an indication of the growth or decline of an area. Each parish was to report the numbers of burials, baptisms, and marriages in various formats since 1700. Sadly, the odds of examining this for your parish are one in ten. The officials reported that no more that 99 parishes out of the 890 parishes in Scotland which made returns actually had regular registers. For more on the value of statistical evidence, see *Census Records for Scottish Families at Home and Abroad*.[1]

If you are searching coastal communities, pay attention to how the enumeration of fishermen and sailors was dealt with in each census. A sailor on board his ship in its home port on census night will be found in the shipping lists at the end of the district. However, if the vessel was at sea or in another port there is a problem, especially prior to 1861. Details of persons on board merchant vessels were recorded and deposited at the next British port of call, where they remained, along with the lists of those on board any vessels in that port on census night. This obviously creates problems when the next port of call is unknown, although the home port of any ship is given.[2] Sailors in foreign waters on board Royal Navy vessels or merchant ships were enumerated from 1861. For 1861, the Family History Department created an overall alphabetical index to the 120,000 people on British vessels. This Surname Index to the 1861 Ships at Sea and in Port is on microfiche. Look for the reference within the Locality section for England. There is an accompanying list of all the ships enumerated. Fortunately, shipping indexes have been included in the 1881 census index project as a distinct segment. So, for 1861 and 1881 it is not necessary to know the name of the seaman's ship. An interesting bonus detail for ships on the high seas is their exact position, i.e., longitude and latitude, at midnight on census day.

The census returns for Scotland are found in the Family History Library (FHL) of The Church of Jesus Christ of Latter-day Saints (LDS) in Salt Lake City and can be ordered on microfilm to be sent to any family history center. Census returns are also in the General Register Office (GRO), New Register House, Edinburgh. In addition, regional archives and many libraries in Scotland, particularly the main library in a town or district, have the films for the local area. The holdings of any archives or library can be ascertained by consulting *Census Records for Scottish Families at Home and Abroad* (Johnson, 1997), *Census Returns 1841-1891 in Microform* (Gibson and Hampson, 1994) and *Exploring Scottish History* (Cox, 1999). Guides issued by regional family history societies are another source of information on local holdings.

Using the Census

Deciding how to access census data for one or more parishes or districts is influenced by efficiency, time, and cost. Some things to keep in mind are the charges incurred in bringing films to the nearest family history center; the daily user fee at New Register House, at least a part of which will be reflected in the charges made by any agent in Edinburgh; fees charged by private research agents in Scotland or in Salt Lake City; and, fees assessed by archives and libraries in Scotland. Finally, consider the distinct advantage in doing this research yourself. You are best qualified to watch for any other relevant information beyond the family entry which is the object of the search.

Using finding aids is efficient. A nominal index could put you right on the mark immediately. If address information is correct, a street index can do the same. With the main entry pinpointed, time is available to search the neighborhood for relatives or for background information about socio-economic conditions.

Begin by investigating what has been done for your parish—what nominal indexes are available and how they are arranged. The 1881 Census Index is on fiche in LDS family history centers and can be purchased on CD-ROM. The GRO has indexed the 1891 census. Work is ongoing in many areas for parts of other enumerations. If you do not already know what is available through membership in a family history society, consult *Scottish Census Indexes 1841-1871* (Murray, 1995) and *Marriage and Census Indexes for Family Historians* (Gibson and Hampson, 1998). Is there a street index? Street indexes are available for the larger towns and cities (usually those of about 40,000 or more) and can be consulted at family history centers. For those of you who are researching Glasgow, additional assistance in sorting out street names is provided in a recent publication of the Glasgow and West of Scotland Family History Society: *A Guide to Glasgow Addresses, 1837 to 1945.* (Miller, 1995). This publication is a key to identifying street name changes and newer street names which incorporated other names, a common occurrence as the city grew.

The 1881 census index is very useful because of the detailed listings (full name, age, relationships, marital status, place of enumeration, occupation, place of birth, head of household) arranged in four section (see Table 4-3). The CD-ROM version consists of a single alphabetical index on eight disks and regional sections on the remaining sixteen. The fiche format is arranged in county sections. Try both as these differences favor certain types of searches; e.g. start with the national index on disk if the location is unknown and the name uncommon.

Each of these indexes is grouped by county. Several Scottish counties had small enough populations at the time that an entire index is on one fiche, so the set of all four sections occupies only four fiche. In these cases, you may want to consider purchasing the fiche from the GRO. It would be prohibitively expensive to acquire even one set for heavily populated counties.

This series of indexes can transform a search of frightening scope into something that is actually possible. The object of the search could be someone with a common name, whether a post-1881 emigrant or the relative of an emigrant who was already in North America. After selecting the county or counties to search, begin by finding the name in question in the Surname Index. There may be several possibilities. Next, look at the listings for these names in the Birthplace and Census Place sections which may, because of the geographic grouping, suggest other possible family members. The final index, Census-as-Enumerated, will reveal who was at the same address on census night. From it, you select the record or records to be viewed (film and page number are on the fiche). For a more complete explanation of the use of these indexes, read the leaflet which describes this finding aid (*1881 Census Indexes Research Online*, 1996), and *British 1881 Census Project Nears Completion* (Federation of Genealogical Societies *Forum*, Spring 1995). The former clearly states the use of each section, content, arrangement, and cautions, while the latter explains the strategic use of the different indexes.

TABLE 4-3
Sections of the 1881 Census Index

Index Type	Arrangement	Basic Purpose
Surname Index	Surname, forename, age (always descending).	Initial selection of individuals to be considered.
Birthplace Index	Surname, birthplace, forename, age.	Used to identify people of the same surname born in the same parish or county.
Census Place Index	Surname, census place, forename, age.	Used to identify people of the same surname living in the same census district.
Census-Record-as-Enumerated Index	Census place, address, surname, forename.	Used to sort out people at the same residence.

Some or all of your census work will be done without the aid of indexes. However, for all but the larger cities, identifying the correct film is a simple matter of consulting the FHLC which now, under each parish listing, includes the census films and the parish number (see figure 4-2). Do not be put off because the place is large and no accurate address is known. If you can identify the parish or district, you select the film in the same manner as for a rural area. If a street index exists for your community (arranged by census year, town, and with streets in alphabetical order), your choice of films will be narrowed. Street indexes are on film, and the Locality entry for a city or town shows the film number. Compare the information from the street index to the details in the finding aid for the Scottish census (the fiche version is identified in appendix A, table A-2).

A word should be said about the search process in Edinburgh. The 1881 and 1891 census indexes are there, as are the street indexes. For other searches, here too it is necessary to know the district number, which may be found in volumes in the search room. One small point which may be confusing is that in Edinburgh a different parish/district number is used for the 1851 census. This creates no real problem as the volumes for looking up the place name for a particular census are clearly labeled, so for 1851 just be sure to look it up—it will not be the same number used for 1861. In the LDS arrangement, the number for 1851 is ignored and never used. If you want to know the 1851 number, it is easy to locate it in the *Detailed List of the Old Parochial Registers of Scotland* (1872). This document is on microfilm and shows both numbers.

Strategy, Tips, and Pitfalls

Embark on a census search with an objective. Understand whether it is a fishing expedition to catch all entries of one surname, a broad-based search for a specific person, or a specific check defined by name, date, and location. Answering several questions can help you to sort this out:

- What name or names are to be noted, and what are the possible spellings?
- Is a name common in the search area?
- On what basis was the census year selected? Is it the best choice?
- On what basis was the location selected and with what degree of certainty?

```
              Family History Library Catalog 23 Feb 1996    *   Page 1
                            **Full Display**

AUTHOR
Scotland.  Census Office.

TITLE
Census returns for Dun (parish 281), 1841-1891.

FORMAT
on 8 microfilm reels ; 35 mm.

NOTES
IN Census returns 1841 ... [et al.] / Scotland.  Census Office.
Microfilm of original records in the New Register House, Edinburgh.
A film may contain more than one parish.
                                                            BRITISH
CONTENTS                                                    FILM AREA
1841  ------------------------------------------------------ 1042673
1841  (another filming) ------------------------------------ 0101799
1851  ------------------------------------------------------ 1042218
1851  (another filming) ------------------------------------ 0103636
1861  ------------------------------------------------------ 0103788
1871  ------------------------------------------------------ 0103940
1881  ------------------------------------------------------ 0203478
1891  ------------------------------------------------------ 0208704

LIBRARY HOLDINGS
There are two filmings for the 1841 and 1851 censuses.  Both filmings
are equally readable.

THIS RECORD FOUND UNDER
     1. Scotland, Angus, Dun - Census


Family History Library Catalog Copyright © 1987, Aug 1995 by
The Church of Jesus Christ of Latter-day Saints.  All Rights Reserved.
```

Figure 4-2. Example of Census Return Entry from the FHLC.

- Is the place or area selected made up of one or more parishes? Which ones?
- How much is known about the individual or the family in this census year?

If the search is based somewhat on conjecture, you may have to repeat it using different parameters. Where information is lacking, you must establish limits for the search—the year or years, the geographic area, the names to be listed, and whether other limiting factors must be created to make the search manageable, such as only certain ages or occupations for anyone of a particular name. If you can use the 1881 index in any way, do so. It will certainly help provide perspective for the distribution of a name, even if ten or twenty years separate 1881 from the date in question.

The selection of a location to search may generate some thought and planning. Those who find their ancestors residing in the same parish in Scotland through three or more census returns are fortunate. Scottish ancestors moved about, often to search for work in a neighboring parish. In large cities, they moved from one lodging to another. They went to Ireland or England and returned, and they came to North America and didn't bother to tell anyone from whence they sprang.

Begin with what is known and attempt to build upon it. If starting from a transatlantic crossing, be sure that you have consulted all possible sources in North America of place of origin. A census return on this side of the Atlantic could be invaluable (see figure 4-3). If no place can be discovered that way, consider what you know about the family that emigrated. How many family members might appear in church registers or civil registration records in Scotland before departure? If the surname is common, can the combination of several Christian names coupled with that surname in a family unit be used to improve the chances of recognition? Remember that civil registration indexes begin in 1855, and that the Scottish Church Records index, the Old Parochial Register Index©, and the International Genealogical Index (IGI; see chapter 5 and appendix B) are all excellent national finding aids. Are any identified family members known to have remained in Scotland around whom you could form a research plan?

Vague geographic clues combined with the choice of a census year which lacks an index make a search more difficult. Before embarking on a

CENSUS RECORD SHEET

date of census __1861__   Ref.No. __C1044__

Province: __Ontario__   County: __Leeds__

Town or Village __Brockville__   Road/Street/etc. __EastWard__

Date of Search __23 Oct '95__   Scope __EastWard only__   Condition of Record __good__

Name and Surname of Each Person	Rela-tionship	Status	Age of M	Age of F	Occupation	Birthplace	Religion
WARDROP John	head	m	43		Contractor	Scotland	FreeChurch
Catherine	wife	m		38		Scotland	"
Euphemia	dau.	s		18		Scotland	"
Robert	son	s	16			Ireland	"
Janett	dau.			14		Ireland	"
Alexander	son		12			Scotland	"
Catherine	dau.			8		Scotland	"
Margaret	dau.			6		Scotland	"
Ellen	dau.			4		Canada	"
John	son		1			Canada	"

Note how the birthplaces of the children identify the years the family was in Scotland, Ireland, and Canada.

Figure 4.3. 1861 Census Return, Brockville, Ontario.

lengthy and possibly futile search through many census returns, examine the usefulness of other records. Once again, the most obvious ones are the indexes to civil registration and the parish register indexes. Directories, valuation rolls, and tax records may also help. Some cities or towns have unique records which could be of use. The Glasgow poor records are an excellent example (see chapter 10). In other words, pause long enough to do your homework, and be sure it includes consulting maps. Obtain a map of the parish boundaries and one for the abutting counties. Be alert to the fact that some parishes straddle county boundaries, but the enumeration for the entire parish will be within the county which included the larger part. In circumstances where you need to build a list of possible names, select a focal point and work methodically outward from there.

Always try to follow a family through more than one census over two, three, or four decades to compare their answers each time. Watch for inconsistencies in ages, children born in different locations, or the presence of a elderly relative, whose birthplace may be a bonus clue. The accuracy of any record is only as good as the information supplied by the informant. If the head of the household gave the answers for other members in one census and got it wrong, you could be working from incorrect data, which may have been given accurately to the enumerator of a subsequent census.

There are several possible explanations as to why an expected record fails to turn up. The individual could have been away census night. The authorities did not ask about absentees as these people would be enumerated at the temporary lodging. For a few locations, a return may simply not exist or the ink may have faded to the extent that the return is not readable. You may have missed the entry because you did not recognize it. Reconsider the possible spelling variations and name alterations. Include in this consideration that a single mother and her child will appear under different names in two returns if she married in the intervening period. Are you looking in the right place? Be prepared to go forward or back one census, to alter the scope of the search, or to check other sources.

If your own direct ancestors are proving elusive, it may be possible to work through the family of a sibling or other close relative. It may be easier, also, if a relatively common surname is offset by an unusual Christian name.

Directories and Electoral Rolls

Long runs of directories can be found for the major cities and towns of Scotland. The Mitchell Library, for example, holds nearly every directory for Glasgow since the first one appeared in 1783. Microfiche copies of these directories are available in the FHL. For the rest of Scotland, directories earlier than the middle of the last century are in short supply. It was not a paying proposition to produce a directory for an area where few people would subscribe or subsequently purchase the publication. Individuals named in these earlier volumes are probably confined to merchants, professional people, more prosperous farmers, and landowners. When consulting directories be sure to read carefully the full description of the contents in the front, examine the layout, and remember that there was a time lag between the time the information was collected and when it appeared in print.

The most obvious fact found in a directory is the address. By the last quarter of the nineteenth century, many more directories were available and they include more people. Hence, they can be viewed as a likely source of an address. If, for example, you particularly want to locate an 1861 or 1871 census record and members of the family failed to produce a birth, marriage or death in, or close to, those years, directories are a logical source to check for a new location.

Other information would include occupation, home and business locations, and good descriptions of the community. The town description may supply useful information, such as the various churches and their denominations, schools, burial grounds, major industries and businesses, and estates. A directory search can be rewarding, whether or not it is a necessary preliminary to a census search, or even if you do not expect to find a humble ancestor within its pages. With the help of a map, you can pinpoint a location, identify cross streets, and pick out features of the neighborhood. It may be possible to identify the neighbors.

A check of the FHLC Locality section at all three levels will elicit what is in that collection. Compare this to what is held by the regional archives or library.

As researchers are always on the lookout for lists which predate civil recording of births, marriages, and deaths, early directories are worthy of note. *In Search of Scottish Ancestry* (Hamilton-Edwards, 1983) includes a list of those lists published before 1860. Two have already been mentioned—*Directory to Gentlemen's Seats, Villages, etc., in Scotland* (Findlay, 1843), and *A Directory of Land Ownership in Scotland circa 1770* (Timperley, 1976). Findlay's book is two complete listings, one alphabetical by the name of the village or estate, and the other by occupant (see figure 4-4). Both of these volumes are available in the FHL, and Findlay's has been reproduced on film and fiche.

Another possible method of checking the presence of an ancestor in a particular community is to consult the voters' lists. The first parliamentary reform bill was passed in 1832. This was a very tentative step toward universal adult suffrage. It took two more such bills in 1868 and 1884 and the Householders of Scotland Act of 1881 to significantly extend the list of male voters and to put women on any lists at all at the local and county council level. Universal suffrage did not occur until 1930. Before 1832, those who were entitled to vote in parliamentary elections were required to meet a property value qualification, which excluded most of the population. The first change in 1832 set the property limit at £10.

Despite the limitations in their scope, voting lists can be useful. First, they were made up on an annual basis; thus, they provide a means of checking how long someone remained in one place. Before 1918 the register explains the qualification to vote. You will find the occupations of those named, whether they are owners or tenants, and property descriptions. Women, able to vote in local elections from 1882, were listed separately. They had to meet the property qualifications and be either unmarried or not living with their husbands.[3] If you are interested in more detail on the reform bills and changing qualifications, read the introduction to *Electoral Registers Since 1832* (Gibson and Rogers, 1989).

From the Union in 1707 until the first Reform Bill in 1832, the vote in the countryside (as opposed to the burghs) was much more restricted in Scotland than in England and Wales. There were fewer than 3,000 voters in 1788 and every one of them, along with the way each voted, was listed in *A View of the Political State of Scotland in the Last Century* (Adam, 1887), which can be found in the LDS collection on microfilm. Similar volumes described the results in 1790, 1811, and 1820. Who voted and how they cast their ballots could be recorded because the vote was public. The secret ballot was not introduced until 1872.

By Place

Villages, Seats, &c.	Post-Town.	County.	Occupants, &c.
Delaies	Nairn	Nairn	Mrs C. Simpson
Delvine House	Dunkeld	Perth	Sir J. M. M'Kenzie, Bt.
Denain	Inverness	Inverness	William Baillie
Denbie House	Ecclefechan	Dumfries	Richard Hetherington
Denbrae House	St Andrews	Fife	Mrs Wemyss
Denboig House	Newburgh	Fife	Mrs Stewart
Denhead	St Andrews	Fife	Village
Denhead	Coupar-Angus	Perth	David Duncan
Denmore	Aberdeen	Aberdeen	George C. Moir
Dennyholm	Denny	Stirling	William Knox
Dennyloanhead	Denny	Stirling	Village
Denock	St Andrews	Fife	T. E. MacRitchie
Denovan	Aberdeen	Aberdeen	William Simpson
Denorulough	Denny	Stirling	Rev. John Dempster
Denny Manse	Denny	Stirling	James G. Adam
Denovan	Peterhead	Aberdeen	William Arbuthnot
Dens	Dunkeld	Perth	Alexander Stewart
Derrall	Ballochroy	Argyle	Village
Derrvuich	Mosaut	Aberdeen	Sir F. Storin, Bart.
Derry Cottage	Tarland	Aberdeen	Sir F. Storin, Bart.
Desery Shiel	Cullen	Banff	Rev. George Innes
Deskford	Ballindalloch	Banff	James Stewart
Deskie	Forfar	Forfar	James Marnie
Deuchar	Aberdeen	Aberdeen	John Blackie
Devaraha	Alloa	Clackmannan	Village
Devon	Dollar	Perth	William Patton
Devonshaw House	Tillicoultry	Clackmannan	Village
Devonside	Ford	Mid-Lothian	Village
Dewartown	Strathaven	Lanark	Rev. Walter M'Leay
Dhucraig	Uphall	Linlithgow	Walter Paris
Dichmont	Lesmahago	Lanark	Village
Dillar Burn	Melrose	Roxburgh	John Murdoch
Dingleton	Portpatrick	Wigtown	A. Maxwell
Dinvin	Lockerbie	Dumfries	Rev. John Ainslie
Dinwiddie Lodge	Haddington	Haddington	Patrick Small
Dirleton Manse	Kirkmichael	Perth	Rev. Dr Geo. Morrison
Dirnanean	Aberdeen	Aberdeen	William Stephen
Diablair	Summerhill	Aberdeen	Evan Baillie
Diablair	Inverness	Inverness	David Fraser
Dochfour	Inverness	Inverness	Alexander Nisbet
Dochgarroch	Lauder	Berwick	Rev. Dr Andrew Mylne
Dods	Dollar	Clackmannan	Robert Haig
Dollar Manse	Dollar	Clackmannan	Anthony Murray
Dollarfield	Crieff	Perth	M'Nab, Brothers, & Co.
Dollarfield	Menstry	Clackmannan	Rev. Dr Alton
Dolla (Distillery)	Noblehouse	Lanark	Richard M'Kenzie
Dolphinton Manse	Dolphington	Haddington	Village
Dolphinton House	Tranent	Haddington	Patrick Firie
Dolphinton	Old Aberdeen	Aberdeen	Village
Don Cottage	Crossgates	Fife	Village
Donibristle	Aberdour	Fife	Grieve & Nasmyth
Donibristle (Colliery)	Aberdour	Fife	Earl Moray
Donibristle Park	Ayr	Ayr	Peter Murdoch
Doonpark	Castle Douglas	Kirkcudbright	John F. Ireland
Doonholme	Ayr	Ayr	William Crawford
Doonside	Inverness	Inverness	Rev. D. Fraser
Dores	Strontian	Inverness	Rev. Ranald Rankin
Dorlin			

By Occupant

Occupants, &c.	Villages, Seats, &c.	Post-Town.	County.
Russell, James	Newtown of Lathisk	Freuchie	Fife
Russell, James	Aden House	Mintlaw	Aberdeen
Russell, James	Kinmid	Linmly	Inverness
Russell, Rev. Robert	Yarrow Manse	Selkirk	Selkirk
Russell, Robert	Hayston	Cupar	Fife
Russell, Robert	Seggie	Milnathort	Kinross
Russell, Walter	Kincraig House	Elie	Fife
Russell, William	Glenduckie	Newburgh	Fife
Russell, Mrs	Kincraig	Elie	Fife
Russell, Miss Isabella	Knottyholm	Canonbie	Dumfries
Rust, Rev. James	Hownam Manse	Elon	Aberdeen
Rutherford, Rev. G. B.	Manse of Slains	Kelso	Roxburgh
Rutherford, George	Channelkirk	Melrose	Roxburgh
Rutherford, Rev. James	Sunnyside	Lauder	Berwick
Rutherford, James	Violet Bank	Annan	Dumfries
Rutherford, Miss J.	Ashiantly Castle	Kirkmichael	Perth
Rutherford, Aw., M.P.	Craiglehall	Cramond	Linlithgow
Rutherford, Wm. Oliver	Edgerton	Jedburgh	Roxburgh
Ruthven, Lord	Freeland	Bridge of Earn	Perth

S

Occupants, &c.	Villages, Seats, &c.	Post-Town.	County.
Sadler, Thomas	Norton Mains	Ratho	Mid-Lothian
Sage, Rev. Donald	Resolis Manse	Cromarty	Cromarty
Saltoun, Lord	Philorth	Fraserburgh	Aberdeen
Saltoun, Lady	Ness Castle	Inverness	Inverness
Samuel, James	Broom House	Winchburgh	Linlithgow
Samwell, Thomas F.	Broomhill House	Lasswade	Mid-Lothian
Sanderson, David	Kirkwood House	Ecclefechan	Dumfries
Sanderson, Mrs	Augustfield	Aberdeen	Aberdeen
Sandford, E. D.	Ardgaith	Kirkcaldy	Fife
Sandilands, Capt. W.	Barneyhill	Dunbar	Haddington
Sandilands, Wm. N.	Couston	Bathgate	Linlithgow
Sandison, William	Auchencloch	Slene	Aberdeen
Sands, Thomas	Swanbister	Kirkwall	Orkney
Sangster, Rev. John	Gerald	Haddington	Haddington
Sawers, Peter	Nether Kirkfield	Neilston	Renfrew
Scarlett, Hon. R. C.	Paydale House	Fort-William	Inverness
Scarth, Robert	Over Innins	Kirkwall	Orkney
Schuler, Arthur	Townhead	Loanhead	Mid-Lothian
Sclater, James	Kalridale	Dornan	Sutherland
Scobie, Mrs Mackay	Ardvar	Asgat	Sutherland
Scobie, Miss H. C.	Greenwells	Melrose	Roxburgh
Scoon, William	Glendouglas	Jedburgh	Roxburgh
Scotland, John	Tullich	Ballaborrow	Banff
Scott, Adam	Glasshellie	Lochcarron	Ross
Scott, Alexander	Craiglockhart	Fort-Augustus	Inverness
Scott, Alexander	Bonkle Manse	Slateford	Mid-Lothian
Scott, Rev. Andrew	Ettrick Bank	Wisham	Lanark
Scott, Andrew	Maleny	Selkirk	Roxburgh
Scott, Carteret George	Hawkhill	Balerno	Lanark
Scott, Charles C.	East Dairy	Largs	Ayr
Scott, David	Inverry	Edinburgh	Mid-Lothian
Scott, Donald	Newton	Chance Inn	Forfar
Scott, Firmaurice	Seggieden	Innergarry	Perth

Figure 4-4. Directory to Gentlemen's Seats, Villages, etc. in Scotland (by James Findlay, Edinburgh, 1843).

The names of electors may appear in lists of freeholders, in lists of voters, or in poll results. Some are regarded as national resources and others as local, so the FHLC Locality entry may appear under either the county or the burgh name, with the topic heading of Voters' Registers. To assess the survival and availability of these records in Scotland, use the resource guides found in the bibliography.

For your purposes, the actual necessity to consult these sources may never arise; however, rather than completely ignore them, consider how they might add to what you already know. There are other lists of inhabitants or heads of households which better fall under the heading of taxes; they are covered in chapter 9.

Newspapers

Newspapers have long been used for their fund of factual information. Dipping into old newspapers is akin to lifting the lid of an ancient trunk in the attic. There is a fascinating mix of fact, opinion, and odd detail which throws considerable light on the lives and viewpoints of our ancestors and their communities. Content and opinion, dictated as they were by a desire to sell newspapers, can become an object of study in themselves. Three small publications are worth reading—*Family History From Newspapers* (McLaughlin, 1992), *Newspapers and Local History* (Murphy, 1991), and *An Introduction to Using Newspapers and Periodicals* (Chapman, 1993). Although not written from a Scottish perspective, they provide historical background and advice on how to make the most of old newspapers.

Scottish publications are described in detail in *The Waterloo Directory of Scottish Newspapers and Periodicals 1800-1900* (North, 1989). This is available in the FHL, or check for it at major university libraries. Comments on the content and point of view of a newspaper may run to several hundred words, and publication dates, present locations, and publishers and editors names are all given.

The *Directory of Scottish Newspapers* (Ferguson, 1984) indicates the location of surviving newspaper files, and The National Library of Scotland maintains a list of the periodicals which it holds. Any one of these sources will guide your search for relevant publications, and an inquiry to the local library in Scotland will produce information on local holdings. Some journals and papers have been indexed. Two examples are: the FHL holds a copy of the index to *The Stirling Journal and Advertiser*, and *Family History Sources in Kirkcaldy Central Library* (Campbell, 1994) mentions a microfiche index to names from the *Fifeshire Advertiser* 1845-1865. Many libraries maintain indexes or clipping files for the local newspaper. A singular incident, or the name of a prominent person, or the construction of a significant building, these are the sorts of things that would have been classified and clipped for deposit in a file. The other source in the United Kingdom for Scottish newspapers is the British Library newspaper collection at Colindale in the north of London. However, a plea has gone out from this heavily used facility that researchers check regional and local holdings first whenever possible.

Scottish newspapers on microfilm can be found in large reference libraries in North America, although holdings vary. Certainly scarce are early issues of the *Scots Magazine* with which many of you may be familiar. It began publication in 1739, and for a considerable time included a section of birth, marriage, and death announcements. A long run from 1739 to 1826 is located in the McLaughlin Library at the University of Guelph, Ontario. Sometimes, much more recent copies show up in used book stores; they are worth browsing through for articles of local history.

Another possible source of information can be found within the pages of genealogical journals. On the simplest level, you could consult the journals collected by the library of the genealogical society where you live. You may have subscribed for some time to the journal of a family history society in Scotland. Have you recently checked your back issues or the index? Most journals issue one every two or three years. Finally, there is the PERiodical Source Index (PERSI), published by the Allen County (Indiana) Public Library Foundation in cooperation with the Genealogical Department of the Allen County Public Library. This index is in two parts, 1847-1985 and 1986 onward. It is based on subject and uses three basic categories, locality, research methodology, and families. It could save time and effort, either through a direct reference to your family or through a how-to article which addresses an important issue. PERSI is available on microfiche at most family history centers (a research outline is available). PERSI is also available in electronic form from Ancestry on CD-ROM and at Ancestry's Web site (www.ancestry.com).

Finally, current newspapers can be of assistance. Editors usually publish letters from overseas requesting a reply from descendants of a local person. Addresses are obtained by reference to *Willings Press Guide*, widely available in reference libraries.

Conclusion

Any one of these resources has the potential to create crucial links with other records and to provide basic genealogical facts. The inhabitants lists may be used to focus on place and time, to check how long someone remained at a location, or to confirm whether or not you are tracking the right person. The records together, and some of them alone, span a considerable period of time, and also provide insights into social history. This in itself is reason enough to incorporate them into your research whenever possible. By the time you have read the *Statistical Accounts*, a book on the history of the town or county, consulted maps and gazetteers, and gleaned what you can from these records, you will have the evidence to recreate a meaningful impression of the lives and times of your nineteenth-century Scottish ancestors.

Notes

1. Johnson, 1997, 1-2.
2. Cory, 1997, 30-31.
3. Sinclair, 1997, 127.

Summary—Census Returns

1. Select the name(s), place, and census year to be searched. Be sure to have the parish number.

2. Is this 1881? If so, use the index to best effect. If not, can it be used to search for relatives or to draw conclusions about distribution of a family name in a region? Again, if not, and if you lack precise guidelines, check for other finding aids—such as an 1851 index, or a street index. *Census Records for Scottish Families at Home and Abroad* (Johnson, 1997), *Scottish Census Indexes 1841-1871* (Murray, 1995), and *Marriage and Census Indexes for Family Historians* (Gibson and Hampson, 1998) will help.

3. Look at the Locality entry for the parish or district in the FHLC. If there are only one or two films, it is easy to search them without an index. Decide whether to order the film or to use a finding aid (you may have to apply to the custodian of the index in Scotland and pay a fee).

4. If exact information about the location of a family over many years is not available, try to use other sources (e.g., church records or civil registration) to narrow the geographic search. If you find the family in the census, always check the same location, in the census returns before and after the one being searched.

5. When the subject fails to appear in the expected location, try logically to expand the area of the search, review again the finding aids for the area, and insure that all possible searches within civil registration or church indexes have been done. It may be necessary to make lists of possible entries and try to eliminate the wrong ones. If the surname is common, look for options, such as a relative with an unusual Christian name, or opt for some reasonable delimiters—area, Christian name, combination of names in a family, age, and/or occupation.

6. If you are doing the search yourself, it could be useful to take the time to look for possible connections and to learn more of the local history. Read through the entire film with a map at hand.

Indexes to the census returns for 1881 and 1891 can also be accessed via the Web site of the General Register Office for Scotland (there is a fee). *See p. 208.*

Summary—Directories, Voters' Lists, and Newspapers

1. Jot down the specific reasons for seeking these records and add whether electoral rolls, directories, or newspapers may supply the desired information. Pay attention to starting dates.

2. Investigate what has survived and what is readily accessible, beginning with a read through the county and parish entries in the Locality section of the FHLC and a check of indefinite loan items in the nearest family history center. Then visit major libraries nearby. Thirdly, check finding aids (e.g., those in the Gibson Guide series) and other publications which list these sources (e.g., Hamilton Edwards, 1983), purchase any source guides for the regional repositories, or write to the institution.

3. Note the record locations, format, and ease of access.

5 • Records of the Church of Scotland

 f your ancestors arrived in North America prior to 1855, the Church of Scotland registers and their finding aids are the first resource to consult. The records of baptism, marriage, and burial of the Church of Scotland—the Presbyterian Church—are referred to as the Old Parochial Registers or the Old Parish Registers (OPRs). You may have heard that access is a simple matter, particularly for births and marriages. This is so because the central collection is located in New Register House and its computer search routine is user-friendly. Also, the International Genealogical Index (IGI) is available, and the Old Parochial Register Index was completed in 1991 on fiche and in 1996 on CD-ROM (Scottish Church Records). Nevertheless, problems may arise. Lost records, gaps in records, cryptic uninformative entries, secessionist groups that are not included, even invented entries—all are likely to create traps for the unwary. This chapter gives a little religious history, describes the records, and discusses possible problems in using them.

Historical Background

Until the middle of the sixteenth century, Scotland was a Roman Catholic country. Bishops, abbots, monasteries (some of you may have seen the magnificent ruins at Jedburgh and Melrose), dioceses, and church courts were the order of the day; however, the church was corrupt and unpopular. The catalyst for change was the return of John Knox from Geneva in 1559. Many years of turmoil followed during the reign of Mary, Queen of Scots. When she went into captivity in England in 1568, the new Protestant religion was firmly established. The Roman Catholic Church had been abolished in 1560. As had been the case in England and Wales a generation earlier, the dissolution of the old system meant massive destruction, including the loss of nearly all the records, paintings, and illuminated manuscripts.

James VI acceded to the Scottish throne in 1567 and that of England, as James I, in 1603. His reign was relatively peaceful, although not free of dispute. King James was a confirmed Protestant who nonetheless believed that the church should be governed by bishops. Astute politically, he accepted for a time in Scotland a system of synods and general assemblies. Once he became king of England as well, James sought to reduce the authority of these organizations and to increase the number of bishops. He died in the midst of this struggle over church governance.

Turmoil returned with the accession of Charles I in 1625. A devout Anglican, hence a supporter of bishoprics and patronage, Charles wanted to bring the Scottish church in line with the Church of England; however, he lacked understanding of the mood of the country, and he was politically inept. His complete insensitivity to the situation was revealed when he finally visited Scotland in 1633. Charles had himself crowned King of Scotland in St. Giles Cathedral according to Anglican rites and went on to appoint a new Bishop of Edinburgh. A prayer book was commissioned to be written for Scotland, and the presbyteries were abolished. In 1637 in Edinburgh, a riot occurred when the new liturgy was used at St. Giles. Soldiers had to be sent north in an attempt to enforce compliance. The Scots responded with the National Covenant, a document which spelled out the Acts of Parliament which had created, what was to them, the true religion. The National Covenant initiated a tremendous common cause amongst the Scottish people at home and abroad. Supporters came to be called Covenanters. Insensitive to the consequences of his actions, Charles persisted in the use of force in what came to be known as the Bishops' Wars, which went on long enough to overlap the opening battles of the English Civil War in 1642.

The place of Scotland in the English Civil War was complex and is outside the scope of this discussion. Suffice to say it was the Scots who turned Charles I over to Oliver Cromwell. Charles was executed in 1649, and by 1652 Cromwell was in control of Scotland. His intention was to allow freedom of worship to all except Anglicans (known in Scotland as Episcopalians—episcopal means "by bishops") and Roman Catholics, a position which angered the General Assembly of the Presbyterian Church. For the people of Scotland, the discontent was directed at the military administration of the country, and when that ended with the restoration of Charles II in 1660, the response was enthusiastic. This good will was short lived. All Scottish legislation back to 1633 was abolished, and rule by bishops returned. Three hundred ministers refused to recognize this action and abandoned their churches. Illegal services, or Conventicles, were held anywhere people could meet. Resistance grew, and positions hardened. The insurrection of the Covenanters was countered severely by the authorities. The 1680s came to be known as "The Killing Time."

Political expediency produced a solution. William and Mary came to the British throne in 1689 at the invitation of Parliament after James II had fled into exile. (James had succeeded his brother in 1685 and was openly a Roman Catholic.) Under William, the Presbyterian system was restored and the established Church of Scotland assumed control of church lands. Episcopalian incumbent ministers were permitted to remain in place if they took the new oath of allegiance. None of the bishops did. In the west of Scotland, two hundred ministers were turned out of their churches with no means of support. In other areas, where Presbyterian sentiment was less strong, transition to new ministers took much longer. The Episcopalian Church of Scotland is considered to date from 1690.

It is interesting to note that the established churches of Scotland and England were different, and both repressed the other faith on either side of the border while at the same time being governed by one monarch and one administration in London. This situation was not altered by the Act of Union in 1707, which guaranteed that Presbyterianism was the established Church of Scotland.

In the wake of the two Jacobite rebellions of the eighteenth century, persecution of Episcopalians grew. They were regarded as supporters of James III (the Old Pretender) and Bonnie Prince Charlie. It was not until one hundred years after it began, and six years after the death of Bonnie Prince Charlie, that the repression finally came to an end in 1792.

The Presbyterian Church experienced internal difficulties in the eighteenth and nineteenth centuries. In a nutshell, the dispute centered around the issue of patronage and whether or not the local church could select its own minister. A number of churches seceded in 1733, and in 1843, a large number of congregations broke away to form the Free Church of Scotland. So significant was this breach, that it became known as the Disruption. These splits had a considerable impact on the comprehensiveness of the records of the Presbyterian Church of Scotland. For the twelve years prior to the introduction of civil registration, the OPRs are unreliable because a large percentage of the population belonged to a secessionist or nonconformist church and did not record their baptisms, marriages, or burials in the OPRs. Not until 1929, did these groups reunite, when the British Parliament at Westminster gave up any authority over the Church of Scotland. A flow chart of church formations, mergers, advances and declines first appeared in *A Church History of Scotland* (Burleigh, 1960) and has since been reproduced in several other volumes including *Tracing Your Scottish Ancestry* (Cory, 1997) and *Collin's Encyclopaedia of Scotland* (J. & J. Keay, 1994).

Index Choices and Preliminary Steps

The Family History Library (FHL) of The Church of Jesus Christ of Latter-day Saints (LDS) and local LDS family history centers have indexes to baptisms/births, and marriages in four forms. The International Genealogical Index (IGI) is available on both CD-ROM and microfiche. The Old Parochial Registers Index is also available on both CD-ROM and microfiche; the CD-ROM format, which is not quite identical, is titled Scottish Church Records (see appendix B, table B-1). You therefore have the option of examining the IGI on fiche or on CD-ROM and indexes to the Old Parochial Registers (OPRs) on fiche or CD-ROM. The features of each are discussed here and in appendix B.

Familiarize yourself with all of these index forms to become aware of the advantages each has to offer; and be flexible. A limited number of computer terminals may mean you must use fiche although you would prefer to use the computer. You will discover that some things can be done in one format and not in the other, and that there are benefits to alternating between them. The indexes cover all of Scotland, although completeness varies, from the beginning (earliest registers date from the sixteenth century) to the start of civil registration in 1855, with a small percentage of entries after that date.

No matter how hard you have tried to discover a place, or even a county of origin, you may be starting your search with only a name and an approximate date, one that is much earlier than civil registration began. In this situation, a computer search is the first choice.

The reason is clear. There is no need to go through the index county by county, as is the case for a search through either index on fiche. In the CD-ROM format of the IGI, the user is prompted to select the region to be searched (in this case, the British Isles). Both computer indexes ask for the event (baptism or marriage), and the name and date. It is possible to narrow the search by filtering. In other words, to request that only those entries that match defined parameters be shown. Parameters can limit the geographic area and/or the years for the search, and specify an exact surname spelling or a combination of names in a marriage. The resulting delay before the narrowed list of entries appears on the screen may be worth the wait.

You will be able to read through all the likely entries, mark those of interest, and subsequently print them or download them onto a disk. If you are fortunate, you will find what you are looking for, one specific entry which is, in all probability, your ancestor. In that case, note the details, in particular, the source of the information, and follow up by ordering the film of the original register.

The most significant advantage of the computer format is the "parent search" option. If you find a marriage, you can immediately call up a list of all children for a couple (or couples) of the specified names. If you find a baptism, it is then possible to input the names of the child's parents to see a list of other children of parents of the same names. This phraseology is deliberate since it is possible that two or more sets of parents had the same names, in which case you must sort out the families. A child may also be missed if either parent is listed differently for an event. With a couple of keystrokes, it is possible to check for the marriage of the individual whose baptism has just been found or for that of his/her parents.

Working back and forth between searching for a single event and for children of a couple, you may be able to build families through several generations. However, a word of caution is needed. These indexes do not link events. You will see no indication that the individual baptized, say in 1751, is the one of the same name who married in the same parish twenty-five years later. Neither do these indexes point out that a child died before reaching adulthood. Using the index is a preliminary step. To be sure of your conclusions, and to be sure that you have all the information contained in the parish register, you must read it for baptism, marriage, and burial records.

The computer search may produce several likely entries, or nothing at all. In these situations you must think about what you have done and what possibilities remain.

If you have been using the IGI on computer, complete the search with a look at the addendum of new entries, and then switch to Scottish Church Records. The latter is more complete for events recorded in the registers of the established Church of Scotland. On the other hand, a first, unsuccessful look at Scottish Church Records would lead you to examine the IGI. It contains many entries from nonconformist and secessionist congregations as well as individual submissions. Scottish Church Records includes a few records of other Scottish churches, but it is based mainly on Church of Scotland registers with some births/baptisms and marriages from kirk sessions. Assuming that success remains elusive, would there be any advantage at this stage in trying a search on microfiche? There might be.

Return to your research in North America. Even if a place of origin was never discovered, the place of first settlement may provide a clue. Local history may state that the settlers were from a region, a county, or even a particular place in Scotland. Equipped with a county name, or several county names in a region, consider using the OPR Index on microfiche.

Set your outside date limits for the search, decide on the name or names, and select one or more counties. If you have already used the IGI, the format of the OPR Index will look familiar. The frames on the fiche are similar, and the source numbers used to access the film of the actual record work the same way. As with the IGI on microfiche, the country is divided into the pre-1974 counties, but in this case there are four sets of fiche per county: given name index to christenings, surname index to christenings, given-name index to marriages, and surname index to marriages. In situations where a computer search results in too many choices, the given-name indexes may provide a breakthrough. Help comes in two ways. Patronymics were in use in some parts of Scotland. The surname changed with each generation according to the name of the father; thus, the son of James McDougall would be Robert Jamieson. In such circumstances, it is easier to use a Christian-name index. In the other situation, you may not know a woman's maiden name. Scottish women retained their birth names, but North American records may not always reveal them. If a woman's surname is not known but the geographic area is, the given-name index can yield a list of names for reference as the search for the surname continues.

Select one of the four name indexes. Are you looking for a baptism or a marriage? In the surname indexes, names are listed alphabetically by actual spellings, but with all Mac, Mc, or M' treated as Mac. Copy the information you find. The source details—batch and serial sheet numbers—can be used to identify and order the film of the parish register in question, or you can look in the Locality section of the Family History Library Catalog (FHLC) to find the film numbers. The OPR Index on microfiche has a supplement known as the Addenda Indexes. These are on three fiches and contain 31,000 birth and marriage entries indexed separately. The organization is by county and then by surname, similar to the main index, except that there are no given-name indexes.

Those of you fortunate enough to be starting an index search with a known name, place, and date can choose whether to begin with a CD-ROM search. You may prefer to; however, if you know the county and parish, or if the name is uncommon, a fiche search is sometimes faster.

The IGI on fiche has its own advantages. This is the only index which shows baptisms and marriages together so you can scan through the listings for one surname, picking out interesting events for both at the same time. This procedure works best when the surname in a particular county does not have a large number of entries. You can gain an impression of the frequency of one surname in a given parish from this format as well.

Whether the search in the IGI or the OPR Index begins with well-defined parameters or just a name, identifiers and boundaries are factors. Identifiers include an unusual given name, perhaps a middle name, the names of siblings, or the mother's maiden name. You may start with some identifiers, based upon what is known about the family after emigration. You may accumulate some as research in Scotland progresses, or you may have to assume some, which may be replaced by others, as you seek to provide method and limits to a search. Keep track of the way you define each search.

This technique also applies to boundaries. They may be limitless at first if no place of origin is known, but before long in church record research you will begin to pay attention to parish names. Is your ancestor's marriage missing from the record? Why does his father not show up in the same registers? Such people may have crossed a boundary. Make sure you are aware of the names of neighboring parishes and counties and use the structure of parish and county lines to help define the stages of a methodical search. Parish boundaries are shown in a series of county maps issued by the North East of Scotland Family History Society and in the new edition of the *Atlas and Index of Parish Registers* (Humphery-Smith, 1995).

Inevitably, the circumstance will arise where an entry cannot be found in the Index. Stop for a moment to think about why this has happened. There may be a gap in the record; in other words, records for the months or years around the time of the search are simply not there. This can be ascertained by looking at the entry for the parish in the Locality section or by reading the notation in the *Key to the Parochial Registers of Scotland* (Bloxham and Metcalfe, 1979; see the note on this in the bibliography). You may have to extend the geographical parameters into a neighboring county. Consider too, the possible ways the name may have been spelled, or transposed, and that the result of human error may mean that there is no index entry at all. Finally, ask yourself whether the years of the search should be adjusted.

There is one more reason why the entry may not be there. It is quite possible that it was never recorded in the registers of the Church of Scotland. Two factors might account for this omission. The brief history at the beginning of this chapter pointed out that some registers begin much later than others, that there were times when the registers may not have been kept at all, and other times when breakaway congregations were so numerous that OPRs are not the most likely source. You can check whether there was a Free Church or other dissenting group in the parish by looking at the entry in the *Ordnance Gazetteer of Scotland* (Groome, 1883-85), or in the second or *New Statistical Account of Scotland* (1845). A second possible cause is that the event was recorded much later. This happened mainly, though not exclusively, with births, which were subsequently registered in retrospect after the beginning of civil registration. They have been combined in the Register of Neglected Entries and record events in the first half of the nineteenth century. A copy of the register is in the FHL. In Edinburgh, these events have been incorporated into the computer indexes at New Register House.

All these wonderful indexes in family history centers give a considerable jump start to your church register searches. It is always wise to do what you can before a research trip, but there are certain attractions to working in the main centers of Edinburgh and Salt Lake City. Some of the advantages of large central facilities include: no need to switch disks in and out of a drive each time you move to another part of the alphabet; the ability to check an index reference in the register immediately; excellent maps close at hand; quick transition to other records, especially census returns and directories. Scottish Church Records and the computer index to OPR registers at New Register House in Edinburgh are derived from the same origin, but there are slight differences in content and more significant differences in function. In either case, instructions are clear and the transition across 1855 is easy. In Edinburgh, all civil indexes and the OPR birth/baptism and marriage indexes are part of the same database, while the IGI gives you twenty years of civil indexes to births and marriages. The IGI is available at New Register House on microfiche.

Appendix B provides more detail on the Indexes, chapter 6 discusses the records of other churches, and chapter 11 provides a framework for solving problems. Do not forget that these resources are only indexes and some difficulties may be resolved when you read the actual registers.

The Registers

The earliest Scottish parish registers date from the sixteenth century, but only a very small number have survived from that era. Twenty-one contain entries before 1600; 100 years later, the number of extant registers reaches a significant proportion (i.e., above a third) of the just over 900 parishes in the country. The starting dates are earlier and the survival rate is greater for Lowland parishes.

Entries in the registers vary from the virtually useless form of many burial notations to the extremely valuable, incorporating details of occupation, address, and relationships. Scotland never had any directives for ministers regarding what was to be noted in the registers. This omission left procedures open to interpretation and personality. A selection of entries illustrating this variety appears in figure 5-1.

Burial, in the parish of Montrose:
With the year noted at the top (1825), three columns gave date, name, and age, but for children only the date and name were given:

      April 29   James Ford   61

Marriage, in the parish of Montrose:
With the year noted at the top (1759), two columns gave date and parties:

      July 29   And^r Ford, Mariner and Katharine
                            Ritchie both of this Parish were
                            contracted

Baptism, in the parish of Dun:
With the name in the margin, entries were extensive:

      James Ford of Finhaven had a daughter born of his wife
      Catharine Aitkin from the Island of St. Croix at Broomley
      Parish of Dun on the 5th February and baptised there on
      the 28th of said month by the Rev. John Aitkin Mrs. Ford's
      uncle of North Tarry, Minister of St. Vigeans
      named Margaret Cornelia Ford

These three transcripts are good examples, showing as they do very little detail in the burial, a fairly typical marriage entry, and the bonus detail that sometimes appears.

Figure 5-1. Sample OPR Entries.

Generally, you will find that a baptismal or birth entry (note which it is) provides the date of the entry, date of birth or baptism (sometimes both), the name of the child, and the names of the parents. Occasionally, occupation is provided. For example, among the nine entries in the register at Dun for the children of William Ford, only once was his occupation mentioned. Sometimes relatives are named, for example the sponsors, and the relationship is shown. In nearly all marriage entries, the parishes of the bride and groom are included, along with their names, the date of proclamation, and/or the date of the marriage. Sometimes included are the occupation of the groom, the name of the bride's father, and (rarely) the name of the groom's father. The unlucky will find merely the name of the groom and the fee paid. In those parishes that recorded them, and not many did, burial entries are pretty much as you see, or you may find reference to the fee paid for the mortcloth (a pall used during burial service, although not for small children, often donated by a prosperous parishioner). The kirk session collected a payment for the use of the mortcloth as a means of raising money for the poor.[1] There is better hope of finding useful information in a monumental inscription.

Missing records, caused by other than the slow start, can be a problem. Fire, vermin, and damp took their toll, but there were other causes of failure to record entries. First, there were the dissenting and breakaway congregations which did not record events in the mainstream registers. After 1843, there were more of these than not. Secondly, there was the eleven-year period when the Stamp Act was in force over the whole of Great Britain (1783-1794). The fee was set at three pence (3d) per entry, and ministers who failed to collect it were liable to be fined. There was a loophole, however. If the minister simply stopped recording in his register, he could not be fined for failure to collect. This was precisely what some ministers did. Third, there was the period from 1633 to 1689 when the church in Scotland was not Presbyterian. Many registers were not kept during this half-century.

For anyone within a convenient distance of an LDS family history center, that is where the OPRs on microfilm may be viewed. The film number will have come either from an IGI or OPR Index search or from consulting the Locality entries for the parish. Some of these entries state that the filmed records are "blotter registers." These were a type of preliminary copy, or notebook, and may be filmed when the original register has not survived.

As you work your way through the entries in a register, keep in mind that recording all the possibilities is better than having to reorder the film some months later. Read through the entire film, as this could help both with handwriting analysis and in the reconstruction of families. It may prove necessary to work out the structure of several families to determine relationships. Watch for, and note, any occupations, locations, or addresses.

Sometimes after collecting entries from one or more registers, there is not a lack of information, but rather too much, and imprecise information at that. Again, considering the family of Fords in Forfar, the problem is apparent. Figure 5-2 shows a summarized list of entries found in three different registers.

Resist the temptation to draw conclusions not founded on fact. In this list, it would be tempting to conclude that Andrew is the son of William Foord and Elizabeth Manne, and likewise, that James, son of Andrew and Katherine, born 1765, is the same person as the father of all those children baptized at Dun. These facts may be used as the basis for further search, but more work must be done to prove such points conclusively.

Many of the registers revealed additional information, such as the lengthy baptism entry shown in figure 5-1. The register volume may also incorporate burials, another possible source of help in family reconstruction. When you have finished, but before you decide that you have extracted every possible baptism, marriage, or burial entry, return to the indexes. Enter the names of couples in a parent search and check your listings against what appears on the monitor. You may have missed an entry or a child may have been born in another parish or county. You never know when a sibling may prove to be the important link to an earlier generation.

Monumental Inscriptions

Visiting graveyards is a common pastime among family historians, and when a visit is impossible, a search for the list of monumental inscriptions becomes the substitute. All graveyards have not been transcribed; many stones have been removed, broken, and worn smooth before their messages could be noted. However, much has been done and is being done to record the cemeteries of Scotland. To learn more about Scottish graveyards, their history, and the types of monuments, look for a copy of *Understanding Scottish Graveyards* (Willsher, 1995).

Churchyards have stories to tell other than those of the deceased. The churchyard area was put to good use perhaps as grounds for a trade fair or to graze the minister's cow, and many churchyards witnessed the actions of the body snatchers—those who stole the bodies of the recently deceased to sell for anatomical and medical examination. Body-snatching became such a problem that many parishes took steps to foil the criminals. They built high walls or morthouses (where the body could be locked away before the service), installed watchtowers, or used mortsafes (a locked coffin case buried with the coffin and removed much later once decomposition was well under way).

1728, June 6	William Foord and Elizabeth Manne (St. Vigeans)
1729, 28 Sep.	David, son of William Foord & Elizabeth Manne, St. Vigeans
1738, Oct. 29	Mary, dau. of William Foord & Elizabeth Manne, St. Vigeans
1759, July 29	And^r. Ford, Mariner, and Katherine Ritchie both of this parish (Montrose)
1760, Aug. 2	David, son of Andrew Ford & Katharine Ritchie, Montrose
1765, May 14	James, son of Andrew Ford & Katharine Ritchie, Montrose
1766, Feb. 14	Jean, dau. of Andrew Ford & Katharine Ritchie, Montrose
1768, Dec. 21	George son of Andrew Ford & Katharine Ritchie, Montrose
1804, 26 Feb.	James Ford & Catharine Aitkin, Montrose*
1804, 28 Feb.	James Ford & Catharine Aitkin, St. Vigeans*
1805, 30 Jan.	Charles, son of James Ford & Catherine Aitkin, Dun
1806, 28 Feb.	Margaret Cornelia, dau, of James Ford and Catharine Aitkin, Dun
1807, 18 Aug.	William, son of James Ford & Catherine Aitkin, Dun
1808, 26 Dec.	Cornelia Beckman, dau. of James Ford & Catharine Aitkin, Dun
1810, 13 June	Georgina, dau. of James Ford & Catharine Aitkin, Dun
1813, 5 Feb.	Catharine, dau. of James Ford & Catharine Aitkin, Dun
1814, 27 April	Elizabeth Duncan, dau. of James Ford & Catharine Aitkin, Dun
1816, 10 Jan.	James, son of James Ford & Catharine Aitkin, Dun
1816, 27 Feb.	Maria Hartley, dau. of James Ford & Catharine Aitkin, Dun

*Proclamations of marriage were commonly read in the parish of the bride and the groom.

Note: These are point-form summaries of the register entries. Among sources to consult next to help sort out these families are kirk sessions for the parishes of Dun, Montrose, and St. Vigeans; testaments; services of heirs; and burgh records for Montrose.

Figure 5-2. Ford/Foord Entries From Three Parishes.

The most informative gravestone inscriptions are found in the lowland parishes. The majority of highland stones were carved only with initials and dates. Burial within the church itself came to an end with the Reformation. Nevertheless, the titled and the wealthy still found ways to create their special monuments, perhaps by adding an aisle or building a vault against the church. The poor of the parish, the stranger poor (e.g., an unknown vagrant), and the unbaptized were usually buried on the north side of the churchyard.

Monumental inscriptions (MIs) are not hard to find. The Scottish Genealogy Society publishes a series of volumes for gravestone inscriptions that predate 1855, and they have a list of those that can be purchased. Sample text is shown in figure 5-3. They will also check for an individual entry for a fee. This series is in the FHL. The same society issues another leaflet, *Burial Grounds in Scotland–An Index of Unpublished Memorial Inscriptions* (Mitchell, 1991), referring to those in the society's library which have not yet been published. For other published inscriptions, consult the family history society in the area (e.g., the Aberdeen and North East Scotland Family History Society publishes several for the northeast). The family history society and the library may also be able to advise on the existence of unpublished recordings of MIs. The Mitchell Library in Glasgow maintains a typescript index to the MIs in its possession.

---

upon a flag s. side of the church. Wm. Ford esq. 3.8.1728 19.6.1816 New Style (see Jervise ms 530 SAS Lib. p. 905): Fords were at one time extensive linen manufacturers here, one of them, possibly a son of the above, bought estate of Finhaven disposed of by his trustees in 1817 - his sister married first Mr. Renny Strachan of Seton, next Mr. Duncan of Parkhill

Extracted from *Pre-1855 Gravestone Inscriptions in Angus, Vol. 2, The Environs of Arbroath and Montrose*. Edinburgh: Scottish Genealogical Society, 1979-84.

Figure 5-3. Text of a Monumental Inscription.

Though not MIs, the death notices in the *Scots Magazine*, 1739-1833, may be similarly useful, although the people listed are mainly from the professional and landed classes (see chapter 4 for more information about this magazine). The magazine is, of course, available in Scottish libraries, in some

North American libraries, and has been filmed by the LDS Family History Department.

You may find that some communities (Glasgow is an example) have what are called bills of mortality. These are statistical statements regarding deaths in a community; they are interesting, and sometimes important if they provide clues about epidemics, crop failure, etc., and thereby suggest reasons for some sudden change in the pattern of an ancestor's life. If your investigation of local sources shows such reports exist, you should note it for possible reference. Sir John Sinclair, in his *Analysis of the Statistical Account of Scotland* (1826)[2] some years after that survey was taken, was very much in favor of the registration of burials and the maintenance of bills of mortality. A few of his reasons are given here, as they give some emphasis to the shortcomings of burial registers.

- All who die are not put upon the register but only those for whom the pall or mortcloth is required. This happens only when the funeral takes place in the parish burying ground.

- It has been the custom to use the mortcloth solely for persons above ten years of age.

- As soon as it was known, that the act imposing a tax on registers, did not oblige any person to record the death, and that the only penalty for neglect was the nonentry of the name, the register of deaths, in many parishes, was totally given up.

- In a medical view such inquiries (i.e., bills of mortality) would suggest the cause of many diseases.

- With a view to morality, the information furnished by bills of mortality, would point out the effects of moral and licentious habits, the situations in which they are most frequent, the circumstances which occasion suicides, and perhaps the means of rendering such disgraceful events more rare.

Kirk Sessions

The kirk session was the lowest administrative level of the Church of Scotland. In descending order, the others were the General Assembly, the Synod, and the Presbytery. They all acted as both courts and administrative bodies. Just as in other parts of the United Kingdom, the parish was the logical unit for local administration, so the kirk session took on many civil responsibilities, in particular care of the poor. Many duties were shared with the heritors, local landowners who because of their greater wealth provided the financial support for community welfare. The session also cooperated with the commissioners of supply in rural areas, and with councils in the burghs (see chapter 9).

The records of the kirk session may provide considerable information on your family and on the social history of the parish. The session was the overseer of the morality and discipline of the parish, it repaired the church fabric, kept lists of communicants, distributed relief, and maintained a careful account of fees and fines collected or disbursements paid. Some are available through the FHL collections, although these tend to be the session records that contain baptism and marriage details. Search the Locality part of the FHLC under SCOTLAND, COUNTY NAME, PARISH NAME.

In Scotland, surviving records are available at regional archives or at the National Archives of Scotland (NAS)[3]. The NAS is turning many of these records over to local authorities, and for many it has retained microfilm copies.

Because of the potential interest and value of session records, every effort should be made to determine what survives for any given parish. This should be done even if an entry has been found in the FHLC, as more may exist than have been collected there on film. Apart from directing a question about holdings to the NAS or to the regional record office, some finding aids outline extant sessions records. The NAS sells on microfiche *Records of the Church of Scotland and Other Presbyterian Churches* (see figure 5-4). This is well worth the small investment as it indicates whether any kirk session records for a given parish are in the NAS with the classification number, and whether the originals have been transferred to a regional archives. If you want to find out in more detail what is in the collection for a parish, order into the nearest family history center the film of the CH2 repertory (SCOTLAND–CHURCH RECORDS–INVENTORIES–REGISTERS, CATALOGS). Here, the NAS holdings of kirk sessions are spelled out (figure 5-5). Armed with this information–you know what survives and where it is–you can give specific instructions to an agent, or make time-saving preliminary plans for a trip of your own.

There is another partial listing of kirk sessions in the *Scottish Genealogist*. Rosemary Bigwood compiled "Pre-1855 Communion Rolls and Other

Listings in Kirk Sessions Records" (June, 1988). Her prefatory remarks tell you that some communion rolls may list only heads of families; others give occupation, residence or even reason for leaving the parish.

Perusal of the accounts or minutes of the local sessions soon makes it apparent that parish administrators were chiefly occupied with morality and revenue and expenditure. Often the two were related. A particular interest in the behavior of parishioners frequently led to the identity of an illegitimate child's father—who could then be pressed to pay for support. Fines imposed for "antenuptial fornication" were a regular and reliable source of parish income until the early 1840s.[4] Where a parish register is missing or particularly brief and uninformative, check the records of the kirk session for such things as the payment of the fee for the proclamation of banns, or the rental of the mortcloth, which indirectly gives at least the date of the event you are seeking. In some parishes, for some years, a separate record of distributions to the poor was maintained. Penance of a couple who had gone through an irregular form of marriage was also recorded here.

---

* Edinkillie, CH2/432 [Moray]
Ednam, CH2/841
Edrom, CH2/1133
Edzell North, CH2/627[1]; OPR 285
          South, CH3/543
Eigg and Canna, CH2/780

Anything with a CH2 reference has kirk session records; those for Edinkillie have been transferred to the regional archives; there is a footnote for Edzell North with further detail; the CH3 reference is for records of a secessionist congregation. From Records of the Church of Scotland and Other Presbyterian Churches. *Scottish Record Office: Edinburgh, 1994.*

Figure 5-4. Sample Format of Entries in *Records of the Church of Scotland and Other Presbyterian Churches.*

In Scotland, it was possible to marry without proclamation of banns or the blessing of the minister. The Church of Scotland denounced these irregular or clandestine marriages and further showed its disapproval by barring the couple from Church privileges. Suitable repentance, such as sitting in church on the "repentance stool" in front of the entire congrega-

```
Reference
CH2      145. ELGIN Kirk Session


1.    Minutes   1584-1598
2.              1598-1605
3.              1613-1622
4.              1622-1629
5.              1629-1640
6.              1640-1648
7.              1648-1675
8.              1682-1712
9.              1712-1733
10.             1733-1770
11.             1767-1779
12.             1780-1783
13.  Collections  1697-1711
     Minutes        1717-1724
14.  Accounts  1780-1825
15.              1827-1843
16.  Poor  Distribution  1842-1849
17.  Young  Men's  Guild  minutes  1892-1901
18.  Sabbath  School  Library  Register
19.  Ladies'  Association  for  female  missionaries
         in  N.  India  1844-1857
```

Note: This example includes a very long run of Minutes and, for some years, separate listings of Collections, Accounts, and Poor Distribution; there is enough information to help you decide whether to make the extra effort to access it. National Archives of Scotland. Repertory of Church of Scotland Records, 1976.

Figure 5-5. CH2 Repertory—The Entry for Elgin.

tion listening to a stern admonition from the pulpit, and the payment of a fine, usually restored the couple to full acceptance. For some, the toleration of irregular marriages was inexcusable (see figure 5-6).

In parts of Scotland the notion of a trial marriage for a year was accepted as normal. Such arrangements were usually made on one of the Term Days—2 February (Candlemas Day), 15 May (Whitsunday), 1 August (Lammas Day), and 11 November (Martinmas Day). Sometimes this was called hand-fasting. If a fine was paid at the time the marriage was regularized, often when the first child was born, it would show in session records. By Scots law, provided the parents were free to marry at the time of birth of an illegitimate child, the child was legitimized by the subsequent marriage of the parents. An individual might have gone by the mother's surname at birth and later in life by the father's.

In former times, too great facilities were given to irregular marriages by the magistrates of Rutherglen, who frequently received a fee for their trouble, and even at this day a Rutherglen marriage is too easily obtained. The form is simple. The couple go before a magistrate, and acknowledge that they have been married without the proclamation of banns by a person unauthorized by the church whose name they do not recollect, and in consequence of this irregularity, they acknowledge a fault, and subject themselves to fine and imprisonment; on which the magistrate fines the parties, remits the imprisonment, and gives an extract of their acknowledged marriage, which is binding in law.

Extracted from "Report for Rutherglen in Lanarkshire," *New Statistical Account of Scotland, Vol. VI, Lanark.* Edinburgh: W. Blackwood, 1845.

Figure 5-6. A Commentary on Irregular Marriages.

When Lord Hardwicke's Act was passed by Parliament at Westminster, it applied to all parts of Great Britain and Ireland except for Scotland and the Channel Islands. Marriage could not occur without the reading of banns or a license, and only Church of England, Jewish or Quaker forms of marriage were legal. Some Presbyterians in England came north for the marriage rites of their faith. Others eloped to Scotland now that clandestine marriages were no longer legal or binding south of the border. The most famous destination was Gretna, but hasty marriages also occurred at several other places. This phenomenon ended in 1856, and it may have been concern for the impact of the railway that led the authorities to eliminate this quick marriage option for English runaways. From that date it became necessary for one of the parties to the marriage to have been resident in Scotland for at least twenty-one days. This was by no means the end of the appeal of Gretna, which was revived as a marriage mart in the twentieth century. The story is told in "Scottish Marriages" (Baird, *Scottish Genealogist*, 1979).

Conclusion

The records of the Church of Scotland are the single most important resource for pre-1855 research. Searching has been facilitated considerably by the availability of the OPR Index on microfiche and CD-ROM (as Scottish Church Records within Family Search).

Two things are essential. Become familiar and at ease with the computer and microfiche formats of the indexes. Then, be certain to identify and know the location of all surviving records of the parishes in your research, whether these records are in the FHL or in Scotland. You can then plan an effective and thorough strategy. When you require the assistance of an agent, this information will mean that you can give specific directions and better assess results.

Be careful about drawing conclusions, or considering the research complete because several generations can be readily followed in the indexes. The indexes are subject to error and you may have identified the wrong person. Always go to the registers; look for corroborative information elsewhere.

Notes

1. Lindsay, 1975, 128.
2. Sinclair, 1997, 189, 192.
3. The Scottish Record Office, at the beinning of 1999, changed its name to the National Archives of Scotland (NAS).
4. Lindsay, 1975, 123.

Summary—Church of Scotland Records

1. Identify the name or names (and variations), the time period (be flexible), and the place (as accurately as possible). Is the place a parish or within a parish of another name? Does it straddle a county boundary? What are the neighboring parishes?

2. Consult the indexes. If problems arise, check for identifiers and ask if you are employing the best index for the task. If you think the entry should be there or if clues seem to support your theory although no actual entry shows in an index, check for gaps in the record (FHLC entry or any one of the books in the bibliography which lists parish records). If a missing part of the register is not the problem, it may be human error (order the register to check), that the event took place in a secessionist church, or it was never recorded (look for alternate sources).

3. Order the appropriate film or films. If the film has been ordered using the batch and serial sheet numbers from the fiche, be sure to check the Locality section of the FHLC under SCOTLAND, COUNTY—PARISH NAME—CHURCH RECORDS to see what you might also order in the way of burial records, MIs, or kirk session records.

4. When you have extracted the entries, go back to the indexes for additional checks using the parent search option on CD-ROM in particular.

5. Write the regional archives or obtain from the area family history society any guides or finding aids for other church records, and assess your researches against what is cataloged. Should additional records in Scotland be researched, and if so, how?

6. When doing the research yourself, take time to study the microfilm carefully. What other records might be cross-referenced against it to verify the tree which is developing? If there are burials or kirk session records, have they produced any special clues to think about?

The indexes to the Old Parochial Registers can also be accessed via the Web site of the General Register Office for Scotland (there is a fee). See p. 208.

6 • Records of Secessionists and Other Denominations

he Old Parochial Registers (OPRs) are the records of the Church of Scotland, that is, the established Presbyterian Church. These registers do not include records of other denominations or records of the breakaway Presbyterian congregations.

Through to the end of the eighteenth century, the strength of the Calvinistic faith kept other denominations from gaining much support in Scotland. Other Protestant faiths which came north with the English armies in the seventeenth century, Independents, Baptists, and Quakers, made little impact at that time. The Episcopalian Church, which was for some years the state supported established church (see the outline of church history in chapter 5) was left weak and without much following because it was suppressed and persecuted for nearly a century. Roman Catholicism, left powerless at the time of the Reformation, did not return to any prominence until the arrival of so many Irish immigrants in the nineteenth century.

When Episcopalians had the upper hand, there were penal laws directed against Presbyterians, and others, designed to keep them from positions of influence, and to keep the dissenting churches weak. When the situation was reversed by William III in 1689, these laws were directed against Episcopalians. Outline histories of the dissenting churches and some interesting comments on the situation in Scotland can be found in the *National Index of Parish Registers*, Vol. XII (Steel, 1970). It states:

> As a result of the alternating supremacy of the Presbyterian and Episcopalian elements within the church, with each change the party in power enforced the penal laws against its dispossessed opponents, who had themselves been responsible for the enactment of the statutes under which they were condemned. Whoever was in power made little difference to the Catholics.[1]

Through the eighteenth and nineteenth centuries, the question of patronage versus the will of a congregation to control the appointment of a minister was a serious source of dissention among Presbyterians. Many congregations quietly left the Church of Scotland to find a new meeting house and arrange for the support of the minister of their choice. In 1843, the matter came to a head with a petition to the Queen, but there was little change. Four hundred and seventy-four ministers, about one third, broke away, gave up their churches and stipends, and formed the Free Church of Scotland (this event is sometimes referred to as the Disruption). In 1847, a large number of other secessionist congregations grouped together as the United Presbyterians. The religious census of 1851 counted more than 1,300 places of worship among these two groups and more than 2,000 that were not Church of Scotland.[2]

None of this helped record keeping. During the Episcopalian period, 1661-1690, The Covenanters did not want their baptisms and marriages recorded in the registers, and Seceders felt so strongly against having events written into the register of the Church of Scotland that they sometimes paid the threepenny tax (between 1783 and 1794) but refused to allow the entry to be made. It should come therefore as no surprise that those ancestors who chose to worship in a different manner may prove to be more difficult to find. There is, therefore, a very good chance that a search in nonconformist registers will become necessary.

Finding the Records

When civil registration was introduced in 1855, the records of the Church of Scotland, the established church, were called in. They are now in the possession of the Registrar General. Most of the records of breakaway

Presbyterian churches came into the possession of the Church of Scotland at or before the time of the reunion in 1929. Roughly thirty years later, these records[3] were turned over to the National Archives of Scotland (NAS)[3]. The NAS has also received many of the surviving records, or microfilm copies, of other denominations. The records of denominations other than the established Church of Scotland can be located in the NAS, in a regional repository, or in the archives of a particular church.

Records of these other denominations are spotty within the collections of the Family History Library (FHL) of The Church of Jesus Christ of Latter-day Saints (LDS). For the majority of parishes, there are only the Old Parochial Registers (OPRs), but some, commonly larger places such as Aberdeen, list several nonconformist registers. Peruse all parts of the Locality section in the Family History Library Catalog (FHLC). At the beginning under SCOTLAND–CHURCH RECORDS is reference to some Quaker sources.

The NAS has some copies of surviving records of Roman Catholic churches (RH21 is their reference). Records remain in local control and survival before the beginning of the nineteenth century is not very likely.

Since chances are good that you will eventually be seeking the registers of a breakaway congregation, it is important to know about the availability of these records in Scotland. Begin with the NAS, the original depository. That same microfiche guide mentioned in chapter 5, *Records of the Church of Scotland and Other Presbyterian Churches*, summarizes the holdings. Figure 5-4 again serves as an example. A further breakdown of material can be found in the other repertories within the CH grouping (for Protestant churches). These can be seen through LDS facilities; the listing is under SCOTLAND–CHURCH RECORDS–INVENTORIES, REGISTERS, CATALOGS. The various churches are split up into sections CH3 through CH16. For example, CH3 is secessionist churches which eventually reunited with the Church of Scotland (see figure 6-1). CH10 is Quaker records, CH11 is Methodist, CH12 is Episcopalian (and there are some filmed copies in RH4), CH13 is United Free Church and CH14 is Congregationalist. Many congregations are not represented in these collections, but microfilm copies for some are being added.

The place in which you are interested may not be included in the finding aid. Before deciding that there are no records for nonconformist

```
Reference
CH3
383. MOTHERWELL First U.P. Church
          (later Brandon Street U.F. Church
          and Brandon Church of Scotland)

 1. Session Minutes         1865-1889
 2.                         1889-1911
 3.                         1911-1928
 4.                         1928-1939
 5.                         1939-59
 6.                         1958-69
 7.                         1969-71
 8.              (scroll)   1928-1931
 9. Congregational and      1865-1896
    Managers' Minutes
10.                         1896-1921
11.                         1921-1947
12. Managers' Minutes       1947-71
13. Baptismal Register      1909-71
14. Proclamations           1962-71
15. Communion Roll          1866-1889
16.                         1939-1946
17. Accounts                1962-70
18. Centenary booklet       (Printed)
```

Note: *The records of this United Presbyterian Church include baptismal registers, communion rolls, and session minutes.*

Repertory of Other Presbyterian Churches, 1971, The National Archives of Scotland.

Figure 6-1. CH3 Repertory—The Entry for Motherwell.

churches, make sure you know what churches actually existed in the area in your ancestor's day. Again, the *Ordnance Gazetteer of Scotland* (Groome, 1885) and the *Statistical Accounts of Scotland* (1799 and 1845) are excellent sources (see figure 6-2). You can check further for location of records by writing regional repositories to request details of these holdings. *Data Sheet No. 6* (SRA, 1994) shows many listings, and there is also the survey of church records, a guide to holdings and locations, held by the National Register of

Larkhall, a Lanarkshire town and *quoad sacra* parish, chiefly in Dalserf parish, but partly in Hamilton. Standing 320 feet above sea-level, $\frac{1}{4}$ mile from the right bank of the Avon, $1\frac{1}{2}$ from the left bank of the Clyde, and $3\frac{1}{2}$ miles SSE of Hamilton, the town has a station on the Lesmahagow branch of the Caledonian railway, $6\frac{1}{4}$ miles S by E of Holytown. With slight exception it began to be built about 1776, and for 15 or 20 years continued to be only a small village. It then was rapidly extended, chiefly by means of building societies, but is less a town, in the ordinary sense of the word, than an assemblage of villages, hamlets, rows of houses, and isolated dwellings. Its inhabitants are principally miners connected with neighbouring collieries, bleachers, and handloom weavers in the employment of Glasgow manufacturers; and Larkhall has a post office, with money order, savings' bank, and telegraph departments, a branch of the Union Bank, gasworks, a *quoad sacra* parish church (1835; 700 sittings), a Free church, a U.P. church (1836; 700 sittings), an Evangelical Union chapel (1876; 420 sittings), St Mary's Roman Catholic church (1872), a subscription library, a masonic lodge, etc. The *quoad sacra* parish is in the presbytery of Hamilton and synod of Glasgow and Ayr; its minister's stipend is £200. Four public schools—Academy, Duke Street, Glengowan, and Muir Street—and a Roman Catholic school, with respective accommodation for 272, 81, 350, 350, and 212 children, had (1881) an average attendance of 284, 81, 422, 501, and 179, and grants of £281, 8s., £50, 11s. 6d., £351, 18s. 6d., £456, 13s., and £147, 10s. Pop. of town (1861) 2685, (1871) 4971, (1881) 6503, of whom 96 were in Hamilton; of *q. s.* parish (1871) 5332, (1881) 7063, of whom 360 were in Hamilton.—*Ord. Sur.*, sh. 23, 1865.

Note: A *quoad sacra* parish is one that is separate for ecclesiastical purposes only.

From the *Ordnance Gazetteer of Scotland*, by F.H. Groome, Vol. 14, 472, Edinburgh, 1883-85.

Figure 6-2. Larkhall: A Community with Several Churches of Different Denominations.

Archives (Scotland). They could advise on the location or survival of records (the address is in appendix D).

The Records

Information in the registers for the various Protestant denominations is not very different from what was found in those of the Established Church. Burials are less likely to be found. For some congregations, administrative records, similar to kirk session records, are also in existence.

Where there are both established church and secessionist congregations in a parish, if an entry fails to show up in the expected source, always check the register of the other. Bear in mind that a secessionist church may have gone through more than one change of faith yet have continued to use the same book as the parish register.

Roman Catholic registers are usually more informative than most. They include records of death that may show name, age, occupation, cause, and marital status. Some marriage registers indicate the home parish of Irish immigrants.[4] Unfortunately, most do not begin until the nineteenth century. Copies of some are available in the NAS which has been copying pre-1855 registers, but many remain in local custody. Boundaries for Catholic dioceses can be found in *Catholic Parishes in England, Wales and Scotland, An Atlas* (Gandy, 1993). They were not set up until 1878. If you have Roman Catholic ancestors in Glasgow, particularly of Irish origin, you will be interested in the St. Andrew's Database. This has been formed from the marriage registers of St. Andrew's Cathedral, 1808-1839. Note the dates, which are prior to the Irish famine. For this period there was no record of people departing from Irish ports for Scotland, so it is a valuable bonus that these registers indicate the parish of origin in Ireland. For further information, see "St. Andrew's Database" (Bayne, *Newsletter of the Glasgow and West of Scotland Family History Society*, Spring, 1992) or consult the Scottish Catholic Archives.

It is abundantly clear that for the majority of dissenting churches you must seek the information in Scotland. For denominations unrelated in any way to the Presbyterian Church, there could be as many as four places to check—the NAS, the local library or archives, the archives of the church head office, or the local church.

Notes

1. Steel, 1970, 102.
2. Steel, 1970, 188.
3. The Scottish Record Office, at the beinning of 1999, changed its name to the National Archives of Scotland (NAS).
4. Sinclair, 1997, 22.

Summary—Other Denominations

1. As usual, first set the parameters of name, date, and place, noting when to be flexible or alert for variations. Study maps and town descriptions for clues about active church congregations.

2. Identify the denomination(s) of interest.

3. See what is available, if anything, through the facilities of an LDS family history center.

4. Investigate overall availability with the help of the CH3-16 repertories or *Records of the Church of Scotland and Other Presbyterian Churches* (NAS, 1994). Or send an inquiry to the NAS, the National Register of Archives (Scotland), the regional archives, or the local library. In some cases you will need to write the main office or local minister of the church concerned.

5. Ask a question on the subject of the area family history society, and/or look through back issues of its journals for articles. This process is not difficult since so many societies in North America exchange journals with societies in Scotland.

7 • Disposition of Goods and Property

he inheritance of moveable goods and the transfer of ownership of land or property in Scotland, whether by inheritance or sale, involved procedure and terminology which will seem strange to North Americans. Also, the methods of accessing these records varies by record type, within record type, and by time period. Neither is there much consistency to the makeup of the finding aids; however, do not be discouraged. The required steps can be described in a straightforward manner. If you can identify the name you are searching for and the approximate place and time period, you can make an outline of the procedure to be followed.

The inheritance of moveable goods was handled separately from the inheritance of land, buildings and mining rights (known as heritable property). When someone died possessed of both moveable and heritable property two records resulted directly (though not necessarily immediately): the testament for the movables and the service of heir or *retour* for the property. Another was generated indirectly by property transfers, the record of sasine. The record of sasine also was generated when land or property changed hands as a result of a sale or when it was used as security against a loan.

Many more people had personal possessions, such as furniture, clothing, tools, or jewelry, than had heritable property. People in remote parts of Scotland and those with few possessions more often than not passed things on without recourse to the legal procedure. It follows that more prosperous people appear in testamentary records and that Lowland entries are more common than Highland.

Testamentary Records

Begin by considering the likelihood of locating a particular ancestor in testamentary records. When was it? Where was it? Was he possessed of sufficient moveable goods to have generated an official record? Some generalizations are possible. The further back in time, the lower the probability of finding a record. The percentage of the population making wills before 1800 is very small indeed. The eldest son may not appear in the testament because he received the heritable property. As already suggested, in remote parts, if only a few personal possessions were involved, there seemed little point in seeking out a court when things could be arranged without. Nevertheless, when assessing the individual's financial condition also ask yourself how sure you are of this conclusion. Do not dismiss the search too readily or forget that you can search for a sibling or other relative instead.

There are two types of testamentary records: a testament *testamentar* included a will; a testament *dative* did not, meaning the individual died intestate. Where the executor was identified in a will, his appointment was confirmed by the court. Where there was no will, the executor was appointed and confirmed by the court. The executor was usually a relative, but was sometimes a creditor. As these confirmations show reasons for appointment, those involving a relative can be useful. A careful examination of the Locality listings will show that confirmations are available on film from 1876 to 1936 and, prior to that, for some probate jurisdictions (the various divisions are explained later in this chapter). The testamentary record should include the anticipated details, such as the name, date of death, and occupation of the deceased. If there is a will, it will be part of the record, along with an inventory of goods and debts, and the identity of the executor.

The testator did not have much freedom to do as he pleased with his personal property. If a widow *and* children survived him, one third went to the widow, one third to the children, and one third to whomever the deceased wished. If a widow *or* children survived, one half went to the survivors and the other half to beneficiaries chosen by the deceased.

Research procedures for finding these records can be conveniently divided into three sections: since 1876, 1823 to 1876, and before 1823. This does not mean that for every jurisdiction the local officials stuck to these cut-off dates in their record keeping. Some of the early registers continue beyond 1823. Some volumes of confirmations, inventories and testaments straddle two periods; however, the dates involved are clearly stated whether you are consulting a National Archives of Scotland (NAS)[1] finding aid or the Family History Library Catalog (FHLC).

For the most recent period the search is an easy one, and because more people made wills in recent times, probably worth doing. *The Calendar of Confirmations and Inventories* covering the years 1876 to 1936 is in the collection of the Family History Library (FHL) of The Church of Jesus Christ of Latter-day Saints (LDS) in book and film formats. The descriptive in the Locality section includes the additional information that beginning in 1895, volumes include *"English and Irish grants of Probate and letters of administration certified, and colonial grants thereof resealed in the Commissariot of Edinburgh."* Don't ignore the hint inherent in this. Some Scots owned property in England, Wales, Ireland, or other parts of the British Empire. From 1858 (when civil probate records began in the rest of Great Britain and Ireland) to 1895, if you think there was any chance your ancestor fell into this group, you should check those indexes; from 1895, there will be an indication of this in the calendars.

These calendars are informative. They are fully alphabetical within each year, though there may be some entries in addenda at the end. A woman is listed under her married name. For each individual listed, the other details are value of the estate, occupation (if known), date and place of death and confirmation, whether testate or intestate, and the name of the executor or executrix, often including the relationship to the deceased. With this information, you can apply to the NAS for a copy of the record, including the will if there was one. If the information as to name, date, and place of death is accurate, it is possible to apply directly to the NAS, dispensing with the index search. In 1996, there is a £3 handling fee to which copy and postage charges are added.

The middle period, from approximately 1823 to 1875 inclusive, is the most complex. The Sheriff courts were created in 1823, but the actual starting dates for all local courts did not exactly coincide. For example, in Aberdeen 1827 is the initial year, while in Angus (Forfar) it is 1823, and in Edinburgh it is 1829. The area of jurisdiction of a sheriff court was in most cases the same as the county area. When the courts were created, there was one court per county except in Perth and Argyll which had two each, and in Angus where a second court was added in 1832. There is a series of printed volumes with the marvelous title *Index to the Inventories of the Personal Estates of Defuncts.* (The word defunct, which means "no longer functioning," is certainly not applied to people in current English usage!) Should the death of your ancestor fit into the times and places covered, your search will not be a difficult one. The volumes apply to the following:

The Lothians (Edinburgh, Haddington, Linlithgow), 1827-1865
Argyll, Bute, Dunbarton, Lanark, Renfrew, 1846-1867
The rest of Scotland, 1846-1867

These are in the FHL and there is a very good chance the films will be on indefinite loan in the nearest LDS family history center. The listings are alphabetical, but for each group of the same surname, the names of the men appear before those of the women. The brief entries are fairly informative because they include the county where the inventory was recorded, the year, if there was a will (i.e., testate or intestate), and the date of death (figure 7-1). This is helpful in picking out the correct entry if the name is common, or in identifying place and date details if it is not.

In these printed indexes to sheriff court records, some years are not covered at the beginning and end of this middle period. All other indexes require the assistance of an agent. The format varies, and if you want to read the details yourself before a trip to Edinburgh they may be found in *Tracing Your Scottish Ancestors* (Sinclair, 1997). As for finding registers of confirmations, inventories, and testaments for this period, check the FHLC under the county. The holdings vary.

Remember that the start date of sheriff court records was not the same in each sheriffdom. Therefore, there is not always a clean division between these records and those of the Commissary Courts which preceded them. The law may have stated that Commissary Courts ceased to exist on 1 January 1824, but this did not always happen. In some places, the records of one court continued after the records of its successor court began. You may find it necessary to check the records of both courts if the subject of your search died in the mid-1820s.

F   186   Hamilton or Gibson, Annabella, wife of Thomas Gibson, Ayr.
          47. A. 15.26.36
E   410   Hamilton, Mrs. Elizabeth, relict of Rev. Adam Hamilton,
          Kilmarnock. 48. A. 6.8.46.
H   120   Hamilton or Jamieson, Elizabeth, spirit-dealer, Irvine.
          57. A. 16.9.54.
G   537   Hamilton or Montgomerie, Lady Jane, relict of Archibald
          Hamilton of Rozelle, Ayr - died at Bath. 60. A. 23.2.60.

The first number after the name is the age at death, the letter A is the county abbreviation, and the last digits are the date of death in order of day, month, year.

Extracted from *Index to the Inventories of the Personal Estates of Defuncts, recorded in the Commissary Court books of Ayr, Kirkcudbright, Wigtown, Dumfries, Roxburgh, Berwick, Peebles, and Selkirk.* Edinburgh: Murray and Gibb for Her Majesty's Stationery Office, 1868.

Figure 7-1. Sample Entries From the *Index to the Inventories of the Personal Estates of Defuncts.*

As to the testamentary records of the earliest period, before 1824, in Scotland the church lost control of testamentary matters with the Reformation in the sixteenth century. At that time, Commissary Courts were established to assume these responsibilities from the church. The jurisdictional boundaries for each of the twenty-two courts (each division is known as a commissariot) were very similar to those of the old Catholic dioceses, which means they are different from the county boundaries. It is an easy matter to discover in which commissariot a given parish falls. You can consult the lists or plans in any one of five sources:

> *In Search of Scottish Ancestry* (Hamilton-Edwards, 1983, which has a list by commissariot and another by parish)
>
> *Tracing Your Scottish Ancestry* (Cory, 1997)
>
> *National Index of Parish Registers Vol. XII* (Steel, 1970)
>
> *Guide to Probate Jurisdictions* (Gibson, 1994)
>
> *Atlas and Index of Parish Registers* (Humphery-Smith, 1995)

If, however, you somehow fail to find one of these references, you won't go too far wrong if you turn directly to the Locality section of the FHLC. As long as you know the county, the catalog limits your choice to only those commissariots that were contiguous with it. Angus is a good example. Three commissariots have part of their territory within that county—St. Andrew's, Brechin, and Dunkeld. If you look under SCOTLAND, ANGUS—PROBATE RECORDS—INDEXES, you will see each of these listed.

The Scottish Record Society published indexes by commissariot to these records up to 1800. These are readily accessible on film through LDS family history centers. They are also available in some large libraries in Scotland, and at The Society of Genealogists' library in London. In these volumes, married women appear according to their maiden names, but they are cross-referenced to their spouses. The index will, of course, confirm whether or not there is a likely entry to be checked. Armed with the date from the index, you can turn to the registers themselves, which have also been filmed (volume and year numbers on each film are included in the Locality listing). In most cases, you will simply have to browse through the identified section, although in a few cases, a list at the beginning may shorten your search. When undertaking your search it is always worthwhile to include the index to the Edinburgh Commissary Court. This was a senior court which could be used by anyone from anywhere in Scotland and which handled the testamentary proceedings of anyone who died out of the country.

Indexes and registers for the 1801 to mid-1820s period are available, although locating them in the FHLC is not quite so simple. For those parts of the country falling within the commissariots of Edinburgh, Glasgow, Peebles, and St. Andrew's, both the indexes and the registers appear with the county listings. For the rest of Scotland (Aberdeen, Argyle, Brechin, Caithness, Dumfries, Dunblane, Dunkeld, Hamilton and Campsie, Inverness, Kirkudbright, Lanark, Lauder, Moray, Ross, Stirling, The Isles, and Wigtown) the index is all on one film found under SCOTLAND—PROBATE RECORDS—INDEXES, titled "Registers of Testaments Index, Various Commissariots 1801-1823." Finding a reference there would lead you to the county listings to check for the records themselves, and, once again, the appropriate commissariot or commissariots will be listed.

You will come across the word commissariot long after the system changed in the 1820s. The term continued to be used to describe the various districts, even though the ancient commissariot boundaries ceased to be used. The text of a confirmation from the latter part of the nineteenth century illustrates this point:

> 20 July.—Confirmation of Elizabeth Brown or Gilchrist, Greenholm, Parish of Gilchrist, who died 9 June 1876, at Kilmarnock, testate, granted at Ayr, to Janet Cameron Gilchrist, her daughter, Executrix nominated in Will or Deed, dated 7 February, 1876, and recorded in Court Books of Commissariot of Ayr, 3 July, 1876. (Calendar of Confirmations and Inventories, 1877.)

Be sure to identify a span of time which you calculate to be the time within which probate would have fallen. Note whether these years are confined to one of the three time periods (before 1823, 1823 to 1876, after 1876) or if it straddles two, consequently requiring a more complex search. Then carefully examine the Locality listings accordingly. The microfiche edition has an advantage in this type of search because it is easy to slip between the national and county portions. Table 7-1 (at the end of this chapter) summarizes the different time periods, the scope of the FHL collection for both finding aids and registers, and alternative locations. For some searches the single best option may be help in Edinburgh.

Services of Heirs

It was not possible to bequeath land before 1868. All land was considered ultimately to be the property of the Crown, so it was necessary for the heir of a deceased landholder to prove that he was indeed entitled to it. Inheritance followed the law of primogeniture, that is, the eldest son inherited or the land was divided among daughters (who sometimes are referred to as "heirs portioner"). Just as there was often a lapse of time between the death of an individual and the creation of the testamentary record, so also many more years might have passed before the heir actually sought to set the record straight. Do not give up on a search too soon; however, it must be emphasized that few people were land owners. Fewer than 3,000 met the property qualifications for parliamentary elections in 1788.

The investigation of the proof of the right of an individual to assume the ownership of his deceased kinsman's land was held before a jury. The result of this inquest was sent back to Chancery in Edinburgh—hence the other name for these records, *retours*. This procedure was also used to appoint a tutor, essentially a guardian, of a fatherless child. The records were written in Latin until 1847, apart from the years 1652 to 1659. The indexes from the beginning of the eighteenth century are very informative, but given the extent of detail that may be in the actual retour, it is recommended that you obtain a copy and have it translated. If you would like to read a good example, refer to *In Search of Scottish Ancestry* (Hamilton-Edwards, 1983).

The information found in entries of the decennial indexes to records of services of heirs is shown in figure 7-2. This series covers the period from 1700 to the end of 1859. Thereafter, there are annual indexes. The listing is alphabetical according to the name of the heir, otherwise referred to as *the person served*. There is an alphabetical list of names of *persons served to*, where that differs from the name of the heir, at the end of each volume or ten-year section, which is helpful if an inheritance involved a distant relative. These *Indexes to the Services of Heirs in Scotland* are on the shelf at the FHL (volumes cover 1700 to 1959) and on microfilm (1700 to 1860). The records themselves have also been filmed for the years 1586-1901 and each volume is individually indexed. Chancery records were generated by the national government, so the Locality entry is under the SCOTLAND–LAND AND PROPERTY section of the FHLC. If you are convinced that there should be a record but cannot find one, turn to *Tracing Your Scottish Ancestors* (Sinclair, 1990) which mentions two sources at the NAS perhaps best described as strays: List of Unrecorded Retours and Index of Retours of General Service.[2] As these lists have been placed among post-1900 records, access requires assistance in Edinburgh.

Names of the Persons Served	Distinguishing Particulars	Date of Recording
Gourlay, Robert	Merchant, St. Andrews, to his Father, Robert Gourlay, Merchant there - Heir General - dated 9th May 1812	1812, June 3
Graham, Ann	at St. Vigeans, to her Uncle William Graham in Newbigging - Heir Portioner General - dated 20th January 1818	1818, Feb. 3

Extracted from the *Decennial Index to the Services of Heirs of Scotland, 1810-1819,* Edinburgh, 1860.

Figure 7-2. Sample Entries from the *Decennial Indexes to Services of Heirs.*

You may come across the word *taillie* or *tailzie* in these decennial indexes. This is the Scottish form of the word entail, by which a land-owner stipulated who would inherit the land for generations to come. If you have landed ancestry and you find reference to this, only limited checks can be done outside Edinburgh. The FHL holds *An Accurate Alphabetical Index of the Registered Entails in Scotland from the Passing of an Act of Parliament in the Year 1685 to February 4, 1784.*

A number of other unusual words will turn up in these records. The sample entry in figure 7-3 is taken from *Services of Heirs, Roxburghshire, 1636-1847*, which was published by the Scottish Record Society in 1934. The terms are explained below.

Service of Elizabeth Marshall, wife of William Johnstone, residing at Bongate near Jedburgh, to her cousin-german John Waugh, feuar in Kelso, in his half tenement of land as particularly bounded and described, lying within the burgh of Kelso, as also another tenement of land, lying at the Chalk cleugh of Kelso, as also particularly bounded and described, lying also within the town of Kelso (in nonentry since the death of her said cousin on the 16th of July 1831).

Expede 30 July 1836 (Six papers.)   R. 12 Aug. 1836

Explanations:
cousin german: a first cousin
feuar: one who holds land in feu (i.e., in perpetual lease)
cleugh: a ravine with steep sides, usually with water (i.e., a gorge)
nonentry: not recorded

Reference was made to several sources to locate these. In addition to the Scottish Genealogist's Glossary *(Burness, 1990),* The Oxford Dictionary on Historical Principles *(Little et al, 1973) is a useful resource.*

Figure 7-3. Sample Entry From *Service of Heirs, Roxburghshire, 1636-1847.*

Should the opportunity arise, take the time to look through the volumes of the *Scottish Historical Review*. They are on microfilm (this type of browsing is best done on site) at the FHL, or you may discover that a nearby university library holds the series. The reason for doing so is that from time to time in the "Communications and Replies" column of this periodical, printed lines of inheritance appear, with frequent reference to the records of services of heirs. An example is shown in figure 7-4.

Colin Campbell of Strachur died in September, 1743 (Services of Heirs), was father of John, who succeeded, and Janet, of whom afterwards.

General John Campbell of Strachur was served heir to his father, July 27, 1744, and January 29, 1800. He died August 28, 1806.

Janet Campbell, afterwards of Strachur, married C. Campbell of Ederline, was served heir to her brother John, March 30, 1807, and died January 8, 1816.

Dugald Campbell of Ederline was served heir to his father, Colin Campbell of Ederline (died June 1780), dated Oct. 16, 1782. He married Mary Campbell, and must have died before 1816. Was probably father of Colin who succeeded to Strachur.

Colin Campbell of Strachur was served heir to his grand uncle, General John Campbell, April 12, 1816, and to his grandmother, Janet Campbell of Strachur, Nov. 21, 1821. He died June 16, 1824.

John Campbell of Strachur was served heir to his father Colin, January 12, 1825.

Extracted from *The Scottish Historical Review*, Volume Four, 234, Glasgow, 1907.

Figure 7-4. The Campbells of Strachur, an Excerpt From *The Scottish Historical Review*.

Register of Sasines

Property transactions were important, so whenever land changed hands, or even if it was used as security, the action was entered in the Register of Sasines. This register has been maintained continuously since 1617. A General Register was set up in Edinburgh and Particular Registers in the localities—in other words, in other areas of the country. Writs could be registered at either. There were separate registers for the royal burghs. In 1868, the Particular Registers were abolished and the General Register was continued with county divisions. The wording of the documents is generally long and repetitive, but often very useful family details are embedded in them.

Searching for a record after 1780 is actually quite easy, aided by the existence of volumes of Abridgements with accompanying indexes to persons and places. All of these volumes are available through a family history center or at the FHL. The persons index covers the period from 1781 to 1868 and the places index, 1781 to 1830. The Abridgements on film are for the years 1781-1868. This is not the end of the Abridgements which, along with indexes, exist for more recent years at the NAS.

To carry out this search, make the usual selection of a name, time period, and county. Whether you select the persons or places index will be determined by the objective. For example, one particular name or all entries in an area for one or more names. There should be no difficulty making a selection from among the listings of volumes of Abridgements as they are categorized by county and date. The Abridgement reveals enough that it may not be necessary to see the entire original wording (figure 7-5). The complete text of a sasine can be obtained from the NAS. It will be long and repetitive and may include Latin words.

The NAS sells a number of the indexes to persons for the registers of sasines prior to 1780. Nine of these include years after 1700: Index to the General Register of Sasines 1701 to 1720; Sheriffdom of Banff 1617-1780; Shire of Berwick and Bailiary of Lauderdale 1617-1780; Sheriffdom of Caithness 1646-1780; Sheriffdom of Dumfries and Stewartries of Kirkcudbright and Annandale 1617-1780; Sheriffdoms of Elgin, Forres and Nairn 1617-1780; Sheriffdoms of Inverness, Ross, Cromarty and Sutherland 1606-1780; Sherifffdom of Lanark 1618-1780; and Sheriffdom of Forfar 1701-1780 (the last one is on fiche). The sensible approach is to look first in the appropriate local record, either the particular or burgh registers, and then in the General Register, because it was open to anyone from anywhere in Scotland. It may, however, be easier to work the other way around. The FHL has on film the index to the General Registers from 1701 to 1720, as well as an index to those from 1617 to 1700.

For a place and time that does not fall within the indexes in the FHL or the list of those which can be purchased, there is a table in *Tracing Your Scottish Ancestors* which shows all existing indexes.[3] Prior to 1780, indexes are not available for all areas or all years. Where these gaps occur, the next best option is to consult minute books, meaning the chronological summaries, or diaries, of the Court of Session. The FHL holds minute books for Particular Registers from 1599 to 1763. Consult them when you know the county and have a fairly accurate date.

If your ancestors lived in a royal burgh, such as Paisley or Montrose, it will be necessary to look in the sasines for the burgh. Some part of these are in the FHL on microfilm. The minute books of sasines for Montrose are listed under SCOTLAND, ANGUS, MONTROSE—LAND AND PROPERTY; others are similarly placed. A list of royal burghs is in Figure 7-6. Be sure to look at maps contemporary to the time of the search so that you are aware of the area covered by the burgh at that time. What is part of a town now may have been out in the country then, and therefore be part of the main body of sasines already de-

1783.   **ABERDEEN.**   **179—203**

(179) Jul. 14. 1783.
JANET, MARION, HELEN, & ELIZABETH FORBES, daughters of William Forbes, Minister at Monedugh, as heirs portioner to William Forbes of Boindlaodach, their great-grandfather, Seised, May 29. 1783,—in BELNABODACH, par. Inverurie;—on Pr. Cl. Con. by James, Earl of Fife, Jan. 6. 1783.
P. R. 30. p. l. 112.

(180) Jul. 15. 1783.
JOHN DAVIDSON of Tillychetly, Seised, Jan. 25. 1783,—in CORRACHRIE in Cromar, comprehending Mains and Nether Corrachrie, Hole, Brachead, Muirhall, Backside, Chesy & Mill of Corrachrie, par. Logie Coldstone; Milltown of Ripachie or Ardgeith; Kippenchy, Ardgeith, Chesnetie & predicles Remalen, Whiteshaul, Craigshaw, Parkhead, Bogforlen, Broomhill and Woodhill of Ripachie, par. Migvie ; Over Kilbatho, Blackfield, Bramhill and Menavie, &c. par. Kilbatho or Towie;—in security of £614. 19s. 4½d.;—on Bond by Robert Lumsden of Corrachrie, Jun. 25. 1783.
P. R. 30. p. l. 113.

(181) Jul. 18. 1783.
CHRISTIAN LESLIE, spouse of Alexander Burnett of Kemnay, Seised, Jul. 12. 1783,—in the Barony of KEMNAY, par. Kemnay ;—in security of a liferent annuity of £136 ;—on Mar. Con. Nov. 13. 1761.
P. R. 30. p. l. 114.

(182) Jul. 18. 1783.
ALEXANDER BURNETT of Kemnay, as heir to George Burnett of Kemnay, his father, Seised, Jul. 12. 1783,—in CRAIGEARN, Salmon Fishings in Don, par. Chapel & Kemnay ;—on Pr. Cl. Con. by Alexander, Duke of Gordon, May 21. 1783.
P. R. 30. p. l. 115.

(183) Jul. 22. 1783.
ROBERT HORN ELPHINSTON of Horn & Logie, & Sir Ernest Gordon of Park, Seised, Jul. 10. 1783,—in the Barony of NEWTON or WRANGHAM, par. Culsamond; Melchside & Teinds; Superiority of parts of Williamston, Mill, &c. & Teinds, par. Culsamond ;—on Disp. by Capt. Alexander Davidson of Newton, Dec. 24. 25. 1782.
P. R. 30. p. l. 116.

(184) Jul. 23. 1783.
SIR WILLIAM FORBES of Pitsligo, gets Reu. Jul. 10. 1783, by Rebecca Forbes, relict of John Forbes of Pitsligo,—of the Barony of PITSLIGO, comprehending Tillanumult & Mill, Old Cake, New Cake, Upper and Nether Cairnywhing, Belmanoor, Fishings & Teinds, par. Tyrie ;—and of her liferent right in Disp. by the said John Forbes, Feb. 28. 1776.
G. R. 406. 85.

(185) Aug. 5. 1783.
WILLIAM ROBERTSON, in Hillhead of Cairngall, Seised, Jul. 28. 1783,—in part of a Tenement in PETERHEAD ;—on Disp. by William Rennie, Shoemaker, Peterhead, Aug. 31. 1782.
P. R. 30. p. l. 117.

rency of KNOCKLEITH, par. Auchterless ;—on Ch. Resig. by Alexander, Duke of Gordon, May 30. 1780.
P. R. 00. p. l. 121.

(190) Aug. 11. 1783.
JOHN DUFF of Hatton, Seised, Jul. 17. 1783,—in WOODTOWN, Old Mill, part of Mill lands of Seggat, par. Turreff ;—on Con. of Resumbion between James, Earl of Findlater & Seafield, and said John Duff, Feb. 21. May 1. 1767.
P. R. 30. p. l. 122.

(195) Aug. 18. 1783.
ALEX. LUMSDEN, son of Alex. Lumsden, Advocate, Aberdeen, Seised, Jul. 31. 1783,—in parts of GILCOMSTON, par. Old Machar ;—on Ch. Resig. by the Master of Kirk & Bridge Works, Aberdeen, Jul. 30. 1783.
P. R. 30. p. l. 123.

(192) Aug. 18. 1783.
MARJORY LOGIE, daughter of Andrew Logie, Merchant, Aberdeen, Seised, Jul. 31. 1783,—in part of GILCOMSTON, par. Old Machar ;—on Ch. Resig. by the Master of Kirk & Bridge Works, Aberdeen, Jul. 30. 1783 (under reservation of the liferent of Marjory Moor, relict of said Andrew Logie).
P. R. 30. p. l. 124.

(194) Aug. 18. 1783.
JAMES CLERK, M. D. Dominies, Seised, Jul. 31. 1783,—in part of GILCOMSTON, par. Old Machar ;—on Ch. Resig. by the Master of Kirk & Bridge Works, Aberdeen, Jul. 30. 1783.
P. R. 30. p. l. 125.

(195) Aug. 18. 1783.
The Boxmaster of the SHOEMAKER TRADE, Aberdeen, Seised, Jul. 31. 1783,—in part of GILCOMSTON, par. Old Machar ;—on Ch. by the Master of Kirk & Bridge Works, Aberdeen, Jul. 30. 1783.
P. R. 30. p. l. 126.

(196) Aug. 18. 1783.
GEORGE SKENE, M. D. Prof. of Philosophy, Marischal College, Aberdeen, Seised, Jul. 31. 1783,—in parts of Gilcomston, to be called FOUNTAINHALL, par. Old Machar ;—on Ch. Resig. by the Master of Kirk & Bridge Works, Aberdeen, Jun. 4. 1783.
P. R. 30. p. l. 127.

(197) Aug. 18. 1783.
SIR ARCH. GRANT of Monymusk, Seised, Jul. 31. 1783,—in BELLVILLE, par. Old Machar ;—on Ch. Resig. by the Master of Kirk & Bridge Works, Aberdeen, Jul. 30. 1783.
P. R. 30. p. l. 128.

(198) Aug. 25. 1783.
JOHN KEMP, Feuar in Gilcomston, gets Resig. and Reu. Aug. 23. 1783,—of part of STOCKET BRAE, & Teinds, par. Old Machar ;—on Proc. Resig. in Disp. by William Mitchell, jun. Merchant, Aberdeen, Aug. 23. 1783.
P. R. 30. p. l. 129.

The designation P.R. means this is a Particular Register, helpful when interested in locating the full document. From The Sasine Abridgements for Aberdeen, Volume 1, 1873, ©The National Archives of Scotland.

Figure 7-5. Sample Entry from *The Sasine Abridgements for Aberdeen.*

scribed. The NAS has quite an extensive collection of burgh sasines, but the availability of indexes is limited, mainly to the years after 1808. Consider checking with local repositories for holdings. For example, the sasines of the royal burgh of Crail to 1804 are at St. Andrews University Library. You may find that a researcher outside Edinburgh charges lower rates and has extensive knowledge of the local collections.

Conclusion

The disposition of goods and property may not have involved a very large number of people, but those people came from many levels of society, and the records have some readily accessible finding aids. The post-1876 testamentary calendars, the indexes to defuncts, the pre-1800 Scottish Record Society indexes, the decennial indexes to Service of Heirs, and the Sasine Abridgement Indexes all allow a researcher to cover a large area, sometimes the entire country, and a lengthy span of years, in a fairly short time. Where information concerning origins on this side of the Atlantic is scarce, this type of finding aid is a bonus. If you have the added luxury of an unusual surname, you can do survey searches, trolling for all references to it.

Notes

1. The Scottish Record Office, at the beginning of 1999, changed its name to the National Archives of Scotland (NAS).

2. Sinclair, 1997, 47.

3. Sinclair, 1997, 53-54.

Figure 7-6. List of Royal Burghs

This list is based on information in the *Ordnance Gazetteer of Scotland* (Groome, 1883-85) and *A Companion to Scottish History from the Reformation to the Present* (Donnachie and Hewitt, 1984).

Aberdeen	Dingwall	Inverness	Peebles
Annan	Dornoch	Irvine	Perth
Anstruther	Dumbarton	Jedburgh	Pittenweem
Arbroath	Dumfries	Kinghorn	Renfrew
Ayr	Dunbar	Kirkcaldy	Rosemarkie and Fortrose
Banff	Dundee	Kirkcudbright	Rothesay
Berwick	Dunfermline	Kirkwall	Roxburgh
Brechin	Dysart	Lanark	Rutherglen
Burntisland	Edinburgh	Lauder	St. Andrews
Campbeltown	ElginFalkland	Linlithgow	Sanquhar
Crail	Forfar	Lochmaben	Stirling
Cromarty	Forres	Montrose	Stranraer
Culross	Glasgow	Nairn	Tain
Cupar	Haddington	New Galloway	Whithorn
Selkirk	Hamilton	North Berwick	Wick
	Inverary		Wigtown

Summary—Testamentary Records

1. Set the parameters for the search and assess the precision and accuracy of known facts.

2. Study table 7-1; if necessary, gather any additional source information, such as the availability of the Calendar of Confirmations and Inventories in the FHL and in local repositories in Scotland.

3. Draft the steps to follow; include which time period the search encompasses (pre-1823, 1823 to 1876, or post-1876), the finding aid, and where the resources can be accessed.

Summary—Records of Services of Heirs

1. Establish the name, dates, and places involved in the search.

2. Consult the decennial indexes if the search falls between 1700 and 1859—available through the facilities of the FHL and its family history centers; outside that period, seek assistance in Scotland (a regional archives may have the indexes for its area well into the twentieth century).

3. Decide whether to locate the main document (these are in Latin until 1847).

Summary—Sasines

1. What leads you to believe an ancestor was involved in land transactions? Did transactions involve property close to home or at a distance from where he lived? When was the most likely time frame for registration?

2. For anything from 1781 to 1868, use the persons or places indexes and the Abridgements of Sasines, all available on film. Also, check for finding aids and records at regional archives. For example, Glasgow City Archives has the Abridgements for the region (and a separate register for the burgh of Glasgow, 1694-1927).

3. Before 1780, look at the list of NAS publications for sale. This purchase could be shared with someone else researching the same area. Also, the index could be donated to a genealogical collection in your area and so help others. If these publications do not fit, examine the FHL holdings for minute books of the particular registers, 1599 to 1793. These books can be used when date information is fairly accurate and no index is available.

4. Check the index list in *Tracing Your Scottish Ancestors* and seek help in Edinburgh; if minute books must be used, weigh the relative costs against the purpose of the search and the availability of other sources which may reveal the same information.

TABLE 7-1
Summary of Testamentary Records

Time Period	Indexes in the FHL	Registers in the FHL	FHLC Locality Locations/Headings	Alternate Location
Before 1801	YES		SCOTLAND - COUNTY NAME - PROBATE RECORDS - INDEXES	These are published volumes of the Scottish Record Society and are in major repositories in Scotland.
		YES	SCOTLAND, COUNTY NAME - PROBATE RECORDS	NAS
1801 to 1823	YES		For the Commissariots of Edinburgh, Glasgow, Peebles, and St. Andrews, the indexes are listed in SCOTLAND - PROBATE RECORDS - INDEXES and in SCOTLAND, COUNTY NAME - PROBATE RECORDS - INDEXES; for the rest of the country, the indexes are all on one film under SCOTLAND - PROBATE RECORDS - INDEXES	NAS
NB: remember, it was not an abrupt change in 1823		YES – a very good collection of testaments and inventories	SCOTLAND, COUNTY NAME - PROBATE RECORDS	NAS
1823 to 1875	SOME		Index to the Inventories of the Personal Estates of Defuncts (dates vary for periods within the years 1827 to 1865) found under SCOTLAND - PROBATE RECORDS - INDEXES	NAS - The assistance of an agent in Scotland is necessary for the years not covered by these indexes.
		SOME: Confirmations, Inventories, and Testamentary records	SCOTLAND, COUNTY NAME - PROBATE RECORDS	NAS
1875 and after to 1936	YES		SCOTLAND - PROBATE RECORDS with Scotland, Sheriff Courts showing as issuing authority	
		NO		Where the date is known within a year or two, a direct inquiry to the NAS may be quickest.

8 • Trades and Occupations

iscovering more about the occupations and living conditions of your ancestors, no matter how humble, has become much easier over the past twenty-five years. There is a greater interest in the everyday lives of ordinary people, and in industrial history. Museums of rural life with working farms using old techniques are now found in many parts of Britain. It is possible to take a ride on an old steam train, to see an ancient mill or mine in working order, or to visit a tenement in Glasgow just as it was at the turn of the nineteenth century. There is also an ever-expanding body of knowledge. Not only are there more books and articles, but genealogists are turning their attention to creating finding aids or writing how-to books devoted entirely to trades and occupations (see the bibliography).

An examination of the trades and occupations of your ancestors may lead into the study of different aspects of economic and social history. Economics was at the root of many historical events which affected people's lives. For example, the Union of 1707 had its roots in economics (the failure of the Darien scheme in South America), as did Scottish emigration to North America in the eighteenth and nineteenth centuries. Some of you will dip into the subject area only enough to learn what the occupation was; others will be drawn into histories of an entire industry, into company records, into asking questions about tools, clothing, pay, working conditions, or the impact of new machinery.

An important part of family history research is to seek understanding of how your ancestors worked and lived. For one thing, it adds a touch of reality, thus reducing the danger of romanticizing their lives. Taking time to discover what someone ate, wore, slept on, and worked at each day brings you closer to viewing them as real people, and, there is a bonus. This type of research usually turns up clues or even hard facts that can further your research.

The occupation of an ancestor, at least in the past 160 years, is not difficult to discover. It appears in census returns, in civil registration records, in testamentary records, in directories, and sometimes in parish registers. This is not an exhaustive list, but it shows that the most commonly used sources for nineteenth century research will probably reveal an occupation. Prior to the first census in 1841, finding an occupation may involve more work. The records which reveal an occupation, such as services of heirs, sasines, and testaments do not encompass a large portion of the population. You may have to address the problem by a roundabout route. What sort of community was it? Did nearly everyone work on the land or in a linen mill or in the fishing fleet? Was there a large house in the vicinity where some individuals may have worked as servants? What sort of record may supply an answer?

The divisions in this chapter are quite arbitrary. The intent is to supply sufficient information about a range of occupations in order to provide guidance for organizing a framework for your research. There are too many different kinds of occupations and businesses to give information for them all. From what is described here and your own research skills you will be able to delve into the employment history of your ancestors.

Government Employees and the Professions
Civilian Government Employees

Senior British government officials for Scotland, particularly in more recent times, are listed in editions of *Whitaker's Almanac*, which has been published annually since 1868. Here you will find Members of Parliament, judges, school principals, senior officials of government departments, senior administrative officers of towns and cities, trade union secretaries, etc. If you have never examined one of these fascinating volumes, take the time to do so. The facts cover all of the United Kingdom and Northern Ireland. Recent editions are available in most large North American libraries, but the number of back issues they hold varies. If you do not find your ancestor here but you know that he or she was a government employee, it will require help in Edinburgh to find out more. The National Archives of Scotland (NAS)[1] holds various pay, pension, and government lists (specifically the registers of the Great Seal and the Privy Seal). *Tracing Your Scottish Ancestors* (Sinclair, 1997) provides details on accessing these sources.

For employees of particular government departments, most records do not begin until into the twentieth century. However, if your ancestor worked for the Post Office or Customs and Excise, you are more fortunate. For roughly one hundred years, from 1803 to 1911, there is at the (NAS) a record of postmasters, postmistresses, and letter carriers.[2] Since the list is arranged by location of the post offices, it is necessary to know the name of the town. For the years since 1830, Customs and Excise officials are listed in the documents held by the Public Record Office (PRO) at Kew, outside London. From 1707 until that date, the NAS has records for these two departments, and a very useful resource, *The List of Members of the Scottish Excise Department 1707 -1830* (a card index), has been filmed by the Family History Department of The Church of Jesus Christ of Latter-day Saints (LDS). With respect to the more recent post-1830 material at Kew, the pension records are likely to be the best bet; however, you will require a researcher on site. For more information on the subject look at *Tracing Your Ancestors in the Public Record Office* (Bevan, 1999) or the leaflet "Customs and Excise Records as Sources for Biography and Family History," issued by the Public Record Office.

Military and Naval Personnel

A disproportionate part of the British Army was made up of soldiers of Scottish origin. All army records from 1707 are at the PRO at Kew, and several useful parts of this massive collection have been filmed by the LDS Family History Department. Before beginning a search in military records, expand your knowledge by studying the list of those held by the Family History Library (FHL). A more complete listing of this collection appears in the Family History Library Catalog (FHLC) under the heading GREAT BRIT-AIN—MILITARY RECORDS (in the fiche version of the FHLC, Great Britain is a small separate set). Compare this to books which describe the records of the British Army in some detail. Those which are generally available are listed in the bibliography.

Some of the most helpful soldiers' records are outlined in this chapter. Follow up with further reading, and take to heart the recommendation to gather all the descriptive information you can about military records. Look closely at figure 8-1, which is two descriptions of the same record group taken from two different listings, the FHLC entry and that in *The Guide to the Public Record Office, Part II* (a section of what is commonly called "Kew Lists"—also in the FHL on microfiche). This supports the recommendation that you should know all you can about what exists and how it is arranged.

W.O. 97
Royal Hospital Chelsea Soldiers' Documents 1760-1913

This is the main series of service documents of soldiers who became in- or out-pensioners of the Royal Hospital Chelsea, giving particulars of age, birthplace, and trade or occupation on enlistment, a record of service including any decorations, and the reason for discharge to pension. For the period from 1760 to 1872 the documents are arranged by regiments, including militia to 1854; from 1873 to 1882 alphabetically under Cavalry, Artillery, Infantry and Corps; from 1883 to 1913, there is one alphabetical sequence for the entire Army. Documents in this latter series usually contain fuller particulars, such as next of kin, marriage, and children.

Extracted from Public Record Office Guide, *Part II, fiche #5, Feb. 1985.*

GREAT BRITAIN - Military Records - Army
Great Britain. War Office.

Soldiers documents: service documents of soldiers containing particulars of age, birthplace and trade or occupation on enlistment, a record of service including any decorations, and the reason for discharge to pension, 1760 -1900—Salt Lake City, filmed by the Genealogical Society of Utah, 1971, 1256 microfilm reels, 35mm. Microfilm of original records in the Public Record Office, London. For the period 1760-1872 the documents are arranged by regiments including militia to 1854.

W.O. 97

Extracted from the Family History Library Catalog, February, 1994. *The lack of any mention of Chelsea Hospital in this FHLC entry may contribute to some confusion. Also, the outside dates in the LDS descriptive, 1760 to 1900, are not reflected in the listing, none of which is later than 1854. By comparing the full entry to the LDS entry, you know the scope of the entire record and to what extent the LDS film collection can help, or whether you will require assistance at the PRO at Kew.*

Figure 8-1. A Comparison of War Office Records Catalog Entries.

For soldier ancestors, you need to know the regiment or at least be able to narrow the choice of regiments to a very few. If there is no knowledge or no immediate evidence of this (a photograph or medals could be the source of this information), consider your dates. The subject of your search may have been caught in a census and the enumerator may have noted the regiment in the occupation column, or it may show up on a certificate of birth, marriage, or death. Without this assistance, and for earlier periods, you must rely on a lucky break in the indexes to the regimental registers of birth (described later in this section) or on fitting your facts with what you can find in books of military history. Do you know where the ancestor served or do you have some information about a particular campaign or battle in which he took part? Nearly every battle or skirmish of the British Army has been described somewhere, including the names of the units involved. Besides looking for a description of the battle, you could browse through any reference books which provide brief histories and battle honors for each regiment. These books are also very useful when you know the regiment but do not know much about the career of your soldier ancestor. *In Search of the Forlorn Hope* (Kitzmiller, 1987), is informative as well as being widely available. Regimental museums are another potential resource.

Many of our ancestors came to North America with the army, stayed on, and often took a land grant near the place of their discharge from the service. A reference to soldier settlers in a local history book might trigger your curiosity. The clue could lead you to discover that an ancestor was a discharged soldier, and the name of his regiment.

Once the regiment or regiments are known, turn to the records. Soldiers' records, in some cases, begin at the turn of the eighteenth century. You will depend upon records such as pension lists, description books and muster rolls. Description books, as the name suggests, include a description of the soldier, which was useful to the authorities when seeking deserters. Muster Rolls are registers of the officers and men of a regiment present at the muster, which was called on a regular basis. The first muster of an individual includes his birthplace and age at enlistment, and sometimes his trade at the time. Each regimental list is by rank and then by order of joining. Muster rolls are available at the PRO at Kew.

Some pension and description book records, however, are in the FHL. The FHL collection includes Soldiers' Documents, classified by the PRO as

War Office 97 and more completely titled *Royal Hospital Chelsea Soldiers'*
Documents (see figure 8-1). These documents include information on all soldiers discharged to pension prior to 1883 and discharged for whatever reason
after 1883. This is probably the best place to begin your search. Those who
were pensioned were actually listed as outpatients of either of the military
hospitals at Kilmainham (near Dublin) and Chelsea (in London). For a
discharge before 1873, the documents are arranged by regiment and thereafter
by alphabetical order within the section of the service. The PRO now has an
index to the years 1760-1854 on computer and in hard copy; from 1855 to
1872 it is necessary to know the regiment. The information revealed is: age at
enlistment (many men who said they were eighteen years old were actually
from only fifteen to seventeen years of age), parish or place of birth, trade, and
physical description. Later, the records may also contain medical history,
conduct sheets and next of kin.

Also in the FHL, there are microfilm copies of Royal Hospital Chelsea
Regimental Registers 1715-1857 (W.O. 120) and Registers of Out-Pensioners
of the Army and Militia 1759-1863 (W.O. 118, mainly for Kilmainham).
The Chelsea records are, as the title suggests, arranged by the regiment in
which the pensioner last served. The Kilmainham record group consists of
entry books (some arranged by date pension awarded), an index to some of
the years, and a register of the pensioners resident abroad who were transferred to the establishment of the Royal Hospital Chelsea in 1822. Other
sources which can help with pensioners resident abroad are W.O. 22
(Royal Hospital Chelsea Pension Returns 1842-1882; must know district of
residence) and *British Army Pensioners Abroad: 1772-1889* (Crowder, 1995).

Depot Description Books 1768-1908 (W.O. 67) are a good source of
information. They give the physical description of each soldier, date and
place of birth, trade, promotions, and the reason why the soldier ultimately ceased to be useful to the army. Some soldiers were not included—
those who transferred to one regiment from another, and those who enlisted where the regiment was stationed rather than at the depot. Regimental Description Books (in W.O. 25) are more extensive but do not begin
until the nineteenth century. Some of both of these classes are in the FHL.

Officers are somewhat easier to trace. In the first place, the *Army List*
includes every officer indicating his regiment, and how long he has been in
his current rank. It is readily available, on film through the FHL, in large

libraries, and in some military museums, particularly in Canada. The *Army List* is also on the shelf at the PRO at Kew and in the library of the Society of Genealogists. Records of Officers Services (W.O. 76) have been included in the FHL collection. This series, although it begins quite early, is not extensive until the nineteenth century, and does not include all regiments. The organization is by regiment, which is not a problem in the case of an officer since you can easily locate this information. As the title implies, details of service and ranks held and some additional personal information, such as date of marriage and births of children, is included. It is possible to follow an officer's career, including any time spent on half-pay. Officers did not have pensions; they either went on half-pay (i.e., when not actively employed by the army) or sold their commissions.

Also worth considering is W.O. 42, simply titled *Certificates of Birth, etc.* If an officer died while on full or half pay, application was sometimes made by the widow for support or on behalf of the children. This series includes certificates of birth/baptism, marriage, and death; probate records; service records; and personal papers during the period from 1755 to 1908. For about one hundred years, from 1776 to 1881, it is arranged alphabetically. The alphabetical portion of this group is listed in the FHLC.

The Highland regiments, and other Scottish regiments are fairly well represented among the books of military history in the FHL. You may find more in public and university libraries. You will also find at the FHL, musters to some pre-1707 regiments, the Blotter Register of the Gordon Highlanders 1803-1881 (births and marriages), and Army Muster Rolls copied from the lists at the NAS for the seventeenth and eighteenth centuries. If you know your ancestor was at a famous battle, such as Waterloo, or the Siege of Sebastopol in the Crimea, you may find a published book listing his name. Two examples are given in the bibliography.

The militia is the reserve force of the army. These soldiers mustered and trained occasionally and were liable to be called up in times of national emergency. This is a source to consider whenever there is a problem locating a name in the usual records, particularly for the early part of the nineteenth century. During the long period of the Napoleonic Wars (1792 to 1815), the militia became very large, and although not everyone was required to muster, a significant percentage of able-bodied men between the ages of 18 and 45, and therefore eligible for service, were listed. Access to militia records at the

NAS or at the PRO at Kew rèquires the assistance of an agent. In fact, the records of military service in the NAS are confined to those that predate 1707 and to units of the militia. A summary list of surviving records of Scottish militia units and their locations is found in *Militia Lists and Musters 1757-1876* (Gibson, 1994).

Within the collections of the General Register Office in London, there is a group of records, separate from the births, marriages, and deaths of England and Wales, which relates to the army. These are registers of army births and marriages from 1761 and of deaths from 1796. The regimental series of births/baptisms and marriages begins in 1761 for home events and in about 1790 for those occurring abroad. The births/baptisms of children born to the wives of soldiers have been indexed, and these indexes include the regiment. The latter fact is important because it may mean that this resource is a tool for finding a soldier's regiment or it may at least narrow the field to a few soldiers with the same name. You must have some idea of when and where children were born. The marriage records are not indexed, so it is necessary to know the regiment and an approximate date. Another set of vital records is called the Chaplain's Returns, 1796-1880. They record births, baptisms, marriages, deaths, and burials, are indexed (regiment not included), and relate to events abroad.

The Scots also went to sea, although not in the same numbers. If they served with the Royal Navy, the records are available through the PRO at Kew. Of that massive collection, the FHL has filmed the Continuous Service Engagement Books 1853-1896. The years from 1853 to 1872 are classified as Admiralty 139, and 1873-1891 as Admiralty 188. Arrangement is by seamen's numbers, but separate indexes are available. The entries show date and place of birth, physical description at enlistment, and details of service. Before the middle of the nineteenth century the main source of information is the ships' musters. These are at the PRO at Kew (1667-1878, Admiralty 36-41); the key to searching these records is the name of the seaman's ship. Determining the ship is a challenge, though not an insurmountable problem, particularly with the help of an experienced researcher. Somewhere between 1828 and 1836 musters acquire "alphabets," which are indexes of surnames grouped by first letter only. About fifty years earlier, a few as early as 1765, the navy pay books (1691-1856, ADM 31-35) have alphabets, and give the seaman's ship. Much of the information in the two record groups is similar (pay books may include mention of next of kin), so that one can be used where the other is missing or speed the search in the other. Research can be hindered by the fact that in the seventeenth and eighteenth centuries a seaman did not always serve his entire career in the navy, but may have been in and out of it and the merchant service. Be sure to read the detailed descriptions in *Naval Records for Genealogists* (Rodger, 1988).

Once again, officers present fewer difficulties. A *Navy List* (issued quarterly since 1814) provides rank, date promoted, ship, and the station to which the ship was attached. (The lists of ships attached to each station can help narrow the search for a seaman's ship if a place of service is known.) Every officer of the rank of lieutenant or above had to have passed his certificate. In ADM 107 are volumes of certificates, supporting documents, and baptismal records. There are indexes. Additional records at the PRO at Kew, which you may want to read more about, are Succession Books (ADM 11 deals with Lieutenants, Commanders and Captains from 1780 to 1847). They are a record of service for commissioned officers arranged by ship. For other ranks there are Certificates of Service, required by a seaman before applying for a medal, a pension, or for entry to the seamen's hospital at Greenwich. First issued in 1790, some references go back forty years earlier (ADM 73). Other records of seamen are discussed under Ships and Railways later in this chapter.

A few of you will discover that the subject of your research was in the Royal Marines (soldiers who served on board ships), or in the Royal Artillery, or in India. If your ancestor was an officer he will show up in the *Navy List* or the *Army List*; Marine officers appear in both. A selection of records of Marine and artillery units can be found in the FHLC under military records. If your ancestor was in India, begin by gaining some understanding of the East India Company, the British Army in India, and the records at the India Office Library. To this end, read *East India Company Ancestry*, an article in the Genealogists Magazine (Vol. XXI, March 1984), and *India Office Library and Records: a Brief Guide to Biographical Sources* (Baxter, 1990). There is a growing collection of records of the East India Company at the FHL.

Professions

The professions include doctors, lawyers, accountants, clergymen, architects, professors, teachers, and engineers, to name the most obvious. Certainly, all occupations such as these have professional associations, some of which have existed for a very long time. As a matter of course, go through the entries found under SCOTLAND–OCCUPATIONS, and SCOTLAND, COUNTY NAME–OCCUPATIONS in the FHLC. *Whitaker's Almanac*, is worth consulting for the name and address of an existing professional association, which may retain membership records that go back a long way. Also at an early stage, check to see whether directories of individuals in the specific profession have been published for the period that interests you. A library close to home may be able to help; otherwise, major libraries in Scotland have such works of reference. Finally, there is a remarkable collection of occupational lists in the library of the Society of Genealogists in London.

The initial volume of *The Medical Register* appeared in 1858 and it has been published annually since. Some of the doctors included in that first edition received their degrees before 1800. Copies can be found in all large libraries in Scotland. Another annual listing is *The Medical Directory*, which has been included in the Index to British and Irish Biographies issued by Chadwyck-Healey on microfiche (see appendix A). The 1856 volume is also in the FHL. For a time before the appearance of the *Register*, address an inquiry to one of the following: Royal College of Physicians, Edinburgh; Royal College of Surgeons, Edinburgh; or Royal College of Physicians and Surgeons, Glasgow (see appendix D).

For lawyers, there is a publication known as *The Law List*, issued since 1848, and also available in main libraries in Scotland. There are several alternative sources. At the top of the legal ladder in Scotland were the judges of the Court of Session and all those from earliest records until 1832 are listed in *An Historical Account of the Senators of the College of Justice* (in the FHL, in book form and on film). Lawyers who could plead at the Court of Session were called advocates. The Scottish Record Society issued *The Faculty of Advocates 1532-1943* (1943); since it is one of their publications, it will be readily available in Scotland and fairly accessible in Canada and the United States. Many solicitors are listed in the pages of *A History of the Society of Writers to Her Majesty's Signet* (in the FHL, in book form and on film) which names everyone in the society to 1832. The Signet is one of the Crown seals of Scotland, and writer is another term for solicitor.

Churches have maintained and usually published the names of their ministers for a considerable length of time. *Fasti Ecclesiae Scoticanae* (Scott et al, 1915-61) is a series of volumes which gives biographical details on all the known ministers of the Church of Scotland. The major breakaway churches are covered by four more titles: *Annals of the Free Church of Scotland 1843-1900*, *Annals and Statistics of the Original Secession Church*, *History of the Congregations of the United Presbyterian Church 1733-1900* and *Fasti of the United Free Church of Scotland*. All in this group are found in the FHL, which also includes a large number of books of church history and a selection of directories and yearbooks for several denominations. You can direct a written inquiry to the administrative office of the specific church.

Society tends to respect and honor its architects, so most communities have some record of who designed the library, the town hall, and the finest houses. Edinburgh is a wonderful example of a city that is proud of its architecture. The New Town to the north of the Castle and Princes Street was a major rebuilding project of the late eighteenth century. Nearly every building is listed (i.e., cannot be altered without planning permission), and information on James Craig, who created the plan, and other architects subsequently involved, is readily available. In search of your architect, look for professional directories, browse through the books of local history and architecture in libraries nearby, and consider writing to the National Monuments Record of Scotland, which maintains files on all significant buildings and monuments. Plans of buildings may be found in local archives or libraries in Scotland or in the extensive collection of plans in West Register House, which has a card index of architects and surveyors associated with it. A free leaflet, *The Register House Plans Collection*, is available from the NAS.

There are sources of information regarding teachers and professors, and their students. Volumes of graduates of various schools and colleges have been published (some are listed in the bibliography), or direct an inquiry to the library in the appropriate region. The Society of Genealogists has many school and university lists and has published a guide to its collection (Society of Genealogists, 1988). *The Growth of British Education and its Records* (Chapman, 1992) includes a chapter on Scottish education records.

Before 1872, local schoolmasters were listed in burgh or town council minutes, as this was the authority which hired them. In rural parishes, decisions to hire masters or mistresses were made by the heritors, so a record of this might survive in the Heritors Records at the NAS. Kirk session records may also reveal a schoolmaster's identity, because in some communities he acted as the session clerk. In the more remote parts of Scotland, teaching was often provided through the Scottish Society for the Propagation of Christian Knowledge. This Society provided schools and teachers in the Highlands from early in the eighteenth century. The masters' names show up in various files, such as school registers, salary books, and inspectors' reports. These records are at the NAS.

Merchants and Manufacturers

This category includes people who operated a business on a larger scale, i.e., were importers and exporters, manufacturers, owners of linen mills or mines, operators of breweries, etc. Some businesses operate to this day. Verify a business' existence by checking telephone directories or by asking the Registrar of Companies at Companies House (address in appendix D). Many records of existing and defunct companies have been deposited with libraries and archives, including the NAS, where they are housed in West Register House. There is a card index. To determine the location of other collections, write to the National Register of Archives (Scotland) or ascertain the holdings of the local public or university library. For example, *Family History Sources in Kirkcaldy Central Library* (Campbell, 1994), mentions material on bookselling, printing, and newspaper publishing in Fife, and two company newsletters. The University of Glasgow has a Business Record Centre, but the staff prefers that you first ask the National Register of Archives (Scotland) about the location of material. Among their holdings are the Clyde Shipyard records. Access requires the assistance of a researcher. Board minutes are not very helpful, but from employee records you will learn about such things as wage rates, and indirectly, about standards of living.

Some industries and businesses have been the subject of a study by the government or the recipients of assistance. Others have been described in books and articles. The *Statistical Accounts* of the parish usually include an account of trade and local manufacturing. The account may not mention anyone by name, but it could be very helpful to know, for example, that the local cotton manufacturer was shut down for many months in 1790 at Langholm in Dumfries.[3] If you become particularly interested in the details of one business, build a bibliography on the subject. Searching through library catalogs and bibliographies will show that much has been written on business history. The linen industry is no exception.

The Ford family, which has been mentioned previously, were usually described as merchants of Montrose. Additional details on their businesses emerged from the SGS volume of Angus monumental inscriptions which noted that the family was active in shipping and linen manufacture. It soon became apparent that much has been written about the linen industry in Scotland and that the government took a considerable interest in its development. An examination of the few books on the subject at the university library in Victoria, B.C., revealed the fact that the Ford mill was sold on July 11, 1817, and produced an interesting description of what went on inside the mill:

> Each piece [of sail-cloth or sail-duck] is 38 yards long and numbered from 8 to 1. No. 8 weighs 24 lb., and every piece, down to No. 1, gains 3 lb. in the piece. The thread for this cloth is spun here, not by the common wheel, but the hands. Women are employed, who have the Flax placed round their waist, and twist a thread with each hand as they recede from a wheel turned by a boy at the end of a great room.[4]

You can conclude from all this that surveying local libraries, reviewing bibliographies and catalogs, and building some knowledge of business records is a worthwhile endeavor. Very likely, either relevant facts or evidence of potentially useful sources will emerge.

Craftsmen and Tradesmen

Some of our ancestors who were in business for themselves in the burghs were recorded in surviving burgh records. Anyone who was a member of a guild or needed a license was mentioned. Small shopkeepers, pedlars, hawkers, and clerks were less likely to appear in minutes and ledgers, but they may be found elsewhere if, for example, they sought poor relief or incurred the displeasure of the authorities. Take the usual steps to determine whether it will be difficult to find out more. Look in the Locality section of the FHLC first under SCOTLAND—OCCUPATIONS, then under the county, and finally under the name of the burgh. The entries may be classified as Public Records, Occupations, or History, but items can generally be found in more than one place if there is any ambiguity. Among the trades and crafts represented are engravers, pewterers, knitters, potters and clockmakers. Explore the stacks in nearby libraries, especially the history and economics sections, and try various keywords in a catalog search.

The burgh council, made up of merchants (or burgesses), was responsible for the affairs of the town. Burghs were originally created to foster trade, but their responsibilities expanded. There was maintenance of, for example, the streets, the bridges, the tollbooths, and the schools. There was administration—organizing the fairs, holding burgh courts, collecting fines, stents (property assessment), and fees and rents. Sometimes the burgh councils got into financial difficulty, borrowed money, fell behind, had to raise fees, etc., and generally became unpopular.

The Scottish Record Society published the lists of burgesses for the cities of Edinburgh (Watson, 1930) and Glasgow (Anderson, 1935). The former are in the FHL and both are in any large library in Scotland. The Central Scotland Family History Society has published, and sells, lists of burgesses for Stirling (see the bibliography). Sometimes, you can track several generations. If you want to pursue this line of research beyond what can be found in the FHLC, look for clues in *Exploring Scottish History* (Cox, 1999), or *Data Sheet No. 6* (SRA, 1994). The entry for the Montrose Public Library indicates that it holds burgh minute books and trade records for such occupations as shoemakers, bakers, hammermen, and weavers in Montrose, and in three or four different communities nearby. You must browse burgh and guild records, which may include council minutes, accounts, licensing records, membership lists and charity, within the appropriate time frame for relevant detail.

Apprenticeships, which bound someone to serve a master for a specified period in return for instruction, food, and lodging, were arranged by private agreement. Survival of the contract is uncertain. There are a few published lists of indentures from the guild records of the large cities, or you may find something in burgh records as was alluded to above. There is, however, another possibility. For about one hundred years, the government at Westminster imposed a stamp duty on apprenticeships throughout Britain, and so kept a record of those who paid. Correctly titled the *Apprenticeship Books of Great Britain* and dating from 1710 to 1811, the records are classified under the Board of Inland Revenue. They are divided into town and county registers and the details recorded were name of the apprentice, date of indenture, name and trade of the master, and duty paid. Until 1754, the parents of the apprentice were also included. These records are at the PRO at Kew, and they have been filmed for the FHL. The Society of Genealogists has indexed them to 1774 (they are also on film) and part of the index to masters can be purchased in microfiche format.

Ships and Railways

For ancestors who went to sea with fishing fleets or the merchant service, records are scattered. The NAS has some records of whalers (1750-1825) and men in the herring fleets (1752-1896). Local libraries in port communities may hold additional material. Once again, the perusal of *Exploring Scottish History* (Cox, 1999) or *Data Sheet #6* (SRA, 1994) will help you judge whether a letter of inquiry is justified.

There are some merchant marine records in the FHL. The merchant marine category shows only four items in the Scotland part of the Locality fiche. As with army items, the best place to look is under Great Britain, where you will find listings for The Registers of Seamen (Board of Trade 112, 113, 116, 120, originals at the PRO at Kew). There are indexes; the years are from 1835 to 1857, and information includes age, birthplace, and voyage details.

The largest collection of merchant service records after 1860 is in the Maritime History Archive at Memorial University of Newfoundland. You cannot simply write to request details about a seaman—there are no alphabetical lists of names. You must know the ship and its number and an approximate date. To find the correct ship number, look in a volume of *Lloyd's Register* at a time the ship was in service. There is a set on fiche (1764-1880), listed under GREAT BRITAIN—MERCHANT MARINE in the FHLC. These volumes list all merchant ships since 1890, appear annually, and give such details as captain's name, port of registry, where built, tonnage, and shipping line. Where the ship is unknown, by using these volumes it may be possible to limit the search to a manageable number of vessels. Using what facts there are, ask a few questions. What was the shipping line? From what port did the ship sail or on what regular run was it? Reference can then be made to some of the many books which have been written about shipping lines, and then back to the information to be gleaned from a study of *Lloyd's Register*.

There is a possibility that a seafaring ancestor or his dependents applied for charitable assistance. The records are known as Trinity House Petitions; the originals are in the possession of the Society of Genealogists, London, and microfilm copies are available through LDS family history centers. Trinity

House has actually been several houses over the centuries, and the organization is known officially as the Corporation of Trinity House on Deptford Strand. It began as a fraternity of mariners and pilots and grew to have broad responsibilities which included lighthouses, lightships, and marker buoys. The surviving petitions, which are arranged alphabetically, begin in the 1780s and continue to 1854 when the Merchant Shipping Act came into force.

Ships' officers after 1845 can be traced through records of certificates of competency, some of which are in the FHL. In addition, there are Lloyd's Captains' Registers, held by the Guildhall Library in London, with microfilm copies in the FHL (they do not circulate to family history centers, except for the fiche copy of the volume for 1869) and in the National Archives of Canada in Ottawa. The registers are alphabetical and include date and place of birth and precise details of certification and ships commanded. A very useful book on the subject of merchant seamen's records is *My Ancestor Was a Merchant Seaman* (Watts, 1988). Other guides to archives holdings are listed in the bibliography.

The surviving records of shipbuilding and shipping companies have, in most cases, been deposited at the nearest library or archives. The Glasgow City Archives has records of shipbuilding on the Clyde, including a detailed index containing information on more than 20,000 ships. The Dundee District Archive and Record Centre has material from the Dundee, Perth and London Shipping Company. For further information, obtain the leaflet on "Maritime History," from the NAS, or contact The National Register of Archives (Scotland). If you are fortunate enough to live in a port city, you may find that a local library or museum has a collection of books, periodicals, plans, etc., that may be useful. For example, there is a very fine collection at the Maritime Museum of British Columbia, a large percentage of which is devoted to ships of British Registry. This museum has a reasonably priced query service and has issued a brief guide to research. One of the larger such museums in the United States with a general maritime history theme and a library is The Mariners' Museum at Newport News, Virginia.

Reading *Was your Grandfather a Railwayman?* (Richards, 1989) is a good place to begin a search for railroad employees. Follow up with a letter to the NAS requesting a copy of their leaflet, "The Scottish Railway Records." Staff records relate to the employees of the railway company, not to those who built the railway lines. Some companies are better represented than others in the collection. If you do not know which company employed your ancestor, a little detective work should produce the answer, unless many different lines operated in the location. *The Ordnance Gazetteer of Scotland* (Groome, 1883-85) mentions the name of the line serving any town which has a railway station, or you may find the information in a regional directory. Contemporary maps usually identify the company that owned the tracks.

Farmers and Laborers

Farmers and laborers is a catchall category for those farming a small-holding, agricultural laborers, weavers, mill workers, miners, etc. Finding names and personal details may be very difficult, but there is certainly a wealth of information describing pay, tasks, and working and living conditions. This information shows up in books, periodicals, government reports, and diaries.

To gain an impression of the tools, techniques and conditions of farming or industry in your ancestor's district, begin by reading the *First* and *New Statistical Accounts*. Follow up with research in local histories, gazetteers and directories.

An FHL review will show a variety of books on farms and farming, coal mining, hand-loom weavers (their distress was the subject of much study), and milling. The NAS has received material from the National Coal Board, which includes records of companies in the last century. Some of these sources list names of employees, anyone injured, or those who borrowed money from the mining company.[5] The Gifts and Deposits at the NAS include many estate papers. These records contain a variety of information related to estate management and industry such as, employees, tenants, farm names, crop rotation books, and volunteer-force muster lists. If you are interested in reports made to the British government, locate *Scottish Economic History in the 19th Century: an analytical bibliography of material relating to Scotland in Parliamentary Papers 1800-1900* (Haythornthwaite, 1993). Further information on Parliamentary Papers is in appendix C.

Conclusion

This topic is different. It lacks precise definition and finite boundaries. When you find a birth record, you have the facts. When you find an occupation, there is so much more to discover. You may be diverted to an entirely new area of research which is as big as you want to make it. The preliminary work which you did in maps and history books will seem more relevant. If you are not yet comfortable with periodical indexes, this might be the time to become so. And if you are happy exploring library listings on the Internet you may turn up book titles, published original records, or student theses which relate to your studies.

Occupational records are not as well represented in the holdings of the FHL as are vital records. Partly for this reason, and partly because this is a topic that draws you to descriptive and secondary sources, you must search harder for information. Record what you do in a little more detail than in other bibliographic entries to guide your research for other ancestors at a later date.

In this discussion, reference has been made to museums. Local history museums, maritime museums, preserved railways, working mills, restored cottages and houses are just some of the institutions that interpret the lives of our ancestors for us. Often, these museums also have libraries and photographic collections. If you cannot plan a trip to do those things yourself, a friend, relative, or agent could visit one to inquire, to buy background material, and to take pictures. A few addresses are included in appendix D.

Remember also that investigating someone's occupation may be the only way to gain enough information to identify an ancestor or to discover his or her date of birth.

Notes

1. The Scottish Record Office, at the beinning of 1999, changed its name to the National Archives of Scotland (NAS).
2. Sinclair, 1997, 101.
3. Sinclair, Vol. IV, 370.
4. Warden, 1864, 575.
5. Sinclair, 1997, 122.

Summary—Trades and Occupations

1. Establish the parameters of the search. Who is the subject? What was the ancestor's trade or occupation, or did he or she have more than one? When did he or she engage in this type of work?

2. If you know the name of the occupation, be sure to look up at least a brief definition if you are unsure of what the job was.

3. Why is the search being made in occupational records? To learn about working conditions and/or the local scene, or to find essential facts that did not turn up in usual resources?

4. List all relevant material in the FHL; check it against repository guide books and finding aids.

5. From the information in this chapter and the bibliography, list (a) any guides, printed lists or bibliographies to examine—be sure to include *Scottish Trades, Professions, Vital Records and Directories* (Torrance, 1998); (b) any finding aids to be consulted.

6. Visit local libraries and browse for occupational lists, local and economic histories, etc. This activity may result in additions to the lists already created, or you may be able to find some of the items in those lists.

7. Write out your research strategy, which may involve applying for titles through interlibrary loan, ordering films from the FHL, or writing to a library, archives, or local authority in Scotland.

9 • Taxes and Contracts

here are times when basic, indexed, and readily accessible resources do not provide the answers. Typical factors are a lack of good base information, a family move, and missing records. When this occurs, consider alternative sources.

Taxation records are sometimes lumped with descriptions of census and census substitutes. Although they can be characterized as a form of enumeration, they are less informative and less inclusive of the local population; however, these shortcomings should not obscure the value of taxation records. They can help you identify ancestors, and the tax information adds another perspective.

The Registry of Deeds is another set of documents to be aware of when you seek supplementary information or when you seem to have reached a dead end. You can consult indexes for most years since 1660, except for a gap in the middle of the eighteenth century. Embarking on a search is something of a fishing expedition, but the catch could be substantial. The deeds relate to marriage contracts, testaments, and an assortment of rather ordinary agreements, incorporating topics such as trade, drainage, and construction. There is obviously potential to find in these documents individuals from all levels of society.

A Word on Local Administration

The first burgh was established in the twelfth century, and by the beginning of the eighteenth century there were nearly 300—seventy-seven royal burghs and about 200 others, the majority known as burghs of barony. The rights and privileges of the burgh, e.g., the tenure of land and the holding of fairs, were spelled out in its charter. The burghs of barony were much smaller, perhaps not even a town as the word is understood today, created with the permission of the Crown by someone who in Scotland would be referred to as a superior or subject superior. Royal burghs were larger, were established by royal charter, held their lands directly from the Crown, and had representation in the pre-1707 Scots parliament. They had exclusive control over foreign trade and elected a council and the magistrates who officiated at the burgh court.[1]

Heritors were local landowners who were taxed or asked to make donations for the maintenance of the church and support of its parish work. Heritors met to resolve issues of parish administration. Some of their minutes and accounts have survived and are located in a separate class in the National Archives of Scotland (NAS)[2]. The commissioners of supply, essentially a committee selected from the landowners, determined the amount of land tax or cess to be paid by each landowner. They were gentry (i.e., landowners without titles), rather than nobility. Later, the commissioners were given other responsibilities, such as roads and schools. They worked with the kirk session, as the responsibilities were not clearly delineated. In the burghs, the kirk sessions cooperated with the burgh administration over such matters as poor relief.

Tax Records

Government was hungry for money in the later Stuart period after 1660. In the years prior to the union, the Scottish parliament borrowed some tax collection techniques from Westminster in the form of the Hearth Tax and the Poll Tax. After the Union, and especially toward the end of the eighteenth century, a number of different taxes were applied to all of Britain. The years of collection for many of these taxes suggest that they were collected to raise funds for the war with France, which went on from 1792 to the defeat of Napoleon at Waterloo in 1815, with only a short-lived period of peace in 1801 and 1802.

In Scotland, the Hearth Tax was imposed in 1691. The levy was based on the householders at that time, although in some areas it was several years before the collection was completed; this is after the time the tax was collected in England and Wales. William III abolished this tax in 1689 south of the border where it had come to be regarded as oppressive. This opinion arose, not surprisingly, from the fact that the tax was imposed on the occupant of the home rather than the owner. The records are arranged by county, by parish, and by occupant's name (see figure 9-1). The number of hearths gives an impression of the size and value of a house.

Somewhat more informative are the poll tax records, levied first in 1694. This was a head tax, payable by everyone, male and female. Only people on charity, anyone under the age of sixteen years, or members of a household whose total tax due was thirty shillings or less, were excused. There were some additional assessments on tradesmen, servants, and tenants. Rates were set for each of the levels of the nobility, for advocates, army officers, etc. These records may name each person in the house for whom the tax was payable, indicating relationship to the head of the household. The last year for the poll tax was 1699.

The Hearth and Poll taxes are found for some areas in the Family History Library (FHL) of The Church of Jesus Christ of Latter-day Saints (LDS). Consequently, begin by examining the Locality listings under taxation, at all three levels—national, county, and parish. If you have access to a copy of *The National Index of Parish Registers*, Vol. XII (Steel, 1970), you will find a list of poll tax records in the NAS. The extensive poll tax rolls for Renfrewshire and Aberdeenshire are worth highlighting. The latter are available in a series of booklets from the Aberdeen and NE Scotland Family History Society. *The Hearth Tax, Other Later Stuart Tax Lists and The Association Oath Rolls* (Gibson, 1996), includes listings for hearth and poll taxes for Scotland.

Of the other levies imposed by revenue-hungry and imaginative mandarins of government, the window tax existed the longest, from 1748 to 1798. The information given is the number of houses in the parish, the number of windows in any houses which had seven or more, and the name of the householder. In some parishes only two or three people are mentioned. To

The
Presbytrie
of
Kirkaltie
&
paroch of Scoonie

Scoonie		Scoonie	
Waltr Strachan	1	Margrt wilky	4
Dab: Hunter	2	Dab: Rouch	1
John Turpy	2	wil: wallace	1
John Strachan younger	2	And: Swine	2
Dab: Strachan	3	Rob: Thomson	1
And: Strachan	1	Janet wallace	1
Jon: Ebr	1	wil: finly	1
Janet Davidson	1	Janet Pittullock	1
Cocknhg & wit: Throp	2	John wood	1
Rob: Nauchton	1	Gro: wilkis	1
Dab: Kilgawr	1	Wil: Morton	2
Tho: Morgan	1	Jam: Turpy	3
Alex wilton	1	Rob: Imbris	1
And: Westwater	1	John Smeton	1
Henry Brigs	2	John Johnston	2
walt: Ball	1	Jam: Girdis	4
Janet Muffat	1	Kat: hunter	1
Wil: Sneggy	1	Dab: Mackie	1
Dab: pity	1	Lodobick Ker	2
John Kilgawr	1	John Gutchr	2
Gro: byird	1	Jam: Ramsay	1
Tho: wilkis	2	John Stedman	1
Tho: Collier	2	John white	1
Alex wallace	1	John walkr	1
Wil: Grundiston	2	wil: wilton	1
John: bowman	1	Dab: henderson	1
Agnes Smith	2	John Breck	1
Dab: prat	1	Jam: Smith in Baobth	3
Rob: prat	1	John prat	1
Dab: Morgan	1	Jam: Lyssils	1
Stiben philps	1	John Balfour	1
John branch	1	wil: french	1
Rob: oyngual	1	wil: Ebr	1
Jam: Littlejohn	1	wil: and Tho: Iyslands	2
		Jam: Gutchr in Scoonie	3

Durys house — 2
Alex Turpy — 3
The Minister Mause —
Jam: Clerk — 2
John wallace & his sub Cotters — 6
Mr John Dwar — 1
Rob: spotter — 4
Jam: Young — 4
wil: Turpy — 1
John wilson — 6
Alex Archibald — 1
Rob: Lawson — 1
Katrin Thomson — 1
Wil: walkr — 1
Rob: Thomson — 1
Jam: Gutchr — 2
Margrt Kilgawr — 1
wil: Craig — 1
And: Buyn — 1
John Stone — 1
Elspet fowols — 1
John Strachan — 1
Alex Anderson — 4
Jam: prat — 2

National Archives of Scotland, Hearth Tax for the County of Fife, E69/10/2, Presbyteries of Kirkcaldy, Cupar, and St. Andrew's, Parish of Scoonie, 1694. By Permission of the Keeper of the Records of Scotland.

Figure 9-1. Hearth Tax for the Parish of Scoonie.

avoid paying this tax, some people boarded up their windows. In burghs it is not usually possible to identify individual houses and their occupants, but in rural parishes this information can often be deduced, particularly for the larger houses. These records are at the NAS.

Tax rolls can be a means of confirming the presence of an individual in a parish. Of the other taxes imposed in the latter part of the eighteenth century, two have a better chance of catching a broader spectrum of the population and, therefore, of being helpful in this regard. The farm horse tax, 1797-98, applied to anyone who used a horse in farming or trade. Carriage and saddle horses were taxed from 1785 to 1798. For a time, the employers of servants were assessed for this perceived luxury. Male servants were taxed from 1777 to 1798. An index to those paying tax on male servants in 1780 is at the Society of Genealogists. Records indicate the name of each servant (sometimes the job too) and the name of the master or mistress. Female servants were added from 1785 to 1792, with the same information noted.

Other objects targeted by the tax gatherers, were carriages, inhabited houses, shops, dogs, clocks, and watches. Sometimes, combined levies were made for two or more taxes. The NAS holds these records, arranged by county, within the collections of the Exchequer.[3]

Land taxes in Scotland have been assessed on a regular basis since the middle of the seventeenth century. Land tax was known as the cess, and after the union, it became an annual tax with valuations of property carried out and recorded under the authority of the commissioners of supply. Whereas the taxes discussed above had a wider application, including occupants as well as owners, the land tax affected only landowners, a much smaller percentage of the population. The existence of valuation rolls before the system was changed by the Valuations of Lands Act in 1855, is very limited and spotty. From 1855, however, the annual valuations are complete and very informative. The property is identified, along with a description of its use, its rateable value, and the names of the proprietor and the occupant, the latter named only if the property was let for more than £4.00 per year (see figure 9-2). These records can be used in conjunction with census returns not only to check back and forth for family locations, but to build up a picture of growth and change in a community.

PARISH OF DUN.

No.	Description and Situation of Subject.	Proprietor.	Tenant.	Occupier.	Inhabitant Occupier not rated (48 Vict. cap. 3, secs. 2 & 9).	Ann. Val. of Dw.-House of Inhabitant Occupier, or Grassum, etc. £ s. d.	Yearly Rent or Value. £ s. d.	Agric. Subjs. etc. Rule of Value. £	No.
1	CRAIGO, ESTATE OF. Woods, Glenskenno	Sir George Macpherson Grant of Ballindalloch, per. Claude Ralston, Factor. Glamis		Proprietor			10 0 0		1
2	Shootings, do.	do		do			10 0 0		2
3	Farm and House, Glenskenno	do	Andrew Spence's Reps.	Tenant			440 0 0	165	3
4	House, Glenskenno	do							4
5	do do	do			Alex. Martin, Grieve	4 0 0			5
6	do	do			James Coutts, Ploughman	4 0 0			6
7	do	do			James Mougi, Gardener	4 0 0			7
8	do	do			Charles Davie, Cattleman	4 0 0			8
9	do	do			Wm. Balfour, Cattleman	4 0 0			9
10	House and Croft, Damside of Glenskenno	do	John Clark	Tenant	Mrs Jane Haxton, Outwrkr.	4 0 0	30 0 0	11	10
11	Farm and Houses, Balyellie & Balillo	do	James Samson	do	Wm. Webster, Farm Servt.	4 0 0	700 0 0	263	11
12	House	do			David Rae, Grieve	5 0 0			12
13	do	do			Chas. Johnston, Gardener	4 0 0			13
14	do	do			John Beattie, Cattleman	4 0 0			14
15	do	do			Geo. Donaldson, Ploughman	4 0 0			15
16	do	do			Joseph Greig, Farm Servant	10 0 0			16
17	do	do			William Torris, Ploughman	10 0 0			17
18	do Balillo	do			Empty				18
19	do Balillo	do			George Walker, Ploughman	4 0 0			19
20	do Balillo	do			George Gouill, Cattleman	4 0 0			20
21	Shootings, Balyrlie and Balillo	do	James Samson, above	Tenant for			15 0 0		21
22	House and Garden, Bridge of Dun	do	do	Tenant	Alex. Craig, Porter		8 10 0		22
23	House, E. Dist. of Dun, Woodside of Balillo	do	A. J. W. H. Kennedy Erskine of Dun Reps.	Tenants			10 0 0		23
24	Farm & House, &c., Woodside of Balillo	do	John Malcolm's Reps.		Peter Leslie, Farm Manager	12 0 0	30 4 0	11	24
25	House	do			Mrs George Greig	4 0 0			25
26	do	do							26
27	do	do							27
28	DUN, ESTATE OF. Mansion House and Garden, Dun	Augustus John William Henry Kennedy Erskine, per Lindsay, Howe & Co., W.S., 32 Charlotte Square, Edinburgh		Proprietor			125 0 0		28
29	Palace, do	do		do			25 0 0		29
30	Shootings	do		do			35 0 0		30
31	House	do							31
32	do	do			David Wood, Coachman	4 0 0	11 0 0		32
33	Woods, Dun	do		do	Andrew Foote, Gamekeeper	4 0 0	516 0 0	119	33
34	Grass Parks, Dun	do			Andrew Lamb, Overseer	5 0 0			34
35	House	do			James Gove, Labourer	4 0 0			35
36	do	do			John Duncan, Gardener	4 0 0			36
37	do	do			Alex. Barrowman, Labourer	4 0 0			37
38	do West Lodge, Dun	do			James Crockatt, Labourer				38
39	Cottage, do	do					3 0 0		39
40	Farm and House, Mains of Dun	do	Proprietor for Robert Rodger's Representatives	Tenants	Robert Rodger, Farmer	25 0 0	740 0 0	282	40
41	Farm House	do			James Karr, Ploughman	4 0 0			41
42	House	do			Empty				42
43	do	do							43

Extracted from *Valuation Roll of the County of Forfar for the year 1904-1905*. Published by direction of the County Council. Dundee: John Leng and Co. Ltd., 1905.

Figure 9-2. Valuation Roll—Parish of Dun.

To use valuation rolls effectively, it is important to refer to maps of the area. This becomes absolutely essential for built-up areas, especially the cities of Edinburgh and Glasgow. If you have access to an index to place names and streets, even if it is for the wrong year for your purpose, it may guide you to the right parish and hence focus your search. For Edinburgh after 1895, it is helpful to know the ward of a particular street; you can find this information in city directories. The difficulty of an urban search is compounded by the fact that the information on a given street may not be located together in an orderly fashion.[4] Even where street name indexes exist, they may not be helpful if they do not explain when name changes occurred. Refer to chapter 1 and the bibliography for a reminder of the maps and other finding aids which may assist.

Some valuation rolls have been filmed and can be viewed through LDS family history centers. There is a complete set of surviving rolls in the NAS, and there are collections in some local Scottish repositories. *Exploring Scottish History* (Cox, 1999) or *Data Sheet No. 6* (SRA, 1994) are helpful in determining local holdings. The latter is more likely to include a specific reference to valuation rolls. Searches through these records for towns and cities, even with maps, may be slow and tedious, so a valuation roll search is a good project for a research trip.

The Registry of Deeds

Any time the parties to an agreement, contract, or transaction chose to ensure the preservation or validity of an undertaking, they sought the backing of a court. The documents or deeds were registered and the volumes of registers of the Court of Session came to be called the Registry of Deeds (the proper term for them was *Books of Council and Session*). There are indexes to the Registry of Deeds, but they are complex. A lack of indexes and few minute books mean no help can be found in records of other courts where deeds could be registered; this was any other court before 1809, the sheriff courts, and the royal burgh courts thereafter.[5]

In his book, *In Search of Ancestry* (1983), Gerald Hamilton-Edwards devotes a chapter to the Registry of Deeds and shows how he constructed a pedigree solely from its records. Would your ancestor have entered into some sort of contract or agreement? This is difficult to predict. He may have repaired the church roof, rebuilt a local bridge after a storm, been party to a marriage contract, or been the beneficiary of a testament. It was not necessary to be of high social standing to do any of those things. Your decision to search these records will be influenced by circumstance and motivation. How important is this line of research? Has it bogged down so that all sources must be tried? Is the family proving so interesting that every piece of information should be found? Is the expenditure of time and/or money a good investment?

Some of these questions can be answered only when you are aware of what it takes to access the Registry of Deeds. The Family History Library Catalog (FHLC) entry (under SCOTLAND—LAND AND PROPERTY) may be confusing because half of it consists of eight names matched to various time periods up to 1770. These people—Scott, Dalrymple, and the rest—were at various times clerks in the Court of Session. There is no way of identifying the clerk who registered a deed, except through the NAS indexes (which, fortunately, are consolidated). For the early period from 1661 to 1696, microfilm copies of the NAS indexes are in the FHL, or you can purchase them from the NAS. They include the names of everyone involved in the contracts. It will still be necessary to obtain a copy of the deed from Edinburgh.

From 1696 to 1770, the indexes relate to only a limited number of years: 1696 to 1711, 1750 to 1752, and 1765.[6] These indexes have not been filmed. The records of the unindexed years must be accessed through the minute books (chronological diaries). There are three sets, and you must search all of them. In 1770, a new continuous series of annual indexes (found under the same Locality heading) begins, but this time based solely on the name of the grantor. If it is more likely that your ancestor was on the other side of the table, it presents a problem to the degree that it might deter your search. The odds can be improved by knowing the names of the local landowners—in other words, look at the entry under the name of each grantor; the name of the grantee is included. Therefore, by searching for each entry in the local landowner's name, you could check then for the name of the subject of your search. Sources for the identity of landowners include the *Statistical Accounts*, the various published returns of owners of land, directories, gazetteers, valuation rolls, and books on local history.

Conclusion

Taxation lists and details of contracts seem less than usually interesting as well as less than usually accessible. They do not have quick and easy finding aids, and they do not touch a major part of the population. Nevertheless, they are worth discussing since a number of you will discover an ancestor who qualifies to be found among those named. Compare the years of collection and the details of the various taxes to your own research to determine if any of them might be a source of useful information. Take a little extra time to survey the neighborhood. It may prove useful to try to reconstruct several families within the parish through, for example, the poll tax records, as this may help you sort out the names in the Old Parochial Registers and determine another generation. An interesting account of this technique can be read in the article "William Edward, Identifying an Eighteenth Century Aberdeenshire Miller" (Hinchliff, *Aberdeen & NE Scotland FHS Journal*, Aug. 1994).

Notes

1. Moody, 1986, 54.
2. The Scottish Record Office, at the beinning of 1999, changed its name to the National Archives of Scotland (NAS).
3. Sinclair, 1997, 96-97.
4. Sinclair, 1997, 63.
5. Sinclair, 1997, 71.
6. Sinclair, 1997, 69-70.

Summary—Taxes and Deeds

1. Match the person, place, and time of your search against the years for which the various taxes were collected or against the years for which Registry of Deeds indexes exist. Also, consider whether the information from the tax record is enough for your purpose.

2. Select the tax record or records that will be worth consulting and then see whether or not it is among the records in the FHLC (look in both the national and country listings).

3. Deeds are at the NAS. You can choose whether to use the indexes for 1661 to 1696 and 1770 to 1851, which are available from the FHL, or to assign the entire search to someone in Edinburgh. Sometimes, the indexes are held by local repositories. For the unindexed portions, remember that someone will have to search through three sets of minute books for a reference. Without a specific date, this could be an expensive undertaking.

10 • Special People

ome of your ancestors undoubtedly attracted the special attention of the church, the courts, or government of one level or another. They may have needed assistance because they fell on hard times, they may have chosen the wrong side in one of the Jacobite rebellions, they may have appeared in court because they broke the law or because they were of an argumentative disposition, or they may have been the unfortunate victims of violent death. In addition, one or more of your ancestors made the difficult decision to leave Scotland and start a new life in North America.

The Poor

Until the middle of the nineteenth century and the adoption of The Poor Law Amendment (Scotland) Act, 1845, two principles guided the system of poor relief. The home parish, or the parish of settlement, of each individual was responsible for that person's assistance, and a distinction was made between able-bodied poor and the destitute. The former required only short-term relief until they could find work; the latter required regular assistance because of infirmity, old age, and the inability of other family members to provide support. Settlement status was acquired by parentage, birth, marriage, or three years residency in the parish. A claimant had to be unable to support him or herself and be without relatives who could offer relief. The destitute sometimes traveled back to the parish of settlement; records show assistance given to beggars on their way home.[1] On the other hand, the same power of removal that was exercised in England was never exercised in Scotland. Paupers frequently stayed in their parishes of choice, even though their assistance might come from another parish.[2] Assistance was not refused to anyone who was not entitled; however, every parish was conscious of its limited resources and tried to avoid paying support when it was not responsible.

In the countryside, the parish, through the kirk session and the heritors, looked after the collection of money for relief of the poor, both the payments, and the moving along of those for whom the parish was not responsible. Money came from voluntary contributions, fines, fees (e.g., for use of the mortcloth, for marriage, or for renting a pew), bequests, collections at the church door, and from a tax on the landholders. If the funds for poor relief came entirely from voluntary contributions, the heritors rarely interfered, leaving decisions about relief to the discretion of the kirk session.[3] Revenue from fines may have been imposed by the magistrates or the kirk session. In some cases, a condition of being placed on the poor roll was to agree to the consignment of personal effects to the kirk session for sale after the person's death. Kirk session records sometimes carefully note the collections made, as in the following example from Fetlar in Shetland:

1852

December 18   David Petrie at Aithness and Molly Sinclair at
                   Funzie contracted this day and were married on
                   the 23rd December, 1852, by the Rev. David
                   Webster. Pd. 2/- to the poor[4]

In towns and burghs, assistance was a more complicated matter. Sometimes, poor relief was doled out by the burgh, usually through the supervision of the magistrates, sometimes by the local church, sometimes by the guilds or the trade organizations. The town was more likely to have a poorhouse or charity workhouse for the very old, the very young, or the sick. Some people belonged to friendly societies (an association or constituted body for the provision of relief during sickness, old age, or widowhood, usually organized by occupation, e.g., foresters or fishermen). Members made payments when they were working, and received help when they were not, rather like a form of unemployment insurance.

With the passage of the Act of 1845, came the beginning of the shift of responsibility away from such a localized system toward the creation of a state bureaucracy to manage social welfare. It was not an abrupt change. Kirk sessions went on giving out assistance long after, but a new system was developing, built around Parochial Boards. Needless to say, this resulted in a new set of records.

Background knowledge of economic history and local history will help you decide whether or not to consult records of the poor. For example, two factors which affected many people over a wide area of Scotland were the potato failure of 1846 (potato failure was not confined to Ireland) and the decline in the linen trade and hand-loom weaving in the first half of nineteenth century. Hand-loom weaving had brought relative comfort to many and relieved the distress of those affected by the changes in agriculture. This occupation made it possible for the old or the widowed to continue earning some income at home. Some weavers earned as much as £2 in four days.[5] The power loom arrived in 1807, and the subsequent competition from mechanically produced cotton led to the disappearance of spinning by 1840. If your ancestor was a hand-loom weaver after 1820, he or she may have required assistance at some time.

Weather reports are a less obvious example of where to find historical information that might point to a search in poor law records. Newspapers, the writings of diarists, and local history books may draw attention to particularly severe winters or other conditions which led to crop failure, hence to a number of people suddenly requiring relief.

Time spent reading about local and national economic conditions will help you determine whether or not these records might be useful. Sample volumes of history with the help of the table of contents and consult the appropriate parish description in the *First* and *New Statistical Accounts*.

The Records of the Poor

Until 1845, the kirk session records are the first source to consider. Some sort of poor roll may also be located with the records of the heritors of the parish. If you are fortunate, the lists of payments, whether regular, occasional, or in kind (e.g., clothing) was compiled in a separate list, but it is far more likely that you will have to plod through the accounts. You may have to know your ancestor's parish of settlement (remembering that the parish of latest residence may not be that from which he or she received relief), and to have selected a reasonable number of years for the search.

Some kirk session records are on microfilm and obtainable through LDS family history centers. Look up the parish in the Locality section of the Family History Library Catalog (FHLC) where you will see a listing like that in figure 10-1. Kirk sessions have been collected by the Family History Library (FHL) of The Church of Jesus Christ of Latter-day Saints (LDS) for baptismal and marriage information, but other details may also be included. Look at the Church of Scotland sessions, even if your ancestor was of another congregation. Some of the breakaway churches gave aid to their poor, but the responsibility for all the poor in a given parish rested with the mainstream Presbyterian church. Anything held by the National Archives of Scotland (NAS)[6], whether from the Church of Scotland or other denominations, will have a reference in the fiche guide to *Records of the Church of Scotland and Other Presbyterian Churches*; additional details of what has survived for an individual parish is found in the CH2 repertory.

The records of the poor in the burghs will vary from place to place depending on how the responsibility was shared. The logical starting point is the kirk session of the appropriate parish. For other burgh records, look under the appropriate Locality section under the categories of PUBLIC RECORDS and COURT RECORDS. The LDS collection is very patchy, so in all likelihood you will have to seek the assistance of someone in Scotland. To build your knowledge of surviving records, consult the listings for the relevant library or archive in *Exploring Scottish History*, (Cox, 1999) or in *Data Sheet No. 6* (SRA, 1994), and then write to that repository for more information. Our ancestors were drawn into towns during hard times, so it may be worthwhile to look in kirk sessions and burgh records for a nearby town.

After 1845, once the change in authority occurred, the location of the records varies. A few are at the (NAS), but mainly, they are in record offices, libraries, and perhaps still in municipal halls. You may also find some assistance through the knowledge of members of the area family history society.

Glasgow has a superb resource due to the efforts of the Strathclyde Regional Archives (now the Glasgow City Archives) and many volunteers,

AUTHOR
Church of Scotland. Parish Church of Carnbee.

TITLE
Old parochial registers, 1646–1855.

PUBLICATION INFORMATION
Salt Lake City : Filmed by the Genealogical Society of Utah, 1979.

FORMAT
on 2 microfilm reels ; 35 mm.

NOTES
Microfilm of original records in the New Register House, Edinburgh.

CONTENTS
Carnbee is parish 413.

	BRITISH FILM AREA
Session book (includes Baptisms 1646–1670, —————————— Marriage proclamations 1646–1699, Mortcloth dues [burial records] 1672–1699); Baptisms 1662–1674, 1693–1819; Marriages 1726–1752, 1761–1819; Mortcloth dues 1782–1792; Burials 1790–1819	1040152 item 2–3.
Session book (includes Marriage proclamations —————————— 1705–1726, Mortcloth dues 1706–1760); Baptisms 1820–1855; Marriages 1820–1848; Burials 1820– 1854	1040153 item 1–2
Another microfilm copy. Salt Lake City : Filmed by the Genealogical Society of Utah, 1951. — 2 microfilm reels ; 35 mm.	
Baptisms (years missing as above) 1662–1855; —————————— Marriages (years missing as above) 1726–1848; Mortcloth dues 1782–1792; Burials 1790–1854; Session book (includes Marriage proclamations and Mortcloth dues as above) 1705–1760	0102171
Session book (includes baptisms, marriage procla- —————— mations and mortcloth dues as above) 1646–1699	0103243

THIS RECORD FOUND UNDER
    1. Scotland, Fife, Carnbee – Church records

Figure 10-1. Example of Kirk Session Record in the FHLC.

largely from the membership of the Glasgow and West of Scotland Family History Society. The applications for poor relief in the parishes of Glasgow (beginning in 1851), Barony (beginning in 1861), Govan (beginning in 1876), and numerous other parishes of the region, have all been indexed. This index is accessible on computer in the Archives. Considerable detail about the individual applicants and their circumstances are revealed in the records.

The Parochial Boards established by the Poor Law Amendment (Scotland) Act had the power to tax and the authority to build a poor house. Some rural parishes could not possibly afford to do this and so banded together with neighboring parishes to find the resources. Support for the poor house was based on the number of inmates from each parish, so the records indicate the home parish, as well as the usual name, occupation, and date of admission.

A postscript to this discussion is the topic of health records. I mention these records because voluntary hospitals and boards of health kept track of their patients, who were often people not recorded elsewhere. A voluntary hospital was one supported by donations and bequests. The earliest ones opened in the eighteenth century. They kept records of their patients, their staff (although not usually the female nurses and servants), and their benefactors. Health records are not readily available because they remain in local custody, but this topic is the subject of a clearly presented booklet, *In Sickness and in Health* (Watson, 1988).

Lawbreakers and Litigants

A few of your ancestors may have found themselves in a court of law because they committed a crime or because of a dispute. The crime may have been major, such as treason or murder, or minor, perhaps breach of a contract or negligence of some form. For the curious, a university law library can provide the opportunity for several hours of unusual and often fascinating research.

These records are complicated. Various courts dealt with different types of cases, and the finding aids at the NAS are not very straightforward. The records for the highest criminal court, the Court of the Justiciary, are unindexed. If, however, you have good reason to believe your ancestor was in court for some reason, there is a way to gently introduce yourself to the material and perhaps to find out more about an actual case. To put it another way, if you are of an inquiring disposition and have a little time to spare, it is not necessary to become an expert on Scottish legal procedure to take an interest in court records. This discussion begins with some information on the Jacobite rebels, about whom much has been written. A review of some of the secondary sources on Scottish cases which might be found in North America follows.

The number of people transported after the Jacobite uprisings of 1715 and 1745 was quite small, and the records, particularly for the latter, are good. David Dobson, who has studied migration from Scotland to America in considerable depth, has compiled a list entitled *Jacobites of the '15* (1993) which includes the names of many known to have been transported. Records of the Jacobites of the '45 are more extensive. Aberdeen University Press published the *Muster Roll of Prince Charles Edward Stuart's Army 1745-46* (Livingstone et al., 1984). The Scottish Historical Society, in its First Series, issued *A List of Persons Concerned in the Rebellion* (1890) and in its Third Series, volumes 13, 14, and 15, the Society reproduced various documents and provided an alphabetical list of the prisoners of the '45, taken from state papers (Seton & Arnot, 1928-29). The forfeited estates of Jacobite sympathizers were administered by the Exchequer, so these records at the NAS are a valuable resource. In fact, the NAS has available for sale on fiche the *Records of the Annexed Estates 1755-1769* and *Statistics of the Annexed Estates 1755-1769*. The former describes conditions in the Highlands; the latter lists tenants of farms on the annexed estates. All of the above resources are available through the FHL, and they may be in some university libraries. Also available through the FHL is the *Jacobite Cess Roll for the County of Aberdeen in 1715* (Taylor, A. & H., 1932).

The published records of the Scottish legal profession are very large. Discussions with staff at the Priestly Law Library, University of Victoria, B.C., produced the statistic that as many as 80 percent of cases heard at the higher levels would gain some sort of mention in published form.

It is best to start from reasonably concrete evidence that one of your ancestors was either tried for a crime or ended up in court over a civil matter. Sources for such evidence might include a newspaper report, family papers or tradition, a clue from a death certificate or a parish register, or mention in a volume of local history. You should know that civil cases were dealt with by the Court of Session or (for lesser cases, commonly debt) the Sheriff Courts, and that criminal cases were the responsibility of either the High Court of the Justiciary (major crimes such as murder, arson, robbery with violence, rape, and appeals from the lower courts) or the Sheriff Courts. The Court of Session was convened only in Edinburgh, while for the High Court of the Justiciary the country was divided into four circuits, each with a circuit town.

At the law library, begin by looking for *The Digest: Annotated British Commonwealth and European Cases* (published from 1950 to the present but containing references to many much earlier cases) The older series titled *The English and Empire Digest* (Halsbury & Chitty, 1919-1932) might also be available. The latter volumes, being from an earlier time, are based on fewer cases, and they also contain a greater proportion of Scottish entries, so odds of finding what you want are better. Each edition has a master index by name of those involved in the cases, which refers you to another volume in the set, which in turn encapsulates the case and indicates the publication in which the court report appears. The law library should have the volumes of case reports. Fishing in this reference material for a common surname is not recommended. Below are described the steps to follow from the index to locating the report.

Chain of Steps to Locating a Case Report

1. Look up the name or names in one of the two index volumes (A-L or M-Z) of *The English and Empire Digest* (Halsbury & Chitty, 1919-32). The entry will look like this:

>Blair v. Blair (Scot.); **44**. Wills. 624, 865.

(NB: Cases which involve the same name on either side are usually more likely to have genealogical information because they are family disputes of some kind.)

2. The number **44** is the volume in the same set with the brief notation on the case; Wills is its title, and the other numbers are pages.

3. On page 865, actually in a footnote at the bottom, there are a few lines which identify this as a disputed will and which report the decision. The year of the case is given (1849) and two references to reports: 12 Dunl. (Ct. of Sess.) 97 and 21 Sc. Jur. 612.

4. Reference to the list of reports cited and their abbreviations at the front of the volume indicates that Dunlop, *Cases Decided in the Court of Session...*volume 12, p. 97, and *The Scottish Jurist*, volume 21, p. 612, should be checked.

5. The report in the former volume was found. *Miss Elizabeth Blair executed a trust-disposition and settlement, by which she conveyed her property to trustees for testamentary purposes. The bulk of the fortune consisted of moveables.* ...The principal beneficiaries are named, viz. William Blair of Blair, Miss Rachael M'Cormick, and Miss Helen M'Cormick. Various other members of the family disputed the provisions of the will. (The summary of the will, the positions of those disputing it, and the judge's decision occupy at least a dozen pages.)

Several series of volumes cover a large proportion of the decisions handed down by judges in cases of the Court of Session. The descriptions make for tedious reading, dealing as they do with judgements and the technicalities of the law; however, these volumes have name indexes. The longest series is the annual volumes of the *Cases Decided in the Court of Session*, beginning in 1821 and running until the present. It would be possible to consult the indexes in these volumes, identify a case, gain some idea of its nature, and, if convinced that it relates to your research, to direct someone in Edinburgh to seek the more detailed proceedings. You can also refer to the minute books (i.e., chronological diaries or summaries) of the Court of Session, which are available as printed volumes or on microfilm at the FHL, 1805-1955, with gaps. Each volume covers roughly twelve months and is indexed. Thus, it is possible to select an entry in the *England and Empire Digest* consolidated indexes, note the year, and locate the summary in the minute books. Refer to the preceding list of steps for an idea of what may be found in a court report. There is a greater emphasis on the arguments advanced by the judge in reaching a decision than on the testimony of witnesses.

Criminal trials of the nineteenth century have been summarized in the writings of nine court reporters, or, after 1874, incorporated into the annual volumes of *Session Cases*. For a list, see *The Scottish Legal System: An Introduction to the Study of Scots Law* (Walker, 1981). A set of five volumes, *Reports of Cases before the High Court and Circuit Courts of Justiciary in Scotland* covers the years from 1852 to 1867, compiled by the court reporter Alexander Forbes

Irvine. These volumes are indexed. Some of the crimes dealt with were poaching, fraud, and cattle-stealing, but there were others, such as culpable and reckless driving of a locomotive (which involved speeds of 25 mph!). The latter report included name, residence, occupation and injury for everyone hurt in the accident. This suggests that you should also consider court records in which your ancestor might be listed a victim or a witness. The forty-five volumes of the *Scottish Jurist* are another significant resource. Further details on these and other secondary sources on criminal cases are included in the bibliography. The procedure is the same as for civil cases. Once you find something, contact a researcher in Edinburgh to find the details of the trial. Also investigate whether a newspaper report exists.

A good, plain-language description of the essentials of the Scottish legal system is found in the third chapter of *Scottish Local History* (Moody, 1986). If you intend to hire someone in Edinburgh to do more work, it is advisable to read the relevant sections in *Tracing Your Scottish Ancestors* (Sinclair, 1990) as well. The complexity of the records comes through in the description, but comprehension increases as interest grows.

Did someone in your family tree die in a significant disaster? There have been numerous disasters in Scotland resulting in loss of life, from a few victims to hundreds. The Spring 1995 issue of the journal of the Glasgow and West of Scotland Family History Society[7] contains an article about the compilation of a list of victims of the major disasters (fifty-nine in all) of the nineteenth century in Scotland. These include the loss of thirty-one Shetland fishing boats in one day in 1832, the Balantyre Pit Calamity in 1877, and the Tay Bridge disaster in 1879.

Migrants

First, heed the warnings in chapter 1 about the origins of your immigrant ancestor. A good knowledge of the lives of the first generation or two in North America and the place or places where they lived is important. There is an excellent chance that this knowledge will narrow your search. A line on the paternal side of my family serves as an example. Alexander Campbell, a Loyalist, brought his family to Canada in 1787 and subsequently sought compensation for his losses in America from the British government. He gave his place of settlement as Fort Edward, New York. Study of the settlement of this area, The Argyle Patent, revealed information about the Campbell origins.

The Argyle Patent was settled by descendants of groups of colonists brought from Argyllshire between 1738 and 1740 by Captain Lauchlin Campbell. A dispute with the governor of New York meant that the promised land grants were never made, and the immigrants dispersed. In 1763, redress was sought, and some of the original colonists, along with the descendants of others, were granted 47,500 acres in Washington County.[8] Historical accounts have identified the parts of Argyllshire from whence the settlers came.

The study of the migration of the Scots has attracted the attention of periodical editors, historians, genealogists, and government officials for a very long time. In the middle of the eighteenth century, the *Scots' Magazine* and the *Gentleman's Magazine* both reported from time to time on the numbers leaving for the New World, occasionally naming names. Also in the eighteenth century, the *Virginia Gazette* reported arrivals in all the colonies, not just Virginia. There are numerous books on the subject in general, most recently *Scottish Emigration to Colonial America* (Dobson, 1994). Other titles of interest are The *People's Clearance* (Bumstead, 1982) and *Colonists from Scotland: Emigration to North America 1707-1783* (Graham, 1956). There is an extensive bibliography of the sources for links between Scotland and America in the eighteenth century in *Scotus Americanus* (Brock, 1982).

The British government took an interest in emigration because of such reasons as worries about depopulation and concern for the conditions in the immigrant ships. A number of parliamentary reports were based on information gleaned from officials—customs officers, sheriffs, and local ministers. These shed considerable light on conditions in Scotland in the nineteenth century. *Voyagers to the West* (Bailyn, 1987) analyses in detail the information collected between 1773 and 1776.

The impetus behind an individual's decision to emigrate is not only interesting to know, but also is likely to suggest further study. Was the migration assisted by an emigration scheme? Some of these schemes were very early, some were privately financed, and others came about through the efforts of the Highlands and Islands Emigration Society, or similar groups, in the nineteenth century. Was your ancestor transported, or an indentured servant? Was he a member of a Highland regiment which was disbanded in North America? Did he come to America because of business or trade? There is considerable literature on the tobacco trade, for example. The local history of the area of settlement should reveal this sort of information and may lead you to further documentation which actually lists the earliest residents. In some cases, your research may involve more than one stage. If you have Loyalist ancestors, you need to know something of the history of the Canadian location and of the place of settlement in the United States prior to 1776, before searching for origins in Scotland.

Effort is continually directed toward the creation of lists and databases of immigrants to North America. For Scottish immigrants, several titles may provide direction to your research, but first, a few words of caution are in order. These publications are indexes, and you should go to the original source to confirm the entry. Second, with many people having the same name, do not hastily jump to the conclusion that a likely entry is definitely your ancestor. Third, read the parameters of the lists which you consult so you know how extensive or how narrowly focused they are. That way, you avoid incorrect conclusions about the thoroughness of your own research. Donald Whyte has compiled *A Dictionary of Emigrants to the USA* (1972) and *A Dictionary of Scottish Emigrants to Canada Before Confederation* (1986 & 1995). P. William Filby produced the *Passenger and Immigrants List Index* in three volumes (1982, with supplementary volumes) and an extensive *Passenger and Immigration Lists Bibliography 1538-1900* (1981). David Dobson is the compiler of a *Directory of Scottish Settlers in North America 1625-1825* (7 vols., 1984-93) and a number of small booklets focused on emigrants from different counties of Scotland. National governments began to keep information about arriving immigrants during the nineteenth century, for the United States from 1820, and for Canada from 1865.

This research into who, where, when, and why paves the way for delving into Scottish records. You hope to be crossing the Atlantic with a full name, and if it is common, also the names of spouse, and/or parents, children, and siblings, to increase the odds of identifying the right people. If your Scottish ancestors were recent enough emigrants, they or their relations can be found in the indexes to civil registration and your task is therefore not too difficult. Immediately prior to 1855 you may be able to identify families through the 1851 or 1841 census returns if you know the area of origin. Before 1855, however, the most likely starting place is the indexes to church records described in chapter 5. If church records do not exist for the time or area that you want to search, you must assess other surviving records and the circumstances surrounding the decision to emigrate. This is where the research in North America will be particularly useful. If you find that your ancestor was part of an emigration scheme, or that most of the people of a town came from one part of Scotland, you quite likely can locate enough detail to create a hypothesis to work from. Look through the appropriate *Statistical Account* to check for corroborative reports of emigration before investigating the existence, availability, and location of other records that contain names.

Conclusion

The information discussed in this chapter is more in the nature of historical research than genealogical research. Along the way, you will have the opportunity to acquire considerable ancillary data about living conditions, or migration or political and economic history. You will also enhance your research skills. Working with these records takes you into new areas of a library and new resources, away from simple searches through indexes and lists.

Notes

1. Lindsay, 1975, 20.
2. Nicholls, 1967, 116.
3. Nicholls, 1967, 114.
4. National Archives of Scotland Kirk Session Records, Fetlar, 1847-55.
5. Hamilton Edwards, 1983, 24.
6. The Scottish Record Office, at the beinning of 1999, changed its name to the National Archives of Scotland (NAS).
7. Cross, 1995, 17.
8. Patten, 1928, 3.

Summary—Records of the Poor

1. If you suspect that your ancestor may appear in records of poor relief, select the most likely time span and read some history of general economic and specific local conditions.

2. Check for the availability of kirk session records, first through the Locality section of the FHLC and then through *Records of the Church of Scotland and other Presbyterian Churches*, the fiche set sold by the NAS (see also chapter 5). If you find a reference, obtain further detail from the CH2 repertory.

3. If you are interested in pursuing post-1845 records of the poor, investigate the whereabouts of records of the Parochial Board by using *Exploring Scottish History* (Cox, 1999) and/or *Data Sheet No. 6* (SRA, 1994), followed by a letter of inquiry to the appropriate repository.

4. For burghs, follow the same routine—the FHLC, the finding aids, and letters of inquiry.

Summary—Court Records

1. Consider the merits of conducting a search in court records— on what do you base your decision to search for a court case?

2. If you are interested in finding out more, read the summary in *Scottish Local History* (Moody, 1986) and the appropriate section in *Tracing Your Scottish Ancestors* (Sinclair, 1997). Lack of indexes will make the search difficult. For lower courts all records are in Scotland.

3. For cases in the Court of Session or the High Court of the Justiciary, whether in Edinburgh or a circuit town, visit the nearest law school library. Check for the *English and Empire Digest* and/or the applicable volumes of cases from those listed in the bibliography.

4. If you find the case, follow up, if necessary, by requesting an Edinburgh agent to research the proceeding. You can also check the reference when appropriate in the minute books of the Court of Session. These books are obtainable on film from family history centers.

Summary—Finding Emigrants

1. Identify the person or persons who left Scotland for North America.

2. Determine the approximate date and the place of settlement.

3. Do some background research into Scottish migration to North America, especially as it relates to your ancestors' time and place.

4. Consult the published lists of emigrants, passengers, and immigrants.

5. Verify that you have consulted every possible source for information about the family and its origins.

6. Work out your research strategy in Scottish records based on (a) how common the name is, (b) how much you know about the identity of other family members, (c) how specific place of origin information is, (d) how many counties must be considered for the search, (e) whether the case is before or after 1855 (the start of civil registration), (f) whether you can use the 1841 or 1851 census returns, and (g) whether a check of one or more parish reports in either the *First* or *New Statistical Accounts* may help confirm the parish.

7. Remember that with twenty years of civil registration in the IGI, any pre-1875 emigrant can be checked for in that index.

8. If a search in the various church record indexes (see chapter 5) has produced no result, determine what other records fit the conditions of your search.

9. If there has been no result but you do not know the place of origin, review the first five points again. Can you search for a different member of the family? Can you return to North American records for identifiers? Can you try other resources?

11 • Problem Solving

epend on it: you will get stuck. Ancestors, ancient clerks, and even computer-assisted indexers of the 1990s have misled every one of us through outright lies, oversight, fatigue, etc. Not only that, we have misled ourselves, perhaps by failing to check the base information, or by jumping to hasty conclusions.

Where the problem is a particularly thorny one, develop some sort of process for diagrammatically and verbally presenting it, one that also suggests a means to a solution. The format in figure 11-1 represents one way of doing this. The problem is clearly defined, and segments of charts place it visually in context. There is a reminder about background information. Possible sources to consult are listed, and space has been left to jot down comments or findings. Implicit in this format are the key questions which form the foundation of any new line of inquiry. Once you have identified the quarry and the parameters (of date and area), it is time to review sources by asking the six questions itemized below about each one in turn. Keep these questions handy, and you will always be able to plan a strategy. This approach does not guarantee a solution at the end, but it does provide a common-sense method that will insure that you have done all you can.

Problem: Extend the Pedigree of Mary Rennie

Pedigree Chart Segment

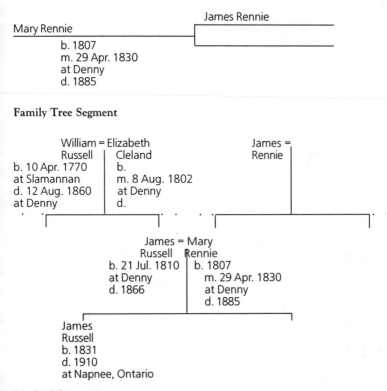

```
                                    James Rennie
                              ┌─────────────────────────────
Mary Rennie
        b. 1807              └─────────────────────────────
        m. 29 Apr. 1830
        at Denny
        d. 1885
```

Family Tree Segment

```
        William = Elizabeth              James =
          Russell │ Cleland              Rennie
b. 10 Apr. 1770  │ b.
at Slamannan     │ m. 8 Aug. 1802
d. 12 Aug. 1860  │ at Denny
at Denny         │ d.
  ·      ·    ┌──────┐   ·    ·    ·   ┌───────────────┐  ·    ·
             │                        │
                  James = Mary
                  Russell │ Rennie
                 b. 21 Jul. 1810 │ b. 1807
                 at Denny        │ m. 29 Apr. 1830
                 d. 1866         │ at Denny
                                 │ d. 1885
              ┌─────────────────────────────┐
          James
          Russell
          b. 1831
          d. 1910
          at Napnee, Ontario
```

Methodology:
1. Boundaries checked? Surname checked (anything been done before, how common in the area)?
2. Death record of Mary Rennie or Russell will provide place and names of both parents.
3. Other accessible records which apply:
   · Church registers (OPR index)
   · Census returns 1841 through 1881, and the 1881 index should be useful; check for 1851 index (?)
4. Civil registration might contain death records of Mary's parents.
5. Testamentary records
6. Kirk session

Notes and Comments

Figure 11-1. A Format for Problem Solving.

1. What time period does the record cover?
2. What geographical area does the record cover?
3. How is the record organized?
4. What information is needed to access the record?
5. What new information will the record supply?
6. Are there finding aids for the record, and where and how can the record be consulted?

Tables 11-1 and 11-2 list roadblocks and solutions. Every genealogical puzzle can be reduced to one or more of these basic generic elements. Once that has been done, you can select possible sources and test their usefulness by applying the questions above.

Problem solving will improve as knowledge and experience grow. Nevertheless, in some instances, only tedious, plodding work offers any hope of producing an answer. Be sure that you have tried all possible short cuts, and that all the facts are gathered and weighed for accuracy. It is sometimes necessary to hypothesize, to assume that one situation was the case and follow through the research on that basis. If it is proven incorrect, the gain is that something has been eliminated, and another theory can be tested.

This is where the concept of reconstruction may come into play. Throughout this book, I have drawn your attention to the importance of the historical and geographical context of the research you are undertaking. Family history is, to some degree, local history; it cannot be studied in isolation from the wider world. If you confine your efforts to the extraction of facts, the results will be deficient, and they may miss the mark. Family history research must incorporate ingenuity and the skillful posing of questions about people, places, and their socio-economic context. Reconstruction of the lives of our ancestors, and of their surroundings, is immensely interesting, satisfying, and potentially rewarding for further research.

A genealogy is only a skeleton, and the most interesting part of family historical work is to paint in the flesh and to catch the breath of the spirit. . . . much can be achieved, particularly in the study of ancestors by proxy, as it were. Thus if one's forbear was a weaver living in Glasgow, one can illuminate his existence through a general study of the life of weavers or of Glasgow at that time, even though one has no direct historical references to the ancestor concerned. In this sense, the family historian is also a local historian, able to point to the buildings and institutions in his or her town and to tell a story of the lives and aspirations of those who built them, lived in them and worked in them.[1]

Meeting the challenge to formulate a research strategy that identifies the necessary records and recognizes the potential of ancillary historical or geographical material is one aspect of family history that keeps us interested. Another aspect is the lucky break.

There are lots of wonderful stories about lucky breaks or inspired guesses and almost spooky visions or impulses which have led researchers to solutions. For everyone who believes that there is a logical explanation for everything, a saying of the ancient Persians may have some appeal: *luck is infatuated with the efficient.* This ties in rather neatly with the idea that you are the instrument of your own fortune (or misfortune), that you make your own luck. Put lots of entries in a surname index, browse libraries every chance you get, talk about your family, follow up on any new leads. People who do these things create their own lucky breaks.

You can post your problem for hundreds, thousands, or more people to see. There are club query pages, surname directories, and the Internet. Personal preference will determine how much you use these vehicles of exchange. Like me, you may follow the "has it been done before?" routine mentioned in chapter 1, and then move on to research, or you may chat by letter, fax, phone, or computer to others, turning up tips and answers. If you choose the latter, be sure to verify anything for which you have not received a definite source reference.

There is, ultimately, the matter of proof, or the establishment of the existence or nonexistence of a fact. When you receive information from another person, critically examine its validity. Have you been given sources, and can you verify some of the facts yourself? There is no doubt that many errors are spread quite innocently and shared through a genuine desire to be helpful; nonetheless, they are errors. Repetition will not make them true. There is a recently written and excellent discussion of the subject of sources, evidence, and the analysis of evidence in *Evidence! Citation and Analysis for the Family Historian* (Mills, 1997). The author stresses the inseparable link between sound analysis and correct documentary references.

I want to leave you with one final reminder. You can never know too much about the records you may use in your search. The quest for knowledge of what records exist should be ongoing. Do not confine your inquisitiveness to only the standard genealogical records. Look beyond to what local, economic, political, and social historians have used. Discover where records are kept, where copies may be found, and in what format. Maintain a file or database of possible sources for future use, especially when the inevitable conundrum arises. Extensive knowledge of source material will keep you in the driver's seat, whether you are planning your own activities or directing an agent. In the end, diversity of sources will create a broader picture. Your family history will be more than a flat, two-dimensional chart; it will have an added vitality. You will have put life into history.

Note
1. Moody, 1988, p. 7.

TABLE 11-1
Roadblocks

For each roadblock, use the solutions suggested to design your strategy.

1. The basic information you are working from may be inaccurate. (B, C, H, J, K)

2. You may not have gathered enough of or the right kind of information for the record. (H, J, K, L)

3. There may be a gap in the records for the particular time and place. (The records may have been damaged or destroyed, may not have been kept for a time, or may be in private hands.) (A, E, I)

4. No listing has been found in the index or finding aid, although you are certain one must be there (could be due to human error in indexing). (A, F, G, I)

5. A search of a record has produced no result, although many other indicators suggest the anticipated entry should be there (may be due to hurried searching, a forgetful minister at the time, deliberate failure to report an event, tax avoidance). (A, D, E, F, I, N)

6. Your research has turned up several possible solutions. (I, J, K, L, M, N)

7. The scale of the search may be too large (too many years to cover, too large an area, too common a name, or a combination of these). (D, I, L, N)

8. There may be a technical problem involving language, handwriting, or organization (e.g., only chronological, not completely alphabetical, or haphazard geographical arrangement). (D, N, O)

TABLE 11-2
Solutions

A. Check the alternate sources that provide similar information.

B. Expand the geographical area of your search, paying close attention to boundaries.

C. Expand the time span of your search.

D. Check that all indexes and finding aids have been identified and checked.

E. Examine another copy of the same source in a different location.

F. Repeat the search.

G. Go directly to the record.

H. Double-check your base information.

I. Carry out the same search for a sibling or other close relative.

J. Try to supplement your base information through additional sources.

K. Improve your historical and geographical background knowledge. Clues found may suggest a different line of inquiry.

L. Create a hypothesis and work through it. You may have to do this more than once.

M. Trace downward from all possible solutions.

N. Check books and periodicals for case studies and talk to other researchers.

O. Hire a professional researcher.

• A •

The Family History Library Catalog (FHLC) is an invaluable research tool. As with any library catalog, it describes the contents of a library, in this case the Family History Library (FHL) of The Church of Jesus Christ of Latter-day Saints (LDS), located in Salt Lake City, Utah. You can consult the catalog in one of two forms: (1) on microfiche or (2) on computer, where it is available as part of Family Search on CD-ROM. The organization of the FHLC makes it very useful. There are four main sections: Author/Title, Subject, Surname, and Locality. The latter two appear in the CD-ROM and fiche versions and are tailor-made to meet the needs of genealogists. Another part of the FHLC is not really a distinct section; it is a native-language version of the Locality section with all of the headings, whether geographic or record type, in the native language of the country concerned.

Because of its organization, the most frequently used part of the FHLC is the Locality section. The organization of sources by place and record category is ideal for family history. The CD-ROM version allows two types of access, Locality Browse and Locality Search. Locality Browse is used when you are unsure of a place or its spelling—helpful when you have a place but no county, or when you do not know the correct spelling. When you input what you know at the prompt, a list of places is displayed. If you know the country, county, and place, use Locality Search as the means of access. The microfiche edition requires you to know the place of interest, but there is an alphabetical place-name list at the beginning of the set of fiche. The microfiche version is available for purchase from the LDS Family History Department (the address is in appendix D). The section for Scotland is very reasonably priced, and if it is likely that any of your ancestors may be listed in the records generated by the British national government at Westminster, consider buying the fiche for Great Britain as well. Microfiche readers are readily available in libraries, and can be purchased new and used; government and business offices regularly sell them. Owning your own copy of the Locality section for Scotland should be a serious consideration if you do not have easy access to an LDS family history center.

The Locality listings are arranged by geographic units, in descending order. For Scotland, this means that records created by the national government in Edinburgh, both before and after the union with England in 1707, and records created at Westminster, or any other records pertaining to the country as a whole, are listed on the microfiche first. As previously mentioned, it is better to search for records of the British government which may include Scottish entries under Great Britain where the listings are more complete (military, naval, and merchant marine in particular). Figure A-1 is an example of national entries. Next the country is broken down into county divisions based on the names used between 1890 and 1974. An example of these entries from fiche and CD-ROM formats is seen in figures A-2 and A-4. Finally, records from the towns or parishes are listed (figure A-4). The geographic region and record classification is clearly visible at the top.

Notice the arrangement of these geographic headings. When you put the first fiche of the Scotland section in a microfiche reader, a list of place names is displayed on the screen. This list is an alphabetical guide to all of the towns and parishes in the index, showing the heading under which each place can be located. The index reminds you of name changes, i.e., to look for Forfar under Angus. The CD-ROM equivalent of the place-name finding aid is the

```
☆☆☆☆☆☆☆☆☆☆☆☆☆☆☆☆☆☆☆☆☆☆☆☆☆☆☆☆☆☆☆☆☆☆☆☆☆☆☆☆☆☆☆☆☆☆☆☆☆☆☆☆☆☆☆☆☆☆☆☆☆☆☆☆☆☆☆☆☆☆☆☆☆☆
SCOTLAND - GENEALOGY

Eyre-Todd, George, 1862-                                        +-------------+
    The highland clans of Scotland : their history and traditions / |BRITISH    |
    by George Eyre-Todd ; with an introduction by A.M.          |FILM AREA    |
    Mackintosh. -- Salt Lake City : Filmed by the Genealogical  |0994038      |
    Society of Utah, 1983. -- on 1 microfilm reel : ill., coats | item 2      |
    of arms, ports. ; 35 mm.                                    +-------------+

    Microreprodiction of original published: London : Heath Cranton
        Limited, 1923.  2 v.
    Index in v. 2.

☆☆☆☆☆☆☆☆☆☆☆☆☆☆☆☆☆☆☆☆☆☆☆☆☆☆☆☆☆☆☆☆☆☆☆☆☆☆☆☆☆☆☆☆☆☆☆☆☆☆☆☆☆☆☆☆☆☆☆☆☆☆☆☆☆☆☆☆☆☆☆☆☆☆
SCOTLAND - GENEALOGY

Eyre-Todd, George, 1862-                                        +-------------+
    The highland clans of Scotland : their history and traditions / |BRITISH   |
    by George Eyre-Todd ; with an introduction by A.M.          |BOOK AREA    |
    Mackintosh. -- Charleston : Garnier, 1969. -- 2 v. in 1 :   |941          |
    coat of arms                                                |H2g          |
                                                                +-------------+
    Reprint.  Originally published in 1923.
    Includes index.

☆☆☆☆☆☆☆☆☆☆☆☆☆☆☆☆☆☆☆☆☆☆☆☆☆☆☆☆☆☆☆☆☆☆☆☆☆☆☆☆☆☆☆☆☆☆☆☆☆☆☆☆☆☆☆☆☆☆☆☆☆☆☆☆☆☆☆☆☆☆☆☆☆☆
SCOTLAND - GENEALOGY

Family histories assembled by the Lord Lyon Registry House,     +-------------+
    Edinburgh, Scotland. -- Salt Lake City : Filmed by the      |BRITISH      |
    Genealogical Society of Utah, 1961. -- 1 microfilm reel ; 35|FILM AREA    |
    mm.                                                         |0277787      |
                                                                +-------------+
    Microreproduction of original.  1 v. (various pagings).

☆☆☆☆☆☆☆☆☆☆☆☆☆☆☆☆☆☆☆☆☆☆☆☆☆☆☆☆☆☆☆☆☆☆☆☆☆☆☆☆☆☆☆☆☆☆☆☆☆☆☆☆☆☆☆☆☆☆☆☆☆☆☆☆☆☆☆☆☆☆☆☆☆☆
SCOTLAND - GENEALOGY

Fraser, Henry.                                                  +-------------+
    Arms drawn with pen and ink for funeral escutcheons, showing|BRITISH      |
    paternal and maternal lines / by Henry Fraser. -- Salt Lake |FILM AREA    |
    City : Filmed by the Genealogical Society of Utah, 1961. -- 1|0277959     |
    microfilm reel ; 35 mm.                                     +-------------+

    Microreproduction of original.

    Includes index.
```

Figure A-1. FHLC: National Entries on Fiche.

☆☆

SCOTLAND, ABERDEEN - PROBATE RECORDS - INDEXES

```
                                                           +--------------+
Grant, Sir Francis J. (Francis James), 1863-              |BRITISH      |
   The commissariot record of Moray : register of testaments, |BOOK AREA |
   1684-1800 / edited by Francis J. Grant. -- Edinburgh : J. |941      |
   Skinner. 1904. -- 29 p. -- (Publications / Scottish Record |B4sr    |
   Society ; v. 20)                                         |v. 20     |
                                                           +--------------+

   With: The commissariot record of Orkney and Shetland / edited by
      Francis J. Grant.

   Also on microfilm. Salt Lake City : Filmed by the        BRITISH
      Genealogical Society of Utah, 1971. on 1              FILM AREA
      microfilm reel ; 35 mm.                               0844771
                                                            item 4
```

☆☆

SCOTLAND, ABERDEEN - PROBATE RECORDS - INDEXES

```
                                                           +--------------+
Index to the inventories of the personal estates of defuncts : |BRITISH   |
   recorded in the Commissary Court books of Aberdeen,    |FILM AREA   |
   Kincardine, Banff, Elgin and Nairn, Inverness, Ross and |1368216    |
   Cromarty, Sutherland Caithness, Orkney, and Zetland. -- | item 2.   |
   Edinburgh : Scottish Record Office, 1985. -- on 1 microfilm +--------------+
   reel ; 35 mm.

   Microfilm of original published: Edinburgh : Printed by
      Murray and Gibb for Her Majesty's Stationery Office, 1869.
   Contents: Index to Defuncts, 1846-1867.
```

☆☆

SCOTLAND, ABERDEEN - PROBATE RECORDS - INDEXES

```
                                                           +--------------+
Scotland. Commissariot (Aberdeen).                        |BRITISH      |
   Register of testaments : 1715-1800. -- Edinburgh : Public |FILM AREA  |
   Library, 1963. -- 1 microfilm reel ; 35 mm. -- (Publications |0334825 |
   / Scottish Record Society ; v. 6)                       +--------------+

   Microreproduction of original published: Edinburgh : [s.n.], 1899.
      69 p.
   Includes records for Banff, Scotland.
```

Figure A-2. FHLC: County Entries on Fiche.

Family History Library Catalog 09 Nov 1995   Page 1
Full Display

CALL NUMBER
BRITISH
FILM AREA
1368216
  item 2.

TITLE
Index to the inventories of the personal estates of defuncts : recorded in
the Commissary Court books of Aberdeen, Kincardine, Banff, Elgin and
Nairn, Inverness, Ross and Cromarty, Sutherland Caithness, Orkney, and
Zetland.

PUBLICATION INFORMATION
Edinburgh : Scottish Record Office, 1985.

FORMAT
on 1 microfilm reel ; 35 mm.

NOTES
Microfilm of original published: Edinburgh : Printed by
Murray and Gibb for Her Majesty's Stationery Office, 1869.

CONTENTS
Contents: Index to defuncts, 1846-1867.

THIS RECORD FOUND UNDER
    1. Scotland - Probate records - Indexes
    2. Scotland, Aberdeen - Probate records - Indexes
    3. Scotland, Kincardine - Probate records - Indexes
    4. Scotland, Banff - Probate records - Indexes
    5. Scotland, Moray - Probate records - Indexes
    6. Scotland, Inverness - Probate records - Indexes
    7. Scotland, Ross and Cromarty - Probate records - Indexes
    8. Scotland, Sutherland - Probate records - Indexes
    9. Scotland, Caithness - Probate records - Indexes
   10. Scotland, Orkney - Probate records - Indexes
   11. Scotland, Shetland - Probate records - Indexes

Family History Library Catalog Copyright © 1987, Aug 1995 by
The Church of Jesus Christ of Latter-day Saints. All Rights Reserved.

Figure A-3. FHLC: County Entry Display—CD-ROM.

☆☆

SCOTLAND, ANGUS, DUNDEE - BUSINESS RECORDS AND COMMERCE

```
                                                              +-------------+
Carmichael, Peter, 1809-1891.                                 |BRITISH      |
    The Dundee textile industry, 1790-1885 : from the papers of |BOOK AREA  |
    Peter Carmichael of Arthurstone / edited by Enid Gauldie. -- |941       |
    Edinburgh : Printed for the Scottish History Society by T.   |B4sc      |
    and A. Constable, 1969, c1969. -- xlii, 268 p., [1] leaf of  |ser. 4    |
    plates : ill., maps, port. -- (Scottish History Society.     |v.   6    |
                                                              +-------------+
    Fourth series ; v. 6)

    Includes index.
```

☆☆

SCOTLAND, ANGUS, DUN - CHURCH RECORDS

```
                                                              +-------------+
Church of Scotland.  Parish Church of Dun.                    |BRITISH    | X
    Parish registers, 1642-1854. -- Salt Lake City : Filmed by the |FILM AREA |
    Genealogical Society of Utah, 1978. -- 2 microfilm reels ; 35  +-------------+
    mm.

    Microfilm of O.P.R. ms. no. 281 in the New Register House, Edinburgh.
    Missing years: Baptisms, Apr. 1690-Feb. 1701 (except for nine entries
    1697-1698); marriages, Apr. 1690-Apr. 1697, Jan. 1698-Feb. 1701, Dec.
    1703-Feb. 1705, Nov. 1706-Nov 1776, Nov. 1793-July 1796, Nov 1807-
    Dec. 1809; burials, Nov. 1675-Nov 1701, Nov. 1706-Jan. 1777, July
    1793-Mar. 1797, May 1798-May 1812.

    Baptisms                  v. 1    1642-1819 ----------------- 0993419    X
    Marriages                          1646-1819
    Burials                            1647-1817
    Marriages and burials     v. 2    1702-1715
    Marriages and burials     v. 3    1716-1727 ----------------- 0993420    X
    Marriages                 v. 4    1727-1755
    Burials                            1727-1748
    Baptisms and Marriages    v. 5    1820-1854
    Burials                            1823-1854

    Another filming.                           BRITISH        X
                                               FILM AREA
                                               0102605-
                                               0102606
```

Reprinted by permission. Copyright © 1987, 1996 by The Church of Jesus Christ of Latter-day Saints.

Figure A-4. FHLC: Parish Entries on Fiche.

Locality Browse feature. Once you find your place, you can then seek particular record types.

When you turn to the record description, you will see, as shown in the examples, that the place information of the heading is paired with one or more words which identify the records. Immediately after the place-name list and still on the first fiche, are the items which are defined as national, categorized by type, and within each type, arranged alphabetically by author or issuing authority where no author is given. Next, the county and local records are listed alphabetically by county sections. In other words, Aberdeen appears first, with county records sorted by type, followed by the alphabetical listings of the parishes and towns of the county according to their appropriate categories. Next, the listings for the county of Angus are listed, and so on through all of the counties. The type of storage format (microfilm, microfiche, book, etc.) and reference number are highlighted to the right.

Generally, you will find that if there is any question about the classification of an item under a given geographic region, it will appear in more than one. Anything which covers several counties is likely to appear in the national portion and also in each of the appropriate county listings. Look again at figure A-2. Since this volume of probate indexes is concerned with more than one county, it will also appear under SCOTLAND–PROBATE and under probate for each county. The computer entry tells you this (figure A-3).

A full entry might include details of organization, date issued or published, location of original records, notation of any indexes, and the extent of the collection. This is, however, a catalog of LDS holdings; therefore, it is not possible to assess the extant records of a particular type from the FHLC entry alone. Military records are a good example. The FHLC shows that it has War Office 25, Regimental Description and Succession Books. This is only a portion of W.O. 25, which the Public Record Office (PRO) titled "Various Registers 1660-1938." Reference to a contents guide, such as *Tracing Your Ancestors in the Public Record Office* (Bevan, 1999), allows comparisons.

The headings for the types of records are taken from a standard list. Occasionally, when unique records do not fit into the standard list, a new heading must be created. More than eighty standard headings and numerous subheadings distinguish indexes and lists. A partial list of main headings is reproduced in table A-1; a more extensive list is included in chapter 2 of *The Library: A Guide to LDS ...* (Cerny and Elliott, 1988).

TABLE A-1
FHLC Subject Headings

Archives and Libraries	Maps
Bibliography	Military History
Biography	Military Records
Business and Commerce	Names—Geographic
Cemeteries	Names—Personal
Census	Newspapers
Church Directories	Nobility
Church History	Obituaries
Church Records	Occupations
Civil Registration	Pensions
Court Records	Periodicals
Description and Travel	Politics and Government
Directories	Poor Houses
Emigration and Immigration	Probate Records
Gazetteers	Public Records
Genealogy	Schools
History	Social Life and Customs
Indexes	Taxation
Inventories and Registers	Vital Records
Land and Property	Voting Registers

The Surname section of the FHLC is the other very useful resource. Consult it early in your research, particularly when you want to determine whether any work has already been done on the family in question. This index lists all compiled family histories alphabetically by surname, when the surname appears either in the title of the item or in the brief description. This index covers a lot of names; nevertheless, many of the names in a family history book will not be listed. If there are multiple entries for one surname, they appear alphabetically by author. The descriptive part of the entry provides information as to place and time. Generally, I prefer to search for entries here using the CD-ROM version as it usually is faster. Also, you can print the selections you have marked for placement in a holding file, which is convenient. If your surname is common, be sure to have some identifiers (forename, place, religion) to reduce the list to scroll through on the monitor.

The Author/Title section of the FHLC is, as you would expect, a strictly alphabetical listing of author names and book titles in the collection. It is on microfiche only. Every item in the FHL is included in this section of the FHLC and in at least one other. The film collection of vital records, for example, appears in this section according to the name of the agency or government department which created it. It is an interesting exercise to look up an item in the Locality section, and then use the agency as the key to a search in this section. On CD-ROM, the Computer # section lists every item in the library by a distinctive record number, which differs from film, fiche, and book numbers.

The portion of the microfiche catalog arranged by Subject is the least used. Usually, it is best to find what you want through the Locality section. Occasionally, when it is difficult to classify a record as to type by the standard catalog list, a search through the subject listings may prove helpful. It is designed to be used in searches by ethnic, religious or political group. The remaining CD-ROM section is a listing by film or fiche number, which is very useful if, for example, you noted an interesting film that was being viewed by someone else and later forgot why it caught your attention.

There are a few tips and suggestions to remember for possible future use. In the CD-ROM format, you can do a keyword search to input an important detail which will perhaps separate the only entry which relates to you from all others of the same name. In both the Locality and the Surname sections on computer, you can use a "wild card" as part to your input. For example, if you remember only part of a place or surname, input the first three or four letters followed by the wild card character, an asterisk (*). Everything that begins with the letters you entered will be displayed. As to spelling, it is worth remembering that in the FHLC, places such as St. Vigeans are sorted as though St. were spelled out as Saint, and M', Mc, and Mac are lumped together, incorporated as they fall rather than separated.

Also, using the CD-ROM version, once you have indicated your place and type of record, you can speed up selection by choosing a listing by author. Read the title information and mark those entries which need to be scrutinized in greater detail. This is preferable to scrolling through the full details of each entry. If a collection is particularly large, you will be warned. Once into a detailed description, press the Enter key to see the exact location in the FHL and a list of which family history centers, if any, have the item on indefinite loan. The indefinite loan list is revised annually, but it is only as complete as the returns submitted by the individual family history centers.

Two significant series of fiche, issued by Chadwyck-Healey of Cambridge, England, can be reviewed best in the Author/Title section of the catalog on fiche. The first is the *National Index of Documentary Sources in the United Kingdom*. Finding aids for many British repositories are summarized, arranged alphabetically by the name of the institution. The National Archives of Scotland and the National Library of Scotland have listings, and these listings state the number of fiche for an item. Generally, these Chadwyck-Healey fiche appear under the appropriate category in the Locality section, but it may be useful to browse the entire consolidated list within the Author/Title section. The other finding aid is *British and Irish Biographies 1840-1940*. Under this heading appear descriptions of hundreds of biographical and professional dictionaries and other lists of individuals. Each has a fiche or film reference. There is an overall alphabetical index to those named in all of these sources, logically titled the *Index to British and Irish Biographies*. The first edition of this index (105 fiche) circulates to family history centers; later, larger editions do not.

Using the FHLC is the best way to understand its organization. During your next visit to an LDS family history center or to the FHL, take time to examine all sections and to explore the headings in the national, county, and local parts of the Locality section. If you are a novice, begin with the fiche edition. Not all searches can be done on the CD-ROM version, and you cannot scan the divisions and headings in the same way. If you are a more experienced researcher, return to the Locality listings regularly to read areas which apply to current research. Not only may this procedure suggest a new source or a line of inquiry beyond the extent of the LDS holdings, but a new edition of the FHLC may have additional entries. It is updated on a regular basis, so keep track of the most recent version consulted.

From time to time, it is necessary to review the details associated with a record type or research problem: parish numbers, gazetteer descriptions, the extent of the LDS collection, to name a few. One way of doing this is to consult the microfiche reprint of the reference work, which quite probably is in your nearest family history center. Table A-2 summarizes several of the most useful items.

Resource Guides describing the FHLC, on microfiche and on CD-ROM, can be obtained from family history centers or from the Family History Department. They are worth reading. *Using the Family History Library Catalog* contains a useful two-page spread on how to match your topic requirements to record-category headings.

> *Getting Started: Family History Library Catalog* (on compact disc)
>
> *Family History Library Catalog* (on compact disc)
>
> *Family History Library Catalog* (on microfiche)
>
> *Using the Family History Library Catalog*

TABLE A-2
Useful Resources Available on Microfiche

Column one is a list of seven different items; across from each in column two is a fiche number and a brief description.

TITLE	NUMBER AND CONTENT
Records of Births, Deaths, and Marriages, Scotland 1855-1875, 1881, 1891, with index 1855-1941	6035516 lists index film numbers and dates, lists of the registers organized as to county and type of event with film numbers
Index to Scottish Census 1841-1891	6035795 microfilm numbers for the census arranged by county, then alphabetically by parish; also has lists of street indexes and instructions
Sasines, Service of Heirs and Deeds Register	6054478 parish boundary maps of each county and detailed lists of FHL holdings arranged by county; chart of the levels of Scottish courts
Scottish Testaments	6054479 commissariot maps and detailed descriptions of FHL holdings arranged by commissariot

TABLE A-2 (cont.)

Key to the Parochial Registers of Scotland	6036348 this is Bloxham and Metcalfe (1979, see bibliography) on fiche
Ordnance Gazetteer of Scotland	6020392-0411 F.H. Groome's very useful work (1883-85, see bibliography) on fiche
Directory of Gentlemen's Seats, Villages, etc.	6026392 James Findlay's cross-referenced listing of landowners and places (1843, see bibliography)

• B •

Indexes to Baptisms and Marriages:
IGI, OPR Index, Scottish Church Records

Research in Scottish church records is unusual because there is a choice of indexes to marriages and baptisms, very similar in layout, but differing somewhat in organization and provenance. The International Genealogical Index (IGI) was created as a means of indexing not only baptisms and marriages, but also the temple ordinance information of The Church of Jesus Christ of Latter-day Saints (LDS). The Old Parochial Registers (OPR) Index for Scotland (available since 1993), was created as a finding aid to the records of baptism and marriage in the registers of the established Church of Scotland. Scottish Church Records, although not exactly the same, is the CD-ROM format of the OPR Index.

Basis of the Indexes

The IGI is an index to more than 200,000,000 names taken from records in roughly 100 countries around the world. The index is not complete and is likely never to be so, a fact that is not surprising when you think about the scale of the undertaking. Record collection is ongoing, and the indexing of collected records is unlikely to ever catch up. The current 1992 edition is supplemented by an Addendum dated 1994. The index is maintained in computer format at the FHL and can be viewed in LDS family history centers around the world in two forms—microfiche and CD-ROM.

In addition to birth/baptisms and marriages of the established church, the IGI includes information from denominations other than the Church of Scotland, submissions by members of the LDS church, and twenty years of records from the indexes to civil registration of births and marriages. In the fiche format, it is organized on a county basis, (baptisms and marriages are listed together); on CD-ROM, it is incorporated into a set which includes all the British Isles (England, Wales, Scotland, and Ireland). Baptisms and marriages are separate listings on CD-ROM, but it is quite easy to move from one type of search to the other.

The OPR Index and Scottish Church records are a fraction the size, each comprising about ten million names. They include the baptisms and marriages recorded in the registers of the Church of Scotland, some baptism and marriage events from kirk sessions, and some entries from other denominations. More of the latter are in Scottish Church Records, some as recent as 1900. The OPR Index introductory information actually states that there are no entries from registers of other denominations; however, spot checks among common names have revealed a few.

There are four indexes within the OPR Index plus the Addenda. For each county entries are arranged into births/baptisms according to surname, births/baptisms by given name, marriages by surname and marriages by given name. The Addenda are on three fiche—separate alphabetical surname listings for births/baptisms and marriages. Sort by given name is not available for the Addenda.

Scottish Church Records is a single, national, alphabetical index which incorporates the listings from the fiche Addenda. Separate searches are utilized to access births/baptisms or marriages, but transition from one to the other is straightforward, requiring only a few keystrokes.

Information in the Indexes

The best way to explain the information available is to illustrate one frame or page of the microfiche version of the IGI and discuss each heading or column in turn (see figure B-1). The same details for each individual entry appear in a slightly different format on the OPR Index fiche (see figure B-2) and again on the monitor when you enter the command to see a full entry. The top line of the page indicates the country, the county, the edition of the IGI, and the page number (which is useful when identifying pages to be copied). Immediately below, are the headings for the eleven columns that appear across the page.

The names in the first column are always listed alphabetically by surname. The IGI uses a system of standard spelling which has been adjusted in the 1992 CD-ROM version to include given names (e.g., Katherine and Catherine appear mixed together). If your surname has been incorporated in a standard grouping but you look it up according to the spelling with which you are familiar, a note will refer you to the correct part of the index. Standard spellings have been utilized less frequently in the most recent edition of the IGI. When a name variation is rare, or when pronunciation or other difficulties have altered the name more than you suspect, the index listing is separate and you must anticipate the possible spelling. Within the same surname, individuals are listed alphabetically by given name (the CD-ROM version ignores middle names). If several individuals have the same surname and given name, the entries appear in chronological order. If a symbol (e.g., #) appears beside a name, it means that some additional information may be included in the record or that the record has been evaluated.

Scottish Church Records similarly uses standardized spellings; however, on the OPR Index fiche, alphabetical lists are by actual spellings with the exception that Mac, Mc, and M' are mixed together. The use of actual spellings means you must be prepared to "jump around" during a search (e.g., other surnames intervene between Foord and Ford).

Column 2 shows the names of parents for baptism entries and the name of the spouse for marriage entries. Column 3 identifies the sex of the individual as male or female (for births or baptisms), or husband or wife (for marriages). Column 4 classifies the type of event. There are nine possible code letters.

A adult christening
B birth
C christening

D death or burial
F birth or christening
M marriage
N census
S miscellaneous
W will or probate

The date of the event appears in column 5, and the place appears in column 6. The place entry may also give the church and/or denomination, if relevant. Columns 7, 8, and 9 provide dates of LDS events. These do not show up on the fiche of the OPR Index.

Columns 10 and 11 provide the key to identifying the original source of the information. The batch number allows you to differentiate, for IGI entries, between those submitted by private individuals and those obtained through the filming program of the LDS Family History Department. Names taken from films of the registers have batch numbers which begin with C or P (usually birth entries), J, K, or M (usually marriage entries, except for M17 or M18), E, 725, 745, and 754. Entries submitted by individuals have batch numbers of all digits, the third digit being smaller than four. Index entries taken from LDS temple records begin with A, M17, or M18. A number beginning with an F indicates that the date is calculated or approximate.

Using the numbers in the last two columns and the Batch Number Index, the precise source of the information can be identified. The Serial Sheet number is the page number for the sheet on which an entry appears. The Batch Number Index is a set of fiche which is with any copy of the IGI. It includes an explanation of the number. Film numbers for church registers can also be found under the name of the parish in the Locality section of the Family History Library Catalog (FHLC).

A comparison of figures B-1 and B-2 quickly shows the similarities between the formats of the two fiche indexes. The three columns of church information on the IGI page have been replaced by a single miscellaneous column on the OPR page. The OPR Index uses batch and serial sheet numbers in the same way as the IGI fiche format. When using the computer, a request for details displays the source references on the screen.

Benefits of the Indexes

The greatest benefit of any of these indexes is the potential to save time and money. Depending on whether you have access to the CD-ROM or microfiche editions, you can check the entire country or selected groupings of counties for a particular name in a matter of minutes or a few hours. Consider how long it would take to read through the registers of many parishes, or how much it might cost to have an agent carry out such a search. Carefully review the summary of features of each index shown in table B-1 before beginning a search. These features are the key to realizing the advantages of each type of index, and of a combined search using more than one (as discussed in chapter 5).

The list of features for the IGI on microfiche is the shortest, but it has one significant advantage over all the others. Using this index, you can view together the baptisms and marriages for all individuals of one name in one county. You can copy individual frames, or pages, from a fiche. You may choose to take copies home and work from them to sort out families within a parish. This arrangement may help you spot connections, and it allows for easy assessment of the presence of a particular surname in one area. None of this is high-tech, but it may work for you.

The OPR Index on microfiche is noteworthy because it presents the baptism and marriage lists in two formats. This is the only tool that provides a given name index, which is especially useful when patronymics are involved or if a woman's maiden name is unknown. There are Addenda of more than 30,000 names that are not in the main index, but sort by given name is not available for these Addenda.

The county arrangement of this index and the IGI fiche edition may sometimes be useful when you have identified the county or have undertaken a methodical, geographically based search.

Computer searches in either the IGI or Scottish Church Records open up interesting possibilities. In the first place, you can look up one name in the listings for the entire country. This procedure is essential to anyone starting research in Scottish records without place of origin information. Second, the "Parent Search" is possible. This search links children who may be from the same family, based on instructing the computer to search for offspring of parents with the selected names. If you suspect that more than one family is

FORRESTER, BESSI

COUNTRY: SCOTLAND COUNTY: ANGUS AS OF MAR 1992 PAGE 6,886

NAME / FATHER / MOTHER OR SPOUSE OR RELATIVE	T/Y/P	EVENT DATE	TOWN, PARISH	B	E	S	BATCH/FILM NO	SERIAL SHEET
FORRESTER, BESSIE								
FOSTER, BESSIE	F C	09JUL1657	ANGUS, DUNDEE	16MAR1983PV	05APR1983PV	15APR1983PV	C112822	4013
ALEXR. FOSTER/ELSPETH FOSTER								
ALEXR. JOHNSTON	U H	05MAR1862	ANGUS, DUNDEE			15JAN1982SL	M112821	6140
FORRESTER, BETSY								
BETSY KIDD	F B	09SEP1861	ANGUS, MONIFIETH	07FEB19800G	15APR19800G	04JUN19800G	C113101	1226
ROBERT FORRESTER/ANN SKIRVING								
BETSY MCKAY	F B	29JAN1870	ANGUS, DUNDEE	10MAR1981SL	20MAR1981SL	25MAR1981SL	C112823	10956
LUNDIE FORRESTER/HELEN KYDD								
FORRESTER, BETTY	U M	01DEC1775	ANGUS, FORFAR			29OCT1981SL	M112882	2714
WILLIAM ALEXANDER								
FORRESTER, BETTY	F C	27MAY1780	ANGUS, CLAMS	05JAN1983PV	21JAN1983PV	28JAN1983PV	C112892	5705
JOHN FORRESTER/								
FORRESTER, BETTY	U M	17NOV1786	ANGUS, DUNDEE			14SEP19920K	M112824	0712
DANIEL MACPHERSON								
FORRESTER, BETTY	U H	18JUN1807	ANGUS, KIRRIEMUIR	05MAR19830G	29MAR19830G	27APR19830G	C112992	12040
DAVID FORRESTER/ELIZ. LOU								
FORRESTER, BETTY	F C	11NOV1814	ANGUS, KIRRIEMUIR	08MAR19830G	29MAR19830G	28APR19830G	C112992	13265
CHARLES FORRESTER/ANN TURNBULL								
FORRESTER, CATHARIN	F C	02MAY1680	ANGUS, MONTROSE	04JUN1983JR	12JUL1983JR	26JUL1983JR	C113122	6454
JOHN ORRE MONRO								
FORRESTER, CATHARINE	U M	30DEC1854	ANGUS, DUNDEE			22FEB1983PV	M112885	20167
ROBERT ANDERSON								
FORRESTER, CATHERINE	U H	15JAN1763	ANGUS, DUNDEE			08OCT1974AL	7330219	14
FORRESTER, CATHERINE	F B	29SEP1866	ANGUS, DUNDEE	15JAN1980PV	26MAR1980PV	22APR1980PV	C112881	47809
JAMES FORRESTER/ALICE GIBB								
FORRESTER, CATHN.	U M	02FEB1763	ANGUS, DUNDEE			01DEC1982PV	M112822	8975
ROBT. ANDERSON								
FORRESTER, CATHREN	U M	11JUN1675	ANGUS, DUNDEE			11NOV1982PV	M112822	2918
DAVID EDGAR								
FORRESTER, CATHREN	U H	02DEC1722	ANGUS, LINTRATHEN	07MAY19820K	17JUN19820K	24JUN19820K	M112822	0244
THOMAS FORRESTER/								
FORRESTER, CHARLES	M C	13DEC1727	ANGUS, OATHLAW	01APR19820G	08JUL19820G	13AUG19820G	C113152	0189
ALEXR. FORRESTER/MARGARET HEY								
FORRESTER, CHARLES	M C	01JUN1752	ANGUS, GLENISLA	08APR1982LG	08MAY1982LG	08JUL1982LG	C112902	0766
WILLM. FORRESTER/								
FORRESTER, CHARLES	U M	17AUG1754	ANGUS, MONTROSE		04NOV1981SL	04NOV1981SL	M113102	2442
ELIZABETH NICOL								
FORRESTER, CHRISTIAN	U H	10APR1743	ANGUS, GLENISLA	16FEB1982LG	14APR1982LG	11JUN1982LG	C112902	0308
JOHN FORRESTER/								
FORRESTER, CHRISTIAN	F C	13OCT1816	ANGUS, DUNDEE	01FEB1983AZ	15FEB1983AZ	09APR1983AZ	C112827	9644
ROBT. FORRESTER/ISABELLA GORDON								
FORRESTER, CHRISTIAN	U M	22NOV1847	ANGUS, DUNDEE			10FEB1983PV	M112825	14486
CHARLES URQUHART								
FOSTER, CHRISTIANE	F C	14MAR1668	ANGUS, DUNDEE	17MAR1983PV	05APR1983PV	15APR1983PV	C112822	7069
JOHN FOSTER/MARGAT. ALLAN								
FORRESTER, CHRISTINA	U M	19SEP1848	ANGUS, DUNDEE			11FEB1983PV	M112825	14998
CHARLES LAWSON								
FORRESTER, CHRISTINA	F B	15OCT1870	ANGUS, COUPAR ANGUS	02DEC1980SE	09JAN1981SE	05FEB1981SE	C112793	0290
JAMES FORRESTER/ANN KENNEDY								
FORRESTER, CHRISTOPHER	M B	16JUL1856	ANGUS, DUNDEE	11DEC1979PV	21MAR1980PV	04APR1980PV	C112821	5657
ALEXANDER FORRESTER/JANET BARKER								
FORRESTER, CLEMENTINA	F C	16OCT1782	ANGUS, GLENISLA	18FEB1982LG	16APR1982LG	16JUN1982LG	C112902	1328
DAVID FORRESTER/								
FORRESTER, CLEMENTINA	U H	06JUN1870	ANGUS, KINGOLDRUM	10MAR1981SL	24MAR1981SL	05JAN1982SL	M112982	0442
JOHN KYD								
DANIEL CAMPBELL	M B	10MAR1870	ANGUS, DUNDEE	10MAR1981SL	24MAR1981SL	26MAR1981SL	C112823	13567
JOHN FORRESTER/ELIZABETH CAMPBELL								
FORRESTER, DAUID	M C	23JAN1672	ANGUS, DUNDEE	15MAR1983PV	30MAR1983PV	08APR1983PV	C112822	8062
GEORG FORRESTER/MARTHA FORRESTER								
FORRESTER, DAVD.	M C	APR1776	ANGUS, KIRRIEMUIR	23FEB19830G	24MAR19830G	12MAY19830G	C112992	7578
JAS. FORRESTER/								
FOSTER, DAVID	M C	12NOV1665	ANGUS, DUNDEE	18AUG1983JR	17SEP1983JR	10NOV1982PV	M112822	2100
GRISSELL WILLIAMSONE								
FORRESTER, DAVID	M C	28DEC1690	ANGUS, DUNDEE			04OCT1983JR	C112824	1951
GEO. FORRESTER/RACHELL YEAMEN								
GEO. FORRESTER…				10MAY19830G	22MAR19830G	10MAY19830G	C112992	1358

Reprinted by permission. Copyright © 1992 by The Church of Jesus Christ of Latter-day Saints.

Figure B-1. IGI Extract—County Angus.

COUNTRY: SCOTLAND	COUNTY: ANGUS			AS OF MAR 1991		PAGE 2 930	
NAME / FATHER/MOTHER OR SPOUSE	SEX	TYPE	EVENT DATE	TOWN, PARISH	MISCELLANEOUS	BATCH	SERIAL SHEET
FORRESTER, ANN TOSH							
FORRESTER, ANN TOSH / ROBERT FORRESTER/ANN MELDRUM	U	C	09NOV1828	DUNDEE		C112828	7299
FORRESTER, ANN TOSH / ROBERT FORRESTER/ANN MELDRUM	U	C	09NOV1828	DUNDEE		C112828	7328
FORRESTER, BARBARA / JAMES FORRESTER/	F	C	22APR1739	GLAMIS		C112892	3422
FORRESTER, BARBARA /	U	C	18MAY1791	DUNDEE		C112826	5330
FORRESTER, BETTY / WILM. FORRESTER/MARGT. SWAN	F	C	21MAY1780	GLAMIS		C112892	5705
FORRESTER, BETTY / JOHN FORRESTER/	U	C	18JUN1807	KIRRIEMUIR		C112992	12040
FORRESTER, BETTY / DAVID FORRESTER/ELIZ. LOW	U	C	11NOV1814	KIRRIEMUIR		C112992	13265
FORRESTER, CATHARINE / CHARLES FORRESTER/ANN TURNBULL	L	C	02MAY1930	MONTROSE	FR14	C113122	4155
FORRESTER, CATHARINE / JOHN FORRESTER/	C	C	02DEC1792	LINTRATHEN	FR93	C113122	0244
FORRESTER, CHARLES / THOMAS FORRESTER/	U	C	13DEC1727	OATHLAW		C113152	0189
FORRESTER, CHARLES / ALEXR. FORRESTER/MARGARET HEY	M	C	01JUN1752	GLENISLA		C112902	0766
FORRESTER, CHRISTIAN / WILM. FORRESTER/	F	C	10APR1743	GLENISLA		C112902	0308
FORRESTER, CHRISIIAN / JOHN FORRESTER/	U	C	13OCT1816	DUNDEE		C112827	9655
FORRESTER, CLEMROBT. FORRESTER/ISABELLA GORDON			16OCT1782	GLENISLA		C112902	1828
FORRESTER, CLEMENTINA / DAVID FORRESTER/	F	C	23JAN1672	DUNDEE		C112822	8062
FORRESTER, DAVD. / GEORG FORRESTER/MARTHA FORRESTER	U	C	APR1776	KIRRIEMUIR		C112992	7578
FORRESTER, DAVID / JAS. FORRESTER	C	C	28DEC1690	DUNDEE		C112824	1951
FORRESTER, DAVID / GEO. FORRESTER/RACHEL YEAMEN	M	C	18JAN1745	KINNETTLES		C112972	0801
FORRESTER, DAVID / DAVID FORRESTER/	U	C	22JAN1756	COUPAR ANGUS		C112794	1652
FORRESTER, DAVID / DAVID FORRESTER/GRIZEL MILLAR	U	C	08JUN1760	DUNDEE		C112825	2058
FORRESTER, DAVID / WILLIAM FORRESTER/MARGARET STRACHAN	M	C	09MAR1779	KIRRIEMUIR		C112992	8023
FORRESTER, DAVID / JNO. FORRESTER/	U	C	16MAY1784	DUNDEE		C112825	12211
FORRESTER, DAVID / WILM. FORRESTER/MARGT. SWAN	M	C	25JAN1789	LINTRATHEN	FR94	C113022	1963
FORRESTER, DAVID / JAS. FORRESTER/MARGT. SMITH	U	C	04NOV1794	DUNDEE		C112825	3391
FORRESTER, ELISABETH / JAMES FORRESTER/MART. STRACHAN	F	C	26JUL1753	GLENISLA		C112902	0814
FORRESTER, ELIZABATH / JOHN FORRESTER/	F	C	19JUL1680	MONTROSE		C113122	6685
FORRESTER, ELIZABETH / DAVID FORRESTER/	F	C	12SEP1707	COUPAR ANGUS		C112792	1297
FORRESTER, ELIZABETH / ALEXR. FORRESTER/	F	C	18JAN1748	GLENISLA		C112902	0550
FORRESTER, ELSPETH / SYLVESTER FORRESTER/	U	C	23FEB1718	LINTRATHEN	FR8	C113022	0045
FORRESTER, ELSPETH / ANDREW FORRESTER/	U	C	12FEB1721	LINTRATHEN	FR1	C113022	0150
FORRESTER, ELSPETH / THOMAS FORRESTER/	U	C	16JAN1653	DUNDEE		C112822	2583
FORRESTER, ALEXANDER FORRESTER/ELSPETH FORRESTER	F	C	10MAR1667	DUNDEE		C112822	6792
FORRESTER, ELSPIT / DAVID FORRESTER/GRISSELL WILLIAMSON	F	C	14MAY1727	CORTACHY AND CLOVA		C113282	2529
FORRESTER, EUPHAM / ALEXR. FORRESTER/	U	C	08OCT1754	DUNDEE		C112825	0543
FORRESTER, GEORG FORRESTER/ISABEL PETRIE	M	C	22DEC1664	DUNDEE		C112822	6187
GEORG FORRESTER/MARTHA FORRESTER							

Figure B-2. OPR Index Extract—County Angus.

TABLE B-1
A Summary of Index Features

IGI on Microfiche	OPR Index on Microfiche	IGI on CD-ROM	Scottish Church Records on CD-ROM
Arranged by county, country then alphabetically using some standardized spellings; chronologically when names are the same.	Arranged by county, then alphabetically, but the alphabetical listing is by actual spelling, with M' and Mc treated as Mac.	Part of British Isles listings, but Scotland, or one (or several) Scottish county(ies) can be specified; alphabetical and chrono. as for IGI on fiche.	Can search entire or specify a particular county or counties; alphabetical as for OPR Index.
Baptisms and marriages are together.	Baptisms and marriages are separate.	Baptisms and marriages are in separate searches, but moving from one to the other is easy.	Baptisms and marriages are in separate searches, but moving from one to the other is easy.
Not as complete as the OPR Index for Church of Scotland; includes many nonconformist tion rejoined the registration indexes, tion indexes, and individual submissions.	Church of Scotland baptisms and marriages, some from kirk sessions and some for entries, 20 years Church of Scotland; the Church of Scotland; Addenda of 31,000 listings are separate.	Not as complete as Scottish Church Records for Church of Scotland; includes many nonconformist entries, nonconformists from civil registra- and individual submissions.	Church of Scotland baptisms and marriages, some from kirk sessions; no nonconformist entries, unless congrega- 20 years from civil bap. or married in OPR Addenda are included.
	Baptism and marriage entries are listed by surname and given name in separate sets of fiche; Addenda do not have a given-name sort.	Parent Search lists together the names of individuals whose parents' names appear the same way.	Parent Search lists together the names of individuals whose parents' names appear the same way.
		Can filter a search to show entries limited by dates, geographic area, or by linkage to another name (or part of a name) in a marriage.	Can filter a search to show entries limited by dates, geographic area, or by linkage to another name (or part of a name) in a marriage.

involved, you must check other details to sort them out (see chapter 5). In either case, the search is focused very quickly and you will have clues about individual identification, family structure, and moves from place to place.

In a similar fashion, it is easy to move to another event for individuals of the same name with just a few keystrokes. For example, when looking at a likely baptism, pressing the appropriate function key for a marriage search moves to the entries without returning to the beginning of the search routine. It is also possible to define a search by geographic region and outside dates and to filter a marriage search by linking certain names. These tools may facilitate the identification of individuals and families or the survey of the numerous entries of a common surname.

The IGI, in either form, has a broader range of entries than the other two, although it is less complete for Church of Scotland items. In fact, remember that on CD-ROM, Scotland is in a combined listing with the rest of the British Isles. This could be useful when dealing with border families. On fiche or CD-ROM, the IGI includes many nonconformist registers and many submissions by individuals. The latter are details submitted by LDS church members. It is possible that one of these entries may reveal new information, but it is also possible that this information may be incorrect or unsubstantiated. Be sure to verify the source or find further proof.

Shortcomings of the Indexes

Remember that any of these indexes is only an index. Any one of them is subject to error and omission. Always order the film of the original parish register to be sure that the index entry was correct, and to check for additional details. Sometimes, it is a good idea to order the film of the register regardless of whether you found the expected index entry in the index. You may find what you are after, you may find other members of the family, and, if there are burial registers, you may find additional clues.

These indexes do not show infant burials or any linkages between events. Do not accept a likely entry without being certain that the individual involved actually lived to adulthood. There is no clue to indicate whether a marriage entry and a birth entry showing the same name (and logical span of years between) actually refer to the same person or coincidentally to two different people with identical names. Names generated by the Parent Search are not necessarily of the same single family.

All the cautionary words about names and places in the pitfalls discussion in chapter 1 apply to these indexes as much as to a record itself. Also, refer to chapter 5 for a discussion of these indexes in the context of your research and to review the reasons for the serious shortcomings in the records of the Church of Scotland and how to overcome the resultant obstacles.

Additionally, practical information about using these indexes and finding the actual register can be found in a series of resource guides, all published by the LDS church. They can be obtained in family history centers or by writing to the LDS Family History Department (see appendix D for the address). You can also purchase sections of the IGI on microfiche from the Family History Department. The General Register Office in Scotland sells the OPR Index on fiche.

Family Search: International Genealogical Index (on compact disc)

Family Search: Scottish Church Records

Finding an IGI source

International Genealogical Index (on microfiche)

Old Parochial Registers (OPR) Index for Scotland

• C •

PARLIAMENTARY PAPERS

This appendix is included as a challenge to those of you who want to find interesting historical detail about a time, a place, an occupation, an economic condition, or—if you are lucky—an individual. The vastness and complexity of the material will deter many researchers. However, Parliamentary Papers are a rich resource for social history in Scotland, and although there is a staggering amount of information, selective dips into them will prove interesting and rewarding.

Published Parliamentary Papers are a fraction of the huge collection of documents generated by the House of Commons and the House of Lords at Westminster in London. Very few libraries have more than a small selection of the thousands of volumes which have been issued over the centuries. A particularly large chunk of this published material was produced by the Irish University Press about twenty-five years ago. More recently, Parliamentary Papers have become available on microcard and microfiche.

Understanding the terminology helps considerably. Definitions of the more commonly used terms follow.

- Royal Commission: The members are usually specialists, not Members of Parliament, appointed to investigate a single subject; once the report is submitted, the Commission disbands.
- Select Committee: A committee of Parliament, sometimes meeting for a limited amount of time to hear evidence on a specific topic of focus, sometimes a standing committee meeting regularly over a long period.
- Blue Books: A name for larger Sessional Papers, usually presented to Parliament inside a blue paper cover.
- White Papers: A name for smaller Sessional Papers, usually presented to Parliament without a cover.
- Sessional Papers: The more formal name for any papers presented to Parliament, originated by an order of the House.
- Command Papers: Those prepared at the Command of the Crown; sometimes, but not always, include the reports of Royal Commissions.
- Parliamentary Papers: The umbrella term for all papers and reports, bills, accounts, and records of debates.

British Parliamentary Papers are in the library of Brigham Young University, at the University of Utah, and a few are in the Family History Library (FHL) of The Church of Jesus Christ of Latter-day Saints (LDS). Format varies. Those at BYU are on microfiche and can be copied; those at the U of U are on microcard and cannot be copied. Inquiries to accessible university libraries will reveal whether you can locate this resource closer to home. Canadian researchers may be more fortunate here because of similar parliamentary traditions. The Papers are in major British libraries, for example, there is a complete set at the Mitchell Library in Glasgow. The headings to use in a catalog search are: Great Britain. Parliament. House of Commons.

Your first step is to discover whether there was a report on a topic of interest. There are official indexes and select guides to help, one of which is devoted entirely to Scotland—*Scottish Economic History in the 19th Century: an analytical bibliography of material relating to Scotland in Parliamentary Papers 1800-1900* (Haythornthwaite, 1993). Other finding aids are listed at the end of this appendix. They provide title, year, volume, and reference number; from this information, it is not difficult to locate a report, whether in a bound volume or on fiche.

A hint of the material to be found in the testimony of witnesses before investigating committees can be obtained by the following excerpts from the questioning of one James Strachan, Land Waiter of the Customs at Burntisland. This account relates many aspects of the herring fishery, from numbers involved to the details of curing:

> In the End of October a vast Collection of Boats, with Fishermen, Nets, and Fishing Materials, repair to Burntisland, not only from all the Ports and Creeks in the Vicinity, but from the North Shore, as far as the Coast of Caithness, from the South Shore, as far as Berwick upon Tweed, and from the West Coasts through the Canal. When all those Bye Boats are assembled, they may amount to from 8 to 900, which when joined by the Boats attached to upwards of 360 Sail of Shipping upon the Fishery, it is a modest Computation to say, that at the throngest Time of the Fishing in some Seasons, the Number of Boats employed at one Time have exceeded 1,200.

> The Herrings being caught and landed fresh, as above mentioned, are commonly gutted, but often are not. The gutting, when thought necessary, being performed by Women and Girls. In either Case, they are taken and roused with Salt in a wooden Vessel, called a Rousing Tub, that is, a Parcel of Fresh Herrings are put into the Tub, and a sufficient Quantity of Salt is sprinkled among the Herrings by the Hand from a Platter, and they are stirred about in the Tub, so as every herring may partake of an equal Portion of the Salt; this also keeps the Herrings asunder when packing as they would otherwise stick together when packed, and would not cure properly; about Half of bushel of Salt is usually expended in rousing.[1]

Parliamentary Papers can be descriptive of an industry, as shown above, or provide statistical evidence (see figure C-1), or reveal personal details about individuals. There are reports on prisons, poor-houses, schools, conditions in factories, the plight of the hand-loom weavers, to name just a few topics. *Scottish Family History* (Moody, 1988) further discusses many possible uses in research; an example of references to a particular family can be found in "British Parliamentary Papers," an article in the *Utah Genealogical Journal* (Wight, 1994). If you are building a social history around your Scottish forebears or want to challenge your research abilities, Parliamentary Papers will serve both purposes well.

Shire of Lanark.

PARISHES, TOWNSHIPS, &c.		Annual Value of the Real Property, as assessed April 1815.	POPULATION.				Aggregate POPULATION of Connected Places (1831.)
		£.	1801.	1811.	1821.	1831.	
AVENDALE	Parish	16,287	3,623	4,353	5,030	5,761	
Biggar	Parish	4,017	1,216	1,376	1,727	1,915	
Blantyre	Parish	4,438	1,751	2,092	2,630	3,000	
Bothwell	Parish	16,053	3,017	3,745	4,844	5,545	
Cadder	Parish	14,439	2,120	2,487	2,798	3,048	
Cambuslang	Parish	8,578	1,558	2,035	2,301	2,697	
Cambusnetham	Parish	6,271	1,972	2,591	3,086	3,824	
Carluke	Parish	8,553	1,756	2,311	2,925	3,288	
Carmichael	Parish	4,236	832	926	963	956	
Carmunnock	Parish	6,002	700	670	637	692	
Carstairs	Parish	4,022	899	875	937	981	
Carnwath	Parish	10,384	2,680	3,789	2,888	3,505	
Cathcart (part of) (*)	Parish	2,827	- -	55	171	200	
Covington	Parish	1,720	456	438	526	521	
Crawford	Parish	16,016	1,671	1,773	1,914	1,850	
Crawfordjohn	Parish	5,014	712	858	971	991	
Culter	Parish	2,769	369	415	467	497	
Dalserf	Parish	5,355	- -	1,660	2,054	2,680	
Dalzell	Parish	2,751	611	758	955	1,180	
Dolphinton	Parish	1,301	231	268	236	302	
Douglas	Parish	7,538	1,730	1,873	2,195	2,542	
Dunsyre	Parish	2,006	352	345	290	335	
Glasford	Parish	5,627	953	1,213	1,504	1,730	
GLASGOW City:							
East, or Outer High	Parish	⎱	5,253	6,159	7,198	9,137	
Enoch, St.	Parish		6,440	7,715	7,038	7,921	
James, St.	Parish		- -	- -	7,263	8,217	
John, St.	Parish		- -	- -	7,965	11,746	
Middle, or St. Andrew's	Parish		4,338	5,250	5,731	5,923	
North, or St. Mungoe's	Parish	234,216	8,089	11,159	8,823	10,295	202,426
North-West, or Ramshorn, now St. David's	Parish		7,401	9,940	6,013	6,268	
South, or Blackfriars	Parish		4,901	5,758	6,266	7,569	
South-West, or St. Mary's	Parish		6,594	8,163	6,865	7,529	
West, or St. George's	Parish	⎰	3,799	4,190	9,603	15,242	
Suburbs:							
Barony	Parish	110,696	26,710	37,216	51,919	77,385	
Gorbals	Parish	31,035	3,896	5,199	29,359	35,194	
Govan (part of) (*)	Parish	14,086	6,701	11,581	3,775	4,967	
Hamilton	Par. & Town	18,863	5,908	6,453	7,613	9,513	
Kibride	Par. & Town	16,363	2,330	2,906	3,485	3,789	
Lamington and Wandell	Parish	3,335	375	356	359	382	
LANARK	Burgh & Parish	3,194 / 6,521	⎱ 4,692	5,667	7,085	7,672	
Lesmohagow	Parish	17,481	3,070	4,464	5,502	6,409	
Liberton	Parish	3,790	706	749	785	773	
Monkland, New	Parish	13,903	4,613	5,529	7,362	9,867	
Monkland, Old	Parish	19,806	4,006	5,469	6,983	9,580	
Pettinairn	Parish	2,082	430	401	490	461	
RUTHERGLEN	Burgh & Parish	5,263 / 4,508	⎱ 2,437	3,529	4,091 / 549	4,741 / 762	5,503
Shotts	Parish	9,012	2,127	2,933	3,297	3,820	
Stonehouse	Town & Parish	5,289	1,259	1,655	2,038	2,359	
Symington	Parish	1,984	308	364	472	489	
Walston	Parish	1,730	383	377	392	429	
Wiston and Roberton	Parish	4,162	757	836	927	940	
SHIRE of **L**ANARK		686,531	146,699	191,752	244,387	316,800	
Increase of POPULATION *in three periods*				31 ⅌ Cent.	27 ⅌ Cent.	30 ⅌ Cent.	

(*) Cathcart Parish is mostly in Renfrewshire, and is wholly entered here in 1801; the entire Parish contains 2,282 Inhabitants.

(*) Govan Parish is partly in Renfrewshire; the entire Parish now contains 5,677 Inhabitants; but if the Population be taken according to its former boundary in 1801 and 1811, it now contains 19,170; the difference of these numbers being added to Gorbals in 1821 and 1831, as a Suburb of Glasgow.

It is interesting to note the population figures for each county and parish in each census year. What was the rate of population growth or decline in the parishes of your ancestors? Why?

Figure C-1. Two Tables from *The Comparative Account of the Population of Great Britain 1801, 1811, 1821, 1831* (London: by Order of the House of Commons, 1831).

SCOTLAND.

COUNTIES OF	1801.	Increase ⅌ Cent.	1811.	Increase ⅌ Cent.	1821.	Increase ⅌ Cent.	1831.
ABERDEEN - - - -	123,082	10	135,075	15	155,387	14	177,651
ARGYLE - - - -	71,859	19	85,585	14	97,316	4	101,425
AYR - - - -	84,306	23	103,954	22	127,299	14	145,055
BANFF - - - -	35,807	2	36,668	19	43,561	12	48,604
BERWICK - - -	30,621	1	30,779	8	33,385	2	34,048
BUTE - - - -	11,791	2	12,033	15	13,797	3	14,151
CAITHNESS - - -	22,609	4	23,419	29	30,238	14	34,529
CLACKMANNAN - -	10,858	11	12,010	10	13,263	11	14,729
DUMBARTON - - -	20,710	17	24,189	13	27,317	22	33,211
DUMFRIES - - -	54,597	15	62,960	13	70,878	4	73,770
EDINBURGH - - -	122,954	21	148,607	29	191,514	15	219,592
ELGIN - - - -	26,705	5	28,108	11	31,162	10	34,231
FIFE - - - -	93,743	8	101,272	13	114,556	12	128,839
FORFAR - - - -	99,127	8	107,264	6	113,430	23	139,606
HADDINGTON - -	29,986	4	31,164	13	35,127	3	36,145
INVERNESS - - -	74,292	5	78,336	15	90,157	5	94,797
KINCARDINE - -	26,349	4	27,439	6	29,118	8	31,431
KINROSS - - -	6,725	8	7,245	7	7,762	17	9,072
KIRKCUDBRIGHT -	29,211	15	33,684	15	38,903	4	40,590
LANARK - - -	146,699	31	191,752	27	244,387	30	316,819
LINLITHGOW - -	17,844	9	19,451	17	22,685	3	23,291
NAIRN - - - -	8,257	—	8,251	9	9,006	4	9,354
ORKNEY AND SHETLAND -	46,824	—	46,153	15	53,124	10	58,239
PEEBLES - - - -	8,735	14	9,935	1	10,046	5	10,578
PERTH - - - -	126,366	7	135,093	3	139,050	3	142,894
RENFREW - - -	78,056	19	92,596	21	112,175	19	133,443
ROSS AND CROMARTY	55,343	10	68,853	13	68,828	9	74,820
ROXBURGH - - -	33,682	11	37,230	10	40,892	7	43,663
SELKIRK - - - -	5,070	16	5,889	13	6,637	2	6,833
STIRLING - - -	50,825	14	58,174	12	65,376	11	72,621
SUTHERLAND - -	23,117	2	23,629	—	23,840	7	25,518
WIGTOWN - - -	22,918	17	26,891	23	33,240	9	36,258
	1,599,068	14	1,805,688	16	2,093,456	13	2,365,807

SUMMARY OF GREAT BRITAIN.

	1801.	Increase ⅌ Cent.	1811.	Increase ⅌ Cent.	1821.	Increase ⅌ Cent.	1831.
ENGLAND - - -	8,331,434	14½	9,551,888	17⅞	11,261,437	16	13,089,338
WALES - - -	541,546	13	611,788	17	717,438	12	805,236
SCOTLAND - - -	1,599,068	14	1,805,688	16	2,093,456	13	2,365,807
ARMY, NAVY, &c. -	470,598	—	640,500	—	319,300	—	277,017
	10,942,646	15¼	12,609,864	14	14,391,631	15	16,537,398

THE Rate of Increase of the Population of Great Britain has not varied much during the last Thirty Years, even when the Increase or Diminution of the Army, Navy, &c. is thus taken into the Calculation; but a more accurate knowledge of the Increase of Population may be obtained by adverting to the Increase of the Female Sex exclusively; thereby virtually omitting throughout the Calculation such of the Army, Navy, and Merchant Seamen as were not domiciled in Great Britain.

1801. Females.	Increase ⅌ Cent.	1811. Females.	Increase ⅌ Cent.	1821. Females.	Increase ⅌ Cent.	1831. Females.
5,492,354	14.15	6,269,650	15.71	7,254,613	15.45	8,375,780

Figure C-1. (cont.)

Note
1. *Sessional Papers of the 18th Century*, vol. 131, 53.

Bibliography

Chaloner, W.H., ed. *Six Reports From the Select Committee on Artisans and Machinery 1824*. London: Cass, 1968.

Comparative Account of the Population of Great Britain in the Years 1801, 1811, 1821, 1831. By Order of the House of Commons, 1831.

Ford, P., and G. Ford, eds. *Hansard's Catalogue and Breviate of Parliamentary Papers 1696-1834*. Shannon: Irish University Press, 1968.

Ford, P., and G. Ford. *A Guide to Parliamentary Papers: What they are, How to find them, How to use them*. Shannon: Irish University Press, 1972.

Ford, P., and G. Ford. *Select List of British Parliamentary Papers 1833-1899*. Rev. ed. Shannon: Irish University Press, 1969.

General Index to the Reports of Select Committees 1801-1852. Printed by Order of the House of Commons. Index #2. Reprint. Shannon: Irish University Press, 1968.

Haythornthwaite, J. A. *Scottish Economic History in the 19th Century: an analytical bibliography of material relating to Scotland in Parliamentary Papers 1800-1900*. Scholarly Press, 1993.

Lambert, Sheila, ed. *House of Commons Sessional Papers of the 18th Century. Volume 131, George III, Food Supply, Fisheries, 1799-1800*. Wilmington, Delaware: Scholarly Resources, 1975.

Lambert, Sheila, ed. *House of Commons Sessional Papers of the 18th Century. Volume 2, George I, Scotland, 1717-1725*. Wilmington, Delaware: Scholarly Resources, 1975. Contains references to the management of the forfeited estates of Jacobites.

Moody, David. *Scottish Family History*. London: B.T. Batsford, 1988. Reprint. Baltimore: Genealogical Publishing Co., 1990.

Powell, W.R. *Local History from Blue Books: A Select List of the Sessional Papers of the House of Commons*. London: Historical Association and Routledge and Kegan Paul, 1962.

Reid, Judith Prowse. *Genealogical Research in England's Public Record Office: A Guide for North Americans*. Baltimore: Genealogical Publishing Company, 1996. Contains a brief section on Parliamentary Papers which lists additional general resources on the subject.

Wight, Judith E. "British Parliamentary Papers—A Source for Family History." *Genealogical Journal* 21, nos. 3-4 (1993): 144-155. Utah Genealogical Association. Describes the arrangement of the Papers, particularly interesting reports, and the author's own study of a Hebrides family.

• D •

LIST OF USEFUL ADDRESSES

Scotland reorganized local government in April 1996. There are thirty-two new councils. Several archives continue to function, albeit in a modified form, and in some areas new archives are being created or planned. Name and organizational changes which are known as of July 1996 are noted in the address list. For other areas, the old regional name has been left in the list. Its use should not prevent delivery of a letter. Some collections will, over time, be moved because of decentralization; materials will relocate from large repositories to smaller, local archives. If you are planning a research trip, write or phone to obtain information about collection location. If a letter comes back to you undelivered, direct an inquiry to the Scottish Records Association, which will keep track of all the changes.

Aberdeen & North East Scotland Family History Society
164 King Street
Aberdeen AB2 3BD Scotland
  Produces an excellent journal and has an extensive publications list.

Aberdeen Central Library
Local Studies Department
Rosemount Viaduct
Aberdeen AB25 1GW Scotland

Aberdeen City Archives
Town House
Aberdeen AB10 1AQ Scotland
  The facility of the Grampian Regional Archives at Old Aberdeen House, Dunbar Street, will be administered by Aberdeen City Archives. Open hours were set provisionally in 1996 at three days a week at each facility. Check before you visit; appointments are advised.

Angus Council Archives
Montrose Public Library
214 High Street
Montrose DD10 8PH Scotland

Argyll and Bute District Archives
Kilmory
Lochgilphead PA31 8RT Scotland

Association of Scottish Genealogists and Record Agents
51/3 Mortonhall Road
Edinburgh EH9 2HN Scotland
  Has available a list of member professional researchers who ascribe to a code of conduct.

Borders Regional Library Service
Archive & Local History Centre
Regional Library HQ
St. Mary's Mill
Selkirk TD7 5EW Scotland

The British Library
Newspaper Library
Colindale Avenue
London NW9 5HE England

Business Records Centre
13 Thurso Street
Glasgow G11 6PE Scotland

Clackmannan District Libraries
Alloa Library
26/28 Drysdale Street
Alloa FK10 1JL Scotland

Companies House (Scotland)
100-102 George Street
Edinburgh EH2 3DJ Scotland
  Maintains lists of registered companies.

Cunninghame District Libraries
Local History Department
(now North Ayrshire Local History Library)
39-41 Princes Street
Ardrossan KA22 8BT Scotland

Dunbarton District Libraries
Dunbarton Public Library
Strathleven Place
Dunbarton G82 1BB Scotland

Dumfries and Galloway Archives
Archive Centre
33 Burns Street
Dumfries DG1 2PS Scotland

Dundee Central Library
The Wellgate
Dundee DD1 1DB Scotland

Dundee City Archives
21 City Square
Dundee DD1 3BY Scotland
  Formerly the Dundee District Archive and Record Centre. This repository will continue to hold core records of the Tayside region; address initial inquiries here.

Dunfermline District Libraries
1 Abbot Street
Dunfermline KY12 7NL Scotland

East Lothian Library Service
Local History Centre
Haddington Branch Library
Newton Port
Haddington EH41 3NA Scotland

Edinburgh City Archives
Department of Administration
City Chambers
High Street
Edinburgh EH1 1YJ Scotland

The Family History Library
35 West North Temple Street
Salt Lake City UT 84150 USA

The Family History Department
50 East North Temple Street
Salt Lake City UT 84150 USA

General Register Office (England and Wales)
St. Catherine's House
10 Kinsway
London WC2B 6JP England
This office is scheduled to relocate in 1997.

General Register Office (Scotland)
New Register House
Princes Street
Edinburgh EH1 3YT Scotland
The GRO sells copies of the OPRs and of the 1841-1891 census returns on microfilm, as well as microfiche copies, by county, of the civil registration indexes; direct inquiries to the microfilm unit at this address.

Glasgow and West of Scotland Family History Society
Unit 15
32 Mansfield Street
Glasgow, G11 5QP, Scotland
Publishes some very useful aids for west of Scotland research.

Glasgow City Archives
Mitchell Library
201 North Street
Glasgow G3 7DN Scotland
Formerly Strathclyde Regional Archives. The Ayr suboffice has closed, but plans are being made for a new joint Ayrshire archive service to be in operation. Direct initial inquiries about Ayrshire here or to the Scottish Records Association.

Highland Council Archives
Inverness Public Library
Farraline Park
Inverness IV1 1NH Scotland

India Office Library and Records
96 Euston Road
London NW1 2DB England

International Society of British Genealogy and Family History
PO Box 3115
Salt Lake City UT 84110-3115 USA
Write to this address for a list of vendors of British resource materials in North America; also produces a quarterly journal devoted to English, Scottish, Welsh, and Irish research.

Inverclyde District Libraries: Watt Library
9 Union Street
Greenock PA16 8JH Scotland

Kilmarnock—East Ayrshire Council Archives
Dick Institute
Elmbank Avenue
Kilmarnock KA1 3BU Scotland

Kirkcaldy District Libraries
Reference and Local Studies Department
Central Library
War Memorial Gardens
Kirkcaldy KY1 1YG Scotland

Kyle and Carrick District Library Service (now South Ayrshire Libraries)
Local Collection
Carnegie Library
12 Main Street
Ayr KA8 8ED Scotland

The Mariners' Museum Library
100 Museum Drive
Newport News VA 23606-3759 USA

Maritime History Archive
Memorial University of Newfoundland
St. John's NF A1C 5S7 Canada

Maritime Museum of British Columbia
28 Bastion Square
Victoria BC V8W 1H9 Canada

McLaughlin Library
University of Guelph
Guelph ON N1G 2W1 Canada

Midlothian Council Archives
Library Headquarters
2 Clerk Street
Loanhead, Midlothian, EH20 9DR, Scotland

National Archives of Scotland
See under National Archives of Scotland

National Library of Scotland
George IV Bridge
Edinburgh EH1 1EW Scotland

National Library of Scotland
Map Library
Causewayside Building
33 Salisbury Place
Edinburgh EH9 1SL Scotland

National Maritime Museum
Manuscript Section
Greenwich
London SE10 9NF England

National Register of Archives (Scotland)
HM General Register House
2 Princes Street
Edinburgh EH1 3YY Scotland
    Operates as a clearinghouse of information about collections in private hands in Scotland, providing advice on whereabouts of papers relating to the enquirer's subject.

North East Fife District Library
County Buildings
St. Catherine's Street
Cupar KY15 5AS Scotland

North Highland Archive
Wick Library
Sinclair Terrace
Wick KW1 5AB Scotland

Orkney Library and Archives
Laing Street
Kirkwall KW15 1NW Scotland

Office of Population Censuses and Surveys
Postal Applications
Smedley Hydro
Southport
Merseyside PR8 2HH England

Perth and Kinross Council Archive
A. K. Bell Library
2 - 8 York Place
Perth PH2 8EP Scotland

Public Record Office
Ruskin Avenue
Kew Richmond
Surrey TW9 4DU England

Renfrew District Council
Local History Department
Central Library
High Street
Paisley PA1 2BB Scotland

Royal College of Physicians and Surgeons
234 St. Vincent Street
Glasgow G2 5RJ Scotland

Royal College of Physicians of Edinburgh
9 Queen Street
Edinburgh EH2 1JQ Scotland

Salt Lake Distribution Center
1999 West 1700 South
Salt Lake City UT 84104-4233 USA
    Write to this address to obtain LDS publications, including fiche.

The Scottish Association of Family History Societies
c/o Aberdeen & NE Scotland FHS
164 King Street
Aberdeen AB2 3BD Scotland
    Has a publications list and can provide current address for contact persons of member societies—any society with its own premises, space in another library, etc. is shown here separately—for the remainder (Borders, FHS, Central Scotland FHS, Dumfries and Galloway FHS, Fife FHS, Hamilton and District FHS, Highland FHS, Largs and N. Ayrshire FHS, and Shetland FHS), write to this office for the name and address of the membership secretary.

Scottish Catholic Archives
Columba House
16 Drummond Place
Edinburgh EH3 6PL Scotland

Scottish Genealogy Society
15 Victoria Terrace
Edinburgh EH1 2JL Scotland
    Library and office; publishes the volumes of MIs; quarterly journal.

The Hon. Treasurer
Department of Scottish History
Edinburgh University
17 Buccleuch Place
Edinburgh, EH8 9LN
    Founded in 1886; the leading publisher of manuscript sources relating to the history of Scotland.

Scottish Maritime Museum
Laird Forge
Gottries Road
Irvine KA12 8QE Scotland

Scottish Mining Museum
Lady Victoria Colliery
Newtongrange EH22 4QN Scotland

Scottish Record Office
now the National Archives of Scotland
HM General Register House
Edinburgh EH1 3YY   Scotland
 Write to this address for the various information leaflets mentioned in the text and for their "List of Publications and Other Items for Sale."

Hon. Secretary
Scottish Record Society
Dept. of Scottish History
University of Glasgow
Glasgow G12 8QQ Scotland
 Created in 1897; publishes an annual volume of records.

The Scottish Records Association
HM General Register House
Princes Street
Edinburgh EH1 3YY Scotland
 Concerned with the preservation and use of public and private records; issues the series of Data Sheets mentioned in the text. Maintains an up-to-date list of all Scottish archives.

Shire Publications Limited
Cromwell House
Church Street
Princes Risborough
Bucks HP27 9AA England

The Society of Genealogists
14 Charterhouse Buildings
Goswell Road
London EC1M 7BA England

Shetland Archives
44 King Harald Street
Lerwick ZE1 0EQ Scotland

Stirling Council Archives
Unit 6
Burghmuir Industrial Estate
Stirling FK7 7PY Scotland
 Formerly Central Region Archives. Write to this address for further information on transfer of materials for Falkirk and Clackmannanshire.

Stirling District Libraries
Central Library
Corn Exchange Road
Stirling FK8 2HX Scotland
Summerlea Heritage Trust
West Canal Street
Coatbridge, Lanarkshire
 Noisiest museum in Scotland—working machinery.

Tay Valley Family History Society
FH Research Centre
179 Princes Street
Dundee DD4 6DQ Scotland

Troon and District Family History Society
c/o Merc
Troon Public Library
South Beach
Troon KA10 6EF Scotland

West Lothian Council Archives
7 Rutherford Square
Bracefield, Livingston
West Lothian EH54 9BU Scotland

To obtain checks in pounds sterling, write or phone:
Ruesch International Financial Services
700 Eleventh Street NW, Suite 400
Washington DC 20001 USA
(800) 424-2923
fax: (202) 408-1211

In Canada, sterling money orders are readily obtainable from banks, credit unions, and post offices.

Web Sites
The following locations provide useful information (e.g., how to contact societies and archives) and links to other Web sites. The World Wide Web and/or membership in a family history society are the best ways to stay current. This selection is based upon two criteria, useful information and/or interesting links. Some URLs will change; if a connection does not work, try one of the main linking sites (such as geuki) or try the root part alone (e.g. www.hmc.gov.uk/)

Aberdeen and North East Scotland Family History Society
www.rsc.co.uk/anesfhs

Angus Archives
www.angus.gov.uk/history/

ARCHON (Archives on Line)
Current contact information, hours, etc.
www.hmc.gov.uk/archon.archon.htm

Dundee City Archive Record Centre
www.dundeecity.gov.uk/dcchtml/a-z/a-z-index.html

Gateway to Scotland
Hundreds of Scottish topics and links.
www.geo.ed.ac.uk/home/scotland/scotland.html

Genealogy site, Church of Jesus Christ of Latter-day Saints
www.familysearch.org

Genealogy UK and Ireland
A good place to start looking for information.
www.genuki.org.uk/

Glasgow City Archvies
www.glasgow.gov.uk/

Guide to Genealogical Resources in Public Libraries, UK and Ireland
www.earl.org.uk/familia/

National Library of Scotland
www.nls.uk/

National Register of Archives
Information on the location of collections.
www.hmc.giv.uk/nra/nra.html

Public Record Office
The catalog and the research outlines are all here.
www.pro.gov.uk/

Registrar General for Scotland
www.open.gov.uk/gros/groshome.htm

Samford University Institute of Genealogy and Historical Research
www.samford.edu/schools/ighr/ighr.htm

Scotland—Internet Signpost
www.scotland.org/

Scottish Association of Family History Societies
www.sol.co.uk/s/scotgensoc/safhs.htm

Scottish Genealogy Society
www.sol.col.uk/s/sscotgensoc/

Scottish Cultural Research Association (SCRAN)
www.scran.ac.uk

Scottish Origins
(indexes to civil registration, census and Old Parochial Registers; fees apply)
www.origins.net/GRO/

The Gazetteer of Scotland
An ongoing project; larger places first; more than 50% complete, with good maps.
www.geo.ed.ac.uk/scotgaz/

• Bibliography •

Some of these sources will not be available in North America. Some will be found in reference libraries; some are in the Family History Library (FHL) of The Church of Jesus Christ of Latter-day Saints (LDS), where they may be available in film or fiche format as well. The International Society of British Genealogy and Family History maintains a list of bookshops and mail order businesses in the United States and Canada with extensive British lists. Also, the Scottish Genealogical Society and the Society of Genealogists have extensive book sale lists and accept charge card orders (the addresses are in appendix D).

Section A—Reference Books

This is a list of how-to books, guides to contents of record offices, encyclopedias, dictionaries, gazetteers, atlases, and related materials. They will be useful throughout your research. Those items preceded by an asterisk (*) are referred to again in individual chapter sections. As the second entry is merely a cryptic reference, the asterisk will help you locate the full-length description.

*Bevan, Amanda ed. *Tracing Your Ancestors in the Public Record Office*. Kew: PRO Publications, 5th edition, 1999. Her Majesty's Stationery Office, 1990. An essential guide for anyone interested in records of the British government.

Bigwood, Rosemary. *Tracing Scottish Ancestors*. Edinburgh: HarperCollins, 1998. A pocket-size guide written by an acknowledged expert.

Burness, Lawrence R. *A Scottish Historian's Glossary*. Aberdeen: Aberdeen and North-east Scotland Family History Society, 1997. There are glossaries in other books, but this is more extensive.

*Campbell, Sheila. *Sources in Kirkcaldy Central Library*. Kirkcaldy District Council, 1994. A good example of a local guide, and the extent of library holdings.

Cerny, J., and J. Elliott. *The Library: A Guide to the LDS Family History Library*. Salt Lake City: Ancestry, 1988. The overview of resources in the Scottish section remains useful; out of print but still available on CD-ROM.

Collins, Ewan K. *Beginners' Guide to Scottish Genealogy*. Dundee: Tay Valley Family History Society, 1992. This little book is of great value, mixing mainly nineteenth-century source information for each of the Scottish regions with remarks on basic records; includes suggested exercises for beginners.

*Cory, Kathleen B. *Tracing Your Scottish Ancestry*. Rev. ed. Edinburgh: Polygon, 1997. Baltimore: Genealogical Publishing Co., 1997. This book offers a detailed presentation of the basic sources in Edinburgh, with a heavy emphasis on civil registration and censuses; some useful appendices, including a case study; with so many changes in recent years, a revised edition would be welcome.

*Cox, Michael. *Exploring Scottish History*. Hamilton: Scottish Library Association, Scottish Local History Forum, and Scottish Records Association, 2nd ed., 1999. A directory of resource centers, this is a reference book which every club library should have. The collections described are in libraries, archives, universities, galleries, and museums.

Diack, H. Leslie. *North East Roots: A Guide to Sources*. 3rd ed. Aberdeen: Aberdeen and North East Scotland Family History Society, 1996. Another helpful guide to regional sources.

Escott, Anne. *Mitchell Library Genealogical Sources, a beginner's list*. Glasgow: Mitchell Library, 1994. This will be most useful if you are planning a trip to Glasgow.

Family History Department. *Scotland Research Outline*. Salt Lake City: The Church of Jesus Christ of Latter-day Saints, 1997. Helpful for basic research techniques; includes outlines of various types of records in the Family History Library, but be sure to read more than this work alone.

*Findlay, James. *Directory To Gentlemen's Seats, Villages, Etc. in Scotland*. Edinburgh: Kennedy, 1843. The subtitle to this adds, "giving the counties in which they are situated—the post-towns to which each is attached—and the name of the resident," so it is a wonderful tool for locating obscure place names; it was reissued in 1852 and 1857, then continued as the *County Directory of Scotland* 1862, 1868, 1872, 1875, 1878, 1882, 1886, 1894, 1902, and 1912 (this last issue included farms).

Foster, Janet, and Julia Sheppard. *British Archives: A Guide to Archive Resources in the United Kingdom.* 3rd ed. London: Macmillan, 1995. This is the largest general reference guide to archives in the United Kingdom. It is arranged alphabetically by town, outlining each repository's collections and finding aids.

*Groome, Francis H. *Ordnance Gazetteer of Scotland: A Survey of Scottish Topography, Statistical, Biographical and Historical.* 6 vols. Edinburgh: T.C. Jack, 1883-85. This may be in the permanent collection (on fiche) of many LDS family history centers; always look up the description of a place in it. The supplementary information is useful too, including brief descriptions of all the religious denominations in Scotland.

*Hamilton-Edwards, Gerald. *In Search of Scottish Ancestry.* 2nd ed. Chichester, England: Phillimore, 1983. This remains useful because of the detailed examples for some records, notably the Registry of Deeds and Sasines.

*Humphery-Smith, Cecil. *Atlas and Index of Parish Registers.* 2nd ed. Chichester, England: Phillimore, 1995. The new edition has been expanded to include Scotland, showing parish and commissariot boundaries.

Index to British and Irish Biographies 1840-1940. Cambridge: Chadwyck-Healey, 1990. A finding aid of more than 6,000 fiche, located at the Family History Library, which incorporates many useful lists of people (about 20% circulates to family history centers; see appendix A).

*Keay, John, and Julia Keay, eds. *Collins Encyclopaedia of Scotland.* London: Harper Collins, 1994. A wonderful source of enlightenment, very readable, sometimes humorous; over 4,000 entries.

Little, William, H.W. Fowler, and J. Coulson. *The Shorter Oxford English Dictionary on Historical Principles.* 3rd ed. Oxford: Clarendon Press, 1973. One can never have too many dictionaries, and this one, showing historical change in usage, is fascinating.

*Miller, Susan. *Strathclyde Sources: A Guide for Family Historians.* 2nd ed. Glasgow: Glasgow and West of Scotland Family History Society, 1995. The new edition of this guide to resources is welcome. Glasgow, Argyll and Bute, Ayrshire, Dunbartonshire, Lanarkshire, Renfrewshire, and part of Stirlingshire are all covered, and the brief opening essay on research is excellent.

*Moody, David. *Scottish Family History.* London: B.T. Batsford, 1988. Reprint. Baltimore: Genealogical Publishing Co., 1990. Not really a handbook but an essay on the importance of incorporating social history into genealogical research; as in his other book, Moody makes you think; essential reading.

*Moody, David. *Scottish Local History.* London: B.T. Batsford, 1986. Reprint. Baltimore: Genealogical Publishing Co., 1990. This is one of my favorites; the source suggestions are endless, and the perspective on local history is very helpful when it comes to considering new approaches to research; extensive bibliography.

National Inventory of Documentary Sources in the United Kingdom. Cambridge: Chadwyck-Healey, various dates, mainly 1980s. This contains summaries of holdings of many repositories in the UK. Usually individual pieces are found in the appropriate part of the Locality section of the FHLC (see appendix A).

New Statistical Account of Scotland. Edinburgh: W. Blackwood, 1845. Undertaken by a committee of the Society for the Benefit of the Sons and Daughters of the Clergy forty-five years after Sinclair's first survey, this series of volumes gives a picture of the parishes of Scotland following a period of considerable change.

*Public Record Office. *Kew Lists. Record Group Guide Part II.* Norwich, England: Her Majesty's Stationery Office, 1985. The complete *Kew Lists* is a guide on 3,542 microfiche to the contents of the PRO; this section, on five fiche, is made up of summary listings of the contents of each record group. *The Current Guide 1996* is now available. It includes many new entries for recent acquisitions, as well as for older records; records on microfiche, with an explanatory handbook, can be purchased from the PRO at Kew.

*Scottish Records Association. *Data Sheet No. 6, Summaries of Archival Holdings.* Edinburgh, 1994. For anyone interested in the location of all sorts of unusual records and/or planning a serious research trip, this is a truly wonderful resource guide which lists contents of records offices and libraries throughout the country. Additions and revisions are made to the list on a regular basis; the summaries can be purchased individually or as a set (address is in appendix D).

Scottish Record Office. *A Short Guide to the Records.* Edinburgh: NAS, 1993. Briefly summarizes the main groups of records.

Sinclair, Cecil. *Tracing Scottish Local History.* Edinburgh: HMSO, 1994. This is the local historians' version of Sinclair's book on Scottish ancestors; you will find the same wording occasionally in both, but this altered perspective is often helpful.

*Sinclair, Cecil. *Tracing Your Scottish Ancestors in the Scottish Record Office.* 2nd ed., Edinburgh: Stationery Office, 1997. Take time to read this book; although the exact instructions of what to do in the NAS are a little tedious at times (you will be glad of them if you make a trip), the source descriptions are invaluable.

*Sinclair, Sir John, Bt. *Analysis of the Statistical Account of Scotland. With an analysis of the history of that country and discussions on some important branches of political economy, in particular a discussion on the various classes into which the inhabitants of Scotland may be divided, e.g., productive, useful and useless.* London: John Murray, 1826. Those far-from-politically-correct terms are actually used in the book; Sinclair's own reflections on the reports from the parishes make very interesting reading.

*Sinclair, Sir John, Bt. *The Statistical Account of Scotland. 1791-99.* Reprint, edited by Donald J. Withrington and I. R. Grant. Wakefield: E.P. Publishing, 1979. Volumes referred to in the text are II, III, IV, and VI. *Always* look up a parish in this; this was followed in the 1830s and 1840s by the *New (or Second) Statistical Account of Scotland* (see above) and in this century by the *Third Statistical Account of Scotland*; interesting comparisons arise when more than one account of a parish is examined.

*Steel, Don. *National Index of Parish Registers. Scotland. Vol. XII.* London: Society of Genealogists, 1970. Do not be deceived by the title or the date. This remains an interesting and useful book that does much more than discuss parish registers.

*Timperley, Loretta R., ed. A *Directory of Land Ownership in Scotland circa 1770*, n.s., vol. 51. Edinburgh: Scottish Record Society, 1976. The usefulness of this volume is fully explained in the text; if you are interested in other volumes published by this society, check university libraries, and use the author/title part of the FHLC, treating Scottish Record Society as an author—there are about 100 entries.

Torrance, D. Richard. *Scottish Personal Names and Place Names—a bibliography*. Edinburgh: Scottish Genealogy Society, 1992. This should provide lots of ideas of other titles to watch for or to try to obtain by interlibrary loan.

Tracing Your Ancestors: Mitchell Library and Archives Sources. Leaflet available from the Mitchell Library and the Glasgow City Archives. Glasgow: 1994.

Whitaker's Almanac. London: J. Whitaker and Sons, published annually since 1868. A good reference resource for finding names and addresses of societies, schools, and associations.

Section B—References by Chapter

Books in this section are arranged according to the chapters in the text. Where a book has already received a full description in section A or an earlier chapter, the reader is asked to refer back to the first entry, which is preceded by an asterisk (*).

Chapters 1 and 2

Anderson, William. *The Scottish Nation: or the surnames, families, literature, honours and biographical history of the people of Scotland*. 3 vols. 1866-77. This covers a wide mix of material and includes lots of interesting people.

Banks, Noel. *Six Inner Hebrides*. Newton Abbot, England: David and Charles, 1977. One of a series of books on islands, this one is about Eigg, Rum, Cann, Coll, Muck, and Tiree; Scottish islands covered in other volumes include Shetland, Orkney, Mull, Bute, Harris, and Lewis.

Black, George F. *The Surnames of Scotland*. New York: New York Public Library, 1973. First printing: 1946. Do more than simply look up a name in this; read the introduction, not only to understand the nature of the study, but for the interesting detail about name origins and use of nicknames in villages where there were only a few surnames between several hundred inhabitants.

Bulloch, John, ed. *Scottish Notes and Queries*. 2nd ser. Aberdeen: Rosemount Press, 1906-07. If you can find any of these, take time to dip into them. The articles may relate to what you are researching, and the queries and answers are often genealogical; long before the age of computers, people seemed to delight in sharing obscure information.

Castleden, Rodney. *Harrap's Book of British Dates*. Bromley, Kent: Harrap, 1991. A chronological dictionary from prehistoric times, arranged by year and category, each with a distinct symbol.

Cory, K. See under section A.

Cox, M. See under section A.

Donaldson, Gordon, and Robert S. Morpeth. A *Dictionary of Scottish History*. Edinburgh: John Donald, 1977.

*Donnachie, Ian, and George Hewitt. A *Companion to Scottish History: From the Reformation to the Present*. New York: Facts on File, 1989. In dictionary form, this book describes or defines significant people, events, and topics, some not found in other works of reference. There is a list of royal burghs with dates of foundation, and county populations through many censuses.

Dorward, David. *Scottish Surnames*. Glasgow: Harper Collins, 1995. Describes over 1000 names with meanings and origins.

Dunbar, John T. *The Costume of Scotland*. London: B.T. Batsford, 1981. Describes the dress of your ancestors and explains the origins of the kilt; illustrated.

Ferguson, Joan P.S., comp. *Scottish Family Histories held in Scottish Libraries*. Edinburgh: Scottish Central Library, 1968. This is useful when surveying what has been done by others.

Findlay, J. See under section A.

Fraser, George Macdonald. *The Steel Bonnets*. London: Barrie and Jenkins, 1971. Still in print in soft cover, this is essential reading for anyone with ancestors in the border counties.

Gillespie, J.D. "Gregorian Calendar." *The Scottish Genealogist* 35, no. 1 (March 1988): 24. Edinburgh: Scottish Genealogical Society.

Graham-Campbell, David. *Portrait of Argyll and the Southern Hebrides*. London: Robert Hale, 1978. A good example of the many books of history, geography, and local history that may be found in used bookshops.

Grant, Sir Francis J., ed. *Index to Genealogies, Birthbriefs and Funeral Escutcheons Recorded in the Lyon Office*. Edinburgh: J. Skinner, 1908.

Groome, F. H. See under section A.

*Hinchliff, Helen. "William Edward, Part 1, Identifying an Eighteenth-Century Miller." *Aberdeen and North East Scotland Family History Society Journal* 53 (November 1994): 6-11. An example of reconstruction of family and community with some excellent examples of how resources outside your time frame can help.

Humphery-Smith, C. See under section A.

Johnson, Keith A., and Malcom R. Sainty. *Genealogical Research Directory*. Melbourne: published by the editors, 1998 (issued annually). Contains listing of subscribers' research interests, and names and addresses; useful for checking who might be researching similar lines.

Keay, J., and J. Keay. See under section A.

Lang, Theo, ed. *The Border Counties*. London: Hodder and Stoughton, 1957. Volume IV of *The Queen's Scotland*, a descriptive series in eight volumes, organized alphabetically by place name.

Lewis, Samuel. *A Topographical Dictionary of Scotland*. London: S. Lewis, 1847. Reprint. Baltimore: Genealogical Publishing Co., 1989. Another informative source of nineteenth-century descriptive detail.

Macdonald, Angus. *The Highlands and Islands of Scotland*. London: Weidenfeld and Nicolson, 1991. Well-illustrated and interesting mix of history, geography, and natural history.

MacLean, Fitzroy. *A Concise History of Scotland*. London: Thames and Hudson, 1973. A readable overview, well-illustrated.

Millman, R.N. *The Making of the Scottish Landscape*. London: B.T. Batsford, 1975. Contains an extensive bibliography of works on the changing face of the Scottish landscape, many on individual parishes; also maps of patterns of growth of Scottish cities.

Ordnance Survey Maps. The government mapping agency began in the late eighteenth century under the authority of the Army Board of Ordnance (which ultimately supplied the army with all its needs, including maps), hence the name. For Scotland, there are reprints of the 1890 series of one-inch-to-one-mile plans, various nineteenth-century town plans, and the modern series. Some of these can be consulted in the FHL; many public libraries hold O/S modern series, and they can be purchased through some family history societies or from some of the vendors on the list maintained by the International Society of British Genealogy and Family History (see appendix D).

Powell, Bob. *Scottish Agricultural Implements*. Princes Risborough, England: Shire, 1988. An interesting survey of machinery from the rudimentary to the complex.

Robinson, Mairi. *The Concise Scots Dictionary*. Oxford: University of Aberdeen Press, 1985.

Rosie, Alison. *Scottish Handwriting 1500-1700: A Self-Help Pack*. Edinburgh: NAS and the Scottish Records Association. This can be purchased from the NAS.

Rhys, Ernest. *A Dictionary of Dates*. Everyman's Library Edition. London: Dent, 1940. A small treasure of information; alphabetical by topic.

Ryan, Michael. *Around the Ancient City*. Privately printed, 1933. Another example of what to watch for in used bookshops.

Sinclair, Sir John, Bt. *Analysis*. See under section A.

Sinclair, Sir John, Bt. *Statistical Accounts*. See under section A.

Smout, Thomas C. *Century of the Scottish People 1830-1950*. London: Fontana, 1987.

Smout, Thomas C. *A History of the Scottish People 1580-1830*. London: Fontana, 1985. Lots of social history and good bibliographies.

Stevenson, David, and Wendy B. Stevenson. *Scottish Texts and Calendars: An Analytic Guide to Serial Publications*. Edinburgh and London: Scottish History Society and Royal Historical Society, 1987. Concentrates on providing notations on the contents of the volumes of private historical societies, but includes some works issued by official bodies. It serves as an update to and partial replacement for *A catalogue of the publications of Scottish Historical and Kindred Clubs and Societies, and of the volumes relevant to*

Scottish history issued by His Majesty's Stationery Office 1780-1908 (C.S. Terry, 1909) and the follow-up of the same title for the years 1908-1927 (C. Matheson, 1928).

Strawhorn, John. *Ayrshire: The Story of a County.* Ayr: Ayrshire Archaeological and Natural History Society, 1975. A very good example of a county history, it covers all aspects of social, economic, and political history, with insights into change, growth, and controversial issues.

Stuart, Margaret. *Scottish Family History: A Guide to Works of Reference on the History and Genealogy of Scottish Families.* Oliver and Boyd, 1930. Reprint. Baltimore: Genealogical Publishing Co., 1994.

Thoyts, E.E. *How to Read Old Documents.* Chichester, England: Phillimore, 1980. Although written at the turn of the century, this remains a useful work on the handwriting, contractions, etc. found in British records.

Timperley, L.R. See under section A.

Torrance, D. R. See under section A.

Way, George, and P. Squire. *Collins Scottish Clan and Family Encyclopaedia.* Glasgow: Harper Collins, 1994. Another recently published, well-illustrated, and informative reference work.

West, T.W. *Discovering Scottish Architecture.* Princes Risborough, England: Shire, 1985. An introductory guide to the built heritage of Scotland.

Wilkes, Margaret. *The Scot and His Maps.* Scottish Library Association, 1991. Written by the Keeper of the Map Library of the National Library, this is an enjoyable read which will be useful background for any genealogist.

Williamson, Elizabeth, Anne Riches, and Malcolm Higgs. *The Buildings of Scotland.* London: Penguin, in association with the National Trust for Scotland, 1980. Selects the buildings which represent the architectural heritage; one of a series.

Wilson, Rev. John. *The Gazetteer of Scotland.* 1882. Reprint. Lovettsville, Va.: Willow Bend Books, 1996. Less extensive than Groome, but mentions every town and village and gives some description; 472 pages, soft cover.

Chapter 3

Bloxham, V. Ben, and D.K. Metcalfe. *Key to the Parochial Registers of Scotland.* See under chapter 4.

Collins, E.K. See under section A.

Cory, K. See under section A.

"Local Registrar's Link with New Register House, Edinburgh." *Tay Valley Family Historian* 43 (January 1996): 5. Dundee: Tay Valley Family History Society. Summarizes the holdings, open hours, and fees at the Dundee registry.

McKirdy, Wayne, and Sue McKirdy. *The McKirdy Index.* As of early 1996, four sections of this index to civil registrations of deaths have been issued: Bute 1855-75, Lanark 1855, Lanark 1856, and Sutherland 1855-75. The intent is to cover all counties, 1855-75.

Miller, Susan. See under section A.

Parishes, Registers and Registrars of Scotland. Scottish Association of Family History Societies, 1993. Contains county maps showing parish boundaries, the addresses for local registrars, and the parish numbers for each parish.

Chapter 4

Abstract of the Answers and Returns Made Pursuant to an Act, Passed in the 41st Year of His Majesty King George III: an act for taking an account of the population of Great Britain and the increase and diminution thereof. London, 1801.

Adam, Sir Charles E., ed. *A View of the Political State of Scotland in the last century: A confidential report on the . . . 2662 County Voters about 1788.* Edinburgh, 1887. Volumes with similar titles appeared again in 1790 (A. Mackenzie, ed.) and 1812 (James Bridges, ed.).

Bigwood, A. Rosemary. "Pre-1855 Communion Rolls and Other Listings in Kirk Sessions Records." *The Scottish Genealogist* 35, no. 2 (June 1988): 73-85. Edinburgh: Scottish Genealogical Society.

*Bloxham, V. Ben, and D.K. Metcalfe. *Key to the Parochial Registers of Scotland.* 2nd ed. Provo, UT: Stevenson Genealogical Supply, 1979. Based on the *Detailed List of the Old Parochial Registers of Scotland* (see below). Each listing includes the parish number and the dates of surviving records; note that the film numbers are from an earlier filming, still available. The second filming is better, but some entries in the earlier filming are not found in the later one (which has numbers of 900,000 or higher).

"British 1881 Census Project Nears Completion." *FGS Forum* 7, no. 1 (Spring 1995): 16-18. Salt Lake City: Federation of Family History Societies.

Campbell, Sheila. See under section A.

Celtic Monthly. A Magazine for Highlanders. First published in October of 1892 by the Glasgow Celtic Press. Some volumes are on film in the FHL.

Chapman, Colin. *An Introduction to Using Newspapers and Periodicals.* Birmingham, England: Federation of Family History Societies, 1993.

Chapman, Colin. *Pre-1841 Censuses and Population Listings in the British Isles.* 4th ed. Dursley, England: Lochin Publishing, 1994. Could be more extensive on the subject of Scottish listings, but useful nonetheless.

Cory, K. See under section A.

Cox, Michael. See under section A.

Ferguson, J.S.P. *Scottish Newspapers Held in Scottish Libraries.* Edinburgh: National Library of Scotland, 1984.

Family History Department. *1881 British Census Indexes Research Outline.* Salt Lake City: Church of Jesus Christ of Latter-day Saints, 1996.

Family History Department. *Periodical Source Index on Microfiche Research Outline.* Salt Lake City: Church of Jesus Christ of Latter-day Saints, 1990.

Gibson, J.S.W. *Poll Books, c. 1695-1872: A Directory to Holdings in Great Britain.* 3rd ed. Birmingham, England: Federation of Family History Societies, 1994. Scottish entries in Gibson guides are invariably brief, and not always complete; however, they are useful; his guides are readily available in North America.

Gibson, J.S.W., and Elizabeth Hampson. *Marriage and Census Indexes for Family Historians.* 7th ed. Birmingham: Federation of Family History Societies, 1998.

Gibson, Jeremy, and Mervyn Medlycott. *Local Census Listings 1522-1930.* 3rd ed. Birmingham: Federation of Family History Societies, 1997. A particularly useful guide.

Gibson, J.S.W., and C. Rogers. *Electoral Registers Since 1832 and Burgess Rolls.* Birmingham, England: Federation of Family History Societies, 1989.

Gilhooley, J., comp. *A Directory of Edinburgh in 1752.* Edinburgh: Edinburgh University Press, 1988.

Hamilton-Edwards, G. See under section A.

*Hinchliff, Helen. "William Edward, Part 1, Identifying an Eighteenth-Century Miller." See under section A.

Johnson, Gordon. *Census Records for Scottish Families at Home and Abroad.* 3rd ed. Aberdeen: Aberdeen and North East Scotland Family History Society, 1997. Packed with useful information about nominal censuses 1841-91 and earlier listings. Also includes a discussion of the value of statistical evidence.

Lumas, Susan B. *Making Use of the Census.* London: PRO Publications, 1993. Interesting background to the census, plus useful tips.

McLaughlin, Eve. *Family History From Newspapers.* Aylesbury, England: McLaughlin, 1993. Informative, with a lighthearted touch.

*Miller, Susan. *A Guide to Glasgow Addresses 1837-1945.* Glasgow: Glasgow and West of Scotland Family History Society, 1993. Will help unravel the changes in street names as the city grew.

Murphy, Michael. *Newspapers and Local History.* Chichester, England: Phillimore, for the British Association for Local History, 1991. More background on the uses of old newspapers, this time from a local history perspective.

Murray, Peter R. *Scottish Census Indexes 1841-1871.* Aberdeen: Scottish Association of Family History Societies, 1995. Lists indexes available for these census returns and their locations.

North, John S. *The Waterloo Directory of Scottish Newspapers and Periodicals 1800-1900.* Vol. I. Waterloo: North Waterloo Academic Press, 1989. All you need to know about old Scottish newspapers.

Parishes, Registers and Registrars of Scotland. See under chapter 3.

Scottish Records Association. See under section A.

Scots Magazine. First published in 1739, now issued monthly from D. and C. Thompson, Dundee. It contains articles of local history, new books about Scotland, and sometimes items or letters genealogical.

Stirling Journal and Advertiser: a local index. Volume 1, 1820-1869. Stirling: University of Stirling, n.d.

The 1881 Census Indexes of Scotland. Salt Lake City: The Church of Jesus Christ of Latter-day Saints, 1994. Guide to the use of these indexes on fiche.

Willings Press Guide. London: James Willing, published annually.

Chapters 5 and 6

Baird, Douglas J. "Scottish Marriages." *The Scottish Genealogist* 26, no. 4 (December 1979). Edinburgh: Scottish Genealogical Society.

Bayne, Gillian. "St. Andrew's Database." *Newsletter* (Spring 1992). Glasgow: Glasgow and West of Scotland Family History Society.

Bigwood, A. Rosemary. "Dissenting Congregations in Pre-Disruption Ayrshire and Their Importance to the Genealogist." *The Scottish Genealogist* 34, no. 2 (June 1987): 238-239. Edinburgh: Scottish Genealogical Society. Proves that a statistical angle on research can be informative.

Bigwood, A. Rosemary. "Pre-1855 Communion Rolls and Other Listings in Kirk Sessions Records." See under chapter 4.

Burleigh, J.H.S. *A Church History of Scotland.* Edinburgh, 1960. The book where the flow chart of Scottish church history first appeared.

The Catholic Directory for Scotland. Edinburgh and Dundee, 1831-35. This continues to be published; the Mitchell library holds volumes from 1836, complete from 1861; some are in the FHL.

Detailed List of the Old Parochial Registers of Scotland. Edinburgh: Murray and Gibb, 1872. List of parishes with their numbers, including the different 1851 numbers.

Gandy, Michael, ed. *Catholic Parishes in England, Wales and Scotland, an Atlas.* London: Gandy, 1993.

Gordon, Anne. *Candie for the Foundling.* Edinburgh: Pentland Press, 1992. A history of kirk sessions and how they influenced the lives of our ancestors.

Groome, F.H. See under section A.

Humphery-Smith, Cecil. See under section A.

Lindsay, Jean. *The Scottish Poor Law: Its Operation in the North East 1745-1845.* Ilfracombe, England: Stockwell, 1975. An absolutely fascinating study, with many interesting examples; well-written.

Mitchell, Alison, ed. *Pre-1855 Gravestone Inscriptions in Angus.* 4 vols. Edinburgh: Scottish Genealogical Society, 1979-1984. Part of a series published by the society.

Mitchell, Angus. *Burial Grounds in Scotland—An Index of Unpublished Memorial Inscriptions.* Edinburgh: Scottish Genealogical Society, 1991. Useful reference list for those not in the above series.

New Statistical Account of Scotland, Volume VI, Lanark. See under section A; this volume includes Rutherglen.

Old Parochial Registers (OPR) Index for Scotland. Salt Lake City: The Church of Jesus Christ of Latter-day Saints, 1994. One of their helpful research guides.

Records of the Church of Scotland and Other Presbyterian Churches. Edinburgh: National Archives of Scotland, 1994. Any society with a number of members researching in Scotland should put this set of microfiche in the club library.

Richardson, Ruth. *Death, Dissection and the Destitute.* London: Penguin, 1989. A gruesome topic, but this study of the trade in bodies for the anatomists of the late eighteenth and early nineteenth centuries makes interesting reading and tells much about values and superstitions of the day.

Scottish Records Association. See under section A.

Sinclair, Sir John, Bt. *Analysis.* See under section A.

Sinclair, Sir John, Bt. *The Statistical Account of Scotland.* (Full details in section A.) Note in particular Vol. III: The Eastern Borders, which includes reference to Lamberton Toll, and Vol. IV: Dumfriesshire, which includes a comment on clandestine marriages at Graitney (informing everyone that the fellow who performs them is without manners or morals and usually drunk).

Steel, Don. See under section A.

The Scots Magazine. See under chapter 4.

Willing, June A., and J. Scott Fairie. *Burial Grounds in Glasgow.* Glasgow: Glasgow and West of Scotland Family History Society, 1986. A guide to burial grounds with date of earliest burial and surviving registers.

Willsher, Betty. *Understanding Scottish Graveyards.* Reprint. Edinburgh: Council for Scottish Archaeology, 1995. Historical background, types of monuments and inscriptions, how to record graveyards.

Chapter 7

Calendar of Confirmations and Inventories Granted and Given Up in the Several Commissariots of Scotland in the Year 1876. Edinburgh: Neil and Co. for HMSO, 1877. This is the first volume of the series.

Donnachie, Ian, and George Hewitt. See under chapters 1 and 2.

Gibson, J.S.W. *Guide to Probate Jurisdictions.* 4th ed. Birmingham, England: Federation of Family History Societies, 1994.

Gouldesborough, P., ed. *Formulary of Old Scots Documents.* Edinburgh: The Stair Society, 1985. Texts of old Scots documents with translations.

Hamilton-Edwards, G. See under section A.

MacLeod, John, ed. *Services of Heirs, Roxburghshire, 1636-1847.* Edinburgh: Scottish Record Society, 1934.

Sinclair, C. *Tracing Your Scottish Ancestors.* See under section A.

Steel, Don. See under section A.

"The Campbells of Strachur." *The Scottish Historical Review* 4 (1907): 234. Glasgow: James Maclehose.

Chapter 8

Adam, Frank. *The Clans, Septs and Regiments of the Scottish Highlands.* 6th ed. Revised by Sir Thomas Innes of Learney. Edinburgh: Johnston and Bacon, 1960.

Addison, W.I. *Roll of Graduates, University of Glasgow, 1727-1897.* Glasgow, 1898. Includes short biographical notes.

Addison, W.I. *The Matriculation Albums of the University of Glasgow 1728-1858.* Glasgow, 1913.

Anderson, James R., ed. *The Burgesses and Guild Brethren of Glasgow 1573-1750.* Edinburgh: Scottish Record Society, 1925.

Anderson, James R., ed. *The Burgesses and Guild Brethren of Glasgow 1751-1846.* Edinburgh: Scottish Record Society, 1935.

Army List. London, annually since 1754.

Barriskill, D. *A Guide to Lloyd's Marine Collection at Guildhall Library and Related Marine Sources.* London: Guildhall Library, n.d.

Baxter, I.A. *India Office Library and Records: A Brief Guide to Biographical Sources.* 2nd ed. London: British Library, 1990.

Bevan, A., and A. Duncan. See under section A.

Campbell, Sheila. See under section A.

Clabburn, Pamela. *Shawls.* Princes Risborough, England: Shire, 1990. The weaving and printing of shawls was a major industry in Paisley in the nineteenth century; this book features the designs, patterns, and fabrics.

Cook, Frank, and Andrea Cook. *The Casualty Roll for the Crimea: the casualty rolls for the siege of Sebastopol and other major actions during the Crimean War 1854-1856.* London: Hayward, 1976. Indexed.

Cox, Michael. See under section A.

Crowder, Norman K. *British Army Pensioners Abroad 1772-1899.* Baltimore: Genealogical Publishing Co., 1995. Especially useful for those who retired from the British Army after serving in Canada or the Caribbean.

Customs and Excise Records as Sources for Biography and Family History. Richmond, England: Public Record Office, 1986. Clear summary of the various record groups for these categories.

Dalton, Charles. *English Army Lists and Commission Registers 1661-1714*. Reprint. London: Francis Edwards, 1960. Many Scottish officers were serving in these regiments.

Dalton, Charles. *The Waterloo Roll Call: with biographical notes and anecdotes*. London: William Clowes, 1890.

Dobson, David. *Scottish Seafarers of the Seventeenth Century*. Aberdeen: Scottish Association of Family History Societies, 1992. One of a series of small booklets listing seafarers and emigrants; David Dobson has also issued a series of booklets on the mariners of several regions of Scotland. A list and prices are available from the Scottish Genealogy Society or the Aberdeen and North East Scotland Family History Society.

Durie, Alastair J. *The Scottish Linen Industry in the Eighteenth Century*. Edinburgh: John Donald, 1979.

Dwelly, E. *A Muster Roll of the British non-commissioned officers and men present at the Battle of Waterloo*. Edinburgh, 1934.

Ewing, William. *Annals of the Free Church of Scotland 1843-1900*. 2 vols. Edinburgh, 1914.

Fasti Academiae Mariscallanae Aberdonensis 1593-1860. 3 vols. Spalding Club, 1889-98. Selections from the records of the Marischal College and University.

Farrington, Anthony. *Guide to the Records of the India Office Military Department*. London: India Office Library, 1982.

Fitzhugh, T.V.H. "East India Company Ancestry." *Genealogists' Magazine* 21, no. 5 (March 1984): 150-154.

Fowler, Simon, and William Spencer. *Army Records for Family Historians*. 2nd ed. Kew: PRO Publications, 1998. Outlines the records of the army in a number of categories such as officers, enlisted men, special branches, corps, and militia.

Frederick, J.B.M. *Lineage Book of British Land Forces*. Wakefield, England: YKS, 1984. A genealogy of British army units, including history and mergers.

Gibson, J. S. W., and M. Medlycott. *Militia Lists and Musters 1757-1876*. 3rd ed. Birmingham, England: Federation of Family History Societies, 1994.

Gilchrist, Alex. "The Use of School Admission Registers for Genealogical Research." *The Scottish Genealogist* 34, no. 4 (December 1987): 402-403.

Grant, Sir Francis J., ed. *The Faculty of Advocates 1532-1943*. Edinburgh: Scottish Record Society, 1943.

Grierson, Lt. Gen. Sir James Moncrieff. *Records of the Scottish Volunteer Force 1859-1908*. London: Frederick Muller, 1972 (facsimile of the 1909 original).

Hamilton-Edwards, Gerald. *In Search of Army Ancestry*. Chichester, England: Phillimore, 1977. Worth reading if you are doing extensive army research.

Harrison, John, ed. *Stirling Burgesses 1600-1699*. Stirling: Central Scotland Family History Society, 1991.

Hawkings, David T. *Railway Ancestors*. Sutton: Stroud, Glos., 1992. This is the most complete account of surviving records of British railways.

History of the Society of Writers to H.M. Signet . . . with List of Members . . . 1594-1890. Edinburgh, 1890.

Hoskins, W.G. *History From the Farm*. London: Faber and Faber, 1968. Probably not widely available, this book describes eighteen farms in England and Scotland in detail (three are in Scotland); very informative on history, farming methods, etc.

Irvine, Sherry. *Researching Seafaring Ancestors*. Victoria: Maritime Museum of British Columbia, 1994. An introduction to naval and merchant marine research focused around the extensive resources of the museum library.

Kitzmiller, John M. *In Search of the Forlorn Hope: a comprehensive guide to locating British regiments and their records 1640 to World War I*. Salt Lake City: Manuscript Publishing Foundation, 1987. A book of considerable detail which can help you narrow a search in army records.

List of the Colonels, Lieutenant Colonels, Majors, Captains, Lieutenants and Ensigns of His Majesty's Forces. London, 1740. Reprint. Society for Army Historical Research, 1931. This provides name, rank, regiment, date of appointment to present rank, and date of first commission.

*Livingstone of Bachuil, Alastair, W.H. Aikman, and Betty Stuart Hart, eds. *Muster Roll of Prince Charles Edward Stuart's Army 1745-1746*. Aberdeen University Press, 1984.

Lloyd's Captains' Registers 1869-1948. Compiled from the records of Lloyd's Underwriters; at the Guildhall Library, London, with copies also at the National Archives of Canada.

Lloyd's Register of Shipping. London: Lloyd's Registry. Published annually since 1760. Includes ships of British registry to 1889 and ships of the world since 1890.

Mackelvie, William. *Annals and Statistics of the United Presbyterian Church*. Edinburgh: Oliphant and Elliot, 1873.

Matthias, Peter, and A.W.H. Pearshall, eds. *Shipping: A Survey of Historical Records*. Newton Abbot, England: David and Charles, 1971.

*McDougall, Ian. *A Catalogue of Some Labour Records in Scotland and Some Scots Records Outside Scotland*. Scottish Labour History Society, 1978.

Medical Directory. 94 vols. London: J. and A. Churchill, 1846-1940. These are available at the Family History Library on fiche within the British and Irish Biographies series issued by Chadwyck-Healey, Cambridge, 1990. Each volume has a separate index for Scotland (and other parts of Britain).

Muniments of the University. Maitland Club, 1854. Graduates, Glasgow down to 1727.

Navy List. London: HMSO, quarterly since 1814.

Officers and Graduates of University and King's College 1495-1860. Aberdeen: Spalding Club, 1893.

Payne, Peter L. *Studies in Scottish Business History*. London: Frank Cass and Co., 1967.

Probert, Eric. D. *Company and Business Records for Family Historians.* Birmingham, England: Federation of Family History Societies, 1994. Informative guide to companies and their records.

Public Record Office. *Kew Lists. Guide Part II.* See under section A.

Raymond, Stuart. *Occupational Sources for Genealogists.* Birmingham, England: Federation of Family History Societies, 1992. A useful bibliography.

Reeks, Lindsay S. *Scottish Coalmining Ancestors.* 1995. Available from the author, US$30, 2013 Westover Drive, Pleasant Hill, CA 94523. Includes information on the history, laws, and social customs relating to coalmining.

Richards, T. *Was Your Grandfather a Railwayman?* 2nd ed. Birmingham, England: Federation of Family History Societies, 1989. How to find railway records.

Ritchie, L.A. *Modern British Shipbuilding: A Guide to Historical Records.* Greenwich, England: National Maritime Museum, Maritime Monographs and Reports No. 48, 1980.

Rodger, N.A.M. *Naval Records for Genealogists.* 2nd ed. Kew: PRO Publications, 1998. Provides extensive detail on the records of the Royal Navy.

School, University and College Registers and Histories in the Library of the Society of Genealogists. 2nd ed. London: Society of Genealogists, 1996. It is worthwhile knowing what is in this collection.

Scott, Hew. *Fasti Ecclesiae Scoticanae: the succession of ministers in the parish churches of Scotland from 1560.* New ed., rev. by W.S. Crockett and Sir Francis J. Grant. 9 vols. 1915-1961.

Scottish Records Association. See under section A.

Sinclair, C. *Tracing Scottish Local History.* See under section A. Contains more extensive information about burgh records than his other book.

Sinclair, C. *Tracing Your Scottish Ancestors.* See under section A.

Sinclair, Sir John, Bt. *Statistical Accounts.* See under section A.

Small, Robert. *History of the Congregations of the United Presbyterian Church 1733-1900.* 2 vols. Edinburgh: D.M. Small, 1904.

Spencer, William. *Records of the Militia and Volunteer Forces 1757-1945.* 2nd ed. Kew: PRO Publications, 1997. Discusses records of militia, volunteers, yeomanry, and the Territorial Army.

Stewart, Charles H. *The Service of British Regiments in Canada and North America.* Ottawa, 1962. Not easy to find, but a useful outline of when and where various regiments served.

Swinson, Arthur, ed. *A Register of the Regiments and Corps of the British Army: the ancestry of every regiment with battle honours.* London: Archive Press, 1972.

Torrance, D. R. *Scottish Trades, Professions, Vital Records and Directories.* Aberdeen: Scottish Association of Family History Societies, 1998.

Warden, Alex. J. *The Linen Trade Ancient and Modern.* London, 1864.

Wareham, Heather, and Roberta Thomas. *A Guide to the Holdings of the Maritime History Archive.* St. John's: Memorial University of Newfoundland, 1991.

Watson, C.B. Boog, ed. *Roll of Edinburgh Burgesses and Guild Brethren 1701-1760.* Edinburgh: Scottish Record Society, 1930.

Watson, C.B. Boog, ed. *Roll of Edinburgh Burgesses and Guild Brethren 1761-1841.* Edinburgh: Scottish Record Society, 1933.

Watts, C.T., and M.J. Watts. *My Ancestor was a Merchant Seaman: How can I find out more about him?* London: Society of Genealogists, 1991.

Watts, C.T., and M.J. Watts. *My Ancestor was in the British Army: How can I find out more about him?* London: Society of Genealogists, 1992 (reprint with addendum 1995).

Whitaker's Almanac. See under section A.

Wise, Terence. *A Guide to Military Museums and Other Places of Military Interest.* 7th ed. Knighton, Wales: Imperial Press, 1992.

Wood, Margaret. *Register of Edinburgh Apprentices 1756-1800.* Edinburgh: Scottish Record Society, 1963.

Chapter 9

Findlay, James. See under section A.

Gibson, J.S.W. *The Hearth Tax, other later Stuart Tax Lists and the Association Oath Rolls.* 2nd ed. Birmingham, England: Federation of Family History Societies, 1996.

Groome, F. H. See under section A.

Miller, Susan. *A Guide to Glasgow Addresses 1837-1945.* See entry under chapter 4.

Moody, David. *Scottish Family History.* See under section A.

Moody, David. *Scottish Local History.* See under section A.

Pollable Persons within the Shire of Aberdeen 1696. 2 vols. Aberdeen: Spalding Club, 1844. Everyone in the county over the age of sixteen, except for the poor. Now reissued in a series of booklets by the Aberdeen and North East Scotland Family History Society.

Return of Owners of Lands and Heritages (Scotland) 1872-1873. Edinburgh: HMSO, 1874.

Scottish Genealogy Society. *Scottish Poll Tax.* Edinburgh, 1991. (Leaflet # 11.)

Semple, David. *The Poll Tax Rolls of the Parishes in Renfrewshire for the Year 1695.* Edinburgh, 1864. The further extension of the title is, "containing the names of the persons in the county with their calling and residence, and the names of their wives, children, and servants."

Sinclair, C. *Tracing Your Scottish Ancestors.* See under section A.

Steel, Don. See under section A.

Timperley, L.R. See under section A.

*Taylor, Alistair, and Henrietta Taylor, eds. *The Jacobite Cess Roll for the County of Aberdeen in 1715.* Aberdeen: Spalding Club, 1932. This list of those paying tax includes details of ownership back to 1696, occupations, and some genealogical details.

Whiteford, J.L., ed. *Stirling Burgesses 1790-1799.* Stirling: Central Scotland Family History Society, 1992.

Whiteford, J.L., ed. *Stirling Burgesses 1800-1902.* Stirling: Central Scotland Family History Society, 1992.

Wood, Margaret, ed. *Edinburgh Poll Tax Returns 1694.* Edinburgh: Scottish Record Society, 1951.

Chapter 10

Bailyn, Bernard. *Voyagers to the West.* New York: Alfred A. Knopf, 1987. The analysis of people departing for the new world 1773-1776—their social station, occupations, points of origin, and ports of departure—makes for fascinating reading; the ports mentioned are Dumfries, Stranraer, Greenock, Kirkwall, Leith, Gigha, Dunstaffnage Bay, Fort William, Lochbroom, Stornoway, Lerwick, Lochindale, Water of Fleet, Kirkcaldy, Kirkcudbright, Wigtown, Campbelltown, Glasgow, and Ayr.

Brock, W. R. *Scotus Americanus—a survey of the sources for links between Scotland and America in the 18th century.* Edinburgh University Press, 1982. Obviously a tedious job putting this together, but wonderful that it was done—an amazing array of sources.

Bumstead, J.M. *The People's Clearance—Highland Emigration to British North America 1770-1815.* Edinburgh University Press, 1982. Still a recognized authoritative account, with over sixty pages of ships' passenger lists.

Cases Decided in the Court of Session, Teind Court, and Court of Exchequer. Vol. XII. Edinburgh: T. and T. Clark, 1850. This series of volumes began appearing in 1821. The recorders and editors changed at intervals, and after 1907 they were issued by the Faculty of Advocates.

Cox, Michael. See under section A.

Cross, William P. "List of Accidents and Disasters." *Journal of the Glasgow and West of Scotland Family History Society* (Spring 1995): 17-18.

Cross, William P. *Hurried Into Eternity.* London: published by the author, 1995. The accident and disaster lists described in the previous item have been compiled into a fifty-six-page booklet. Check with a family history society to obtain a copy.

Dickson, J.W., W.H. Dunbar, and J. Rymer, eds. *The Scottish Jurist.* Vol. 2. Edinburgh: M.A. Anderson, 1829. (Editors and publishers changed from time to time over the years.) The subtitle explains the contents—containing reports of cases decided in the House of Lords, Court of Session, Teinds, Exchequer, and the Jury and Justiciary Courts.

Dobson, David. *Directory of Scots Banished to the American Plantations 1650-1775.* Baltimore: Genealogical Publishing Co., 1983.

Dobson, David. *Directory of Scottish Settlers in North America 1625-1825*. 7 vols. Baltimore: Genealogical Publishing Co., 1984-1993.

Dobson, David. *Jacobites of the '15*. Aberdeen: Scottish Association of Family History Societies, 1993. A partial list taken from official records.

Dobson, David. *Scottish American Heirs*. Baltimore: Genealogical Publishing Co., 1990.

Dobson, David. *Scottish Emigration to Colonial America*. Athens: University of Georgia Press, 1994. Lots to learn from this one, and it focuses on the earlier periods.

Donnachie, Ian, and George Hewitt. See under chapters 1 and 2. If your ancestors left Scotland because of the Highland Clearances, you will want to read the brief summary of that unhappy period, and the explanation of the role of tacksmen.

European Immigration into Scotland. Glasgow and West of Scotland Family History Society, 1993. Four papers presented at the fourth conference of the Scottish Association of Family History Societies, including one on Irish immigration and one on Glasgow poor law records.

Filby, P. William, with Mary K. Meyer. *Passenger and Immigration Lists Index: a guide to published arrival records of about 500,000 passengers who came to the United States and Canada in the 17th, 18th and 19th centuries*. Detroit: Gale Research, 1981. There have been a number of supplements.

Filby, P. William. *Passenger and Immigration Lists Bibliography 1538-1900: being a guide to published lists of arrivals in the United States and Canada*. Detroit: Gale Research, 1981.

Ford, Percy, and Grace Ford. *Select List of British Parliamentary Papers, 1833-1899*. Blackwell, 1953.

Gentleman's Magazine. Published from 1731 to 1908, it contained birth, marriage, and death notices to 1861, and some obituaries. Some parts have been indexed.

Graham, Ian C.C. *Colonists from Scotland: Emigration to North America 1707-1783*. Kennikat Press, 1956.

Halsbury, The Rt. Hon. Earl of, and Sir Thomas W. Chitty, eds. *The English and Empire Digest*. London, 1919-1932. Indexes and abstracts to cases heard in British courts.

Hamilton-Edwards. See under section A.

Harper, Marjory. *Emigration from North-East Scotland*. 2 vols. Aberdeen: Aberdeen University Press, 1988.

Haythornthwaite, J. *Scottish Economic History in the 19th Century: an analytical bibliography of material relating to Scotland in Parliamentary Papers 1800-1900*. Scholarly Press, 1993. The key to identifying the most useful Parliamentary Papers.

Irvine, Alexander Forbes. *Reports of Cases Before the High Court and Circuit Courts of Justiciary in Scotland*. Vol. 1. T. and T. Clark, 1855.

Lawson, James. *The Emigrant Scots*. Aberdeen: Aberdeen and North East Scotland Family History Society, 1990. Describes records of Scottish immigrants in the National Archives of Canada.

List and Index Society. *Scottish Record Office Court of Session Productions 1760-1840*. Vol. 23, special series. London: HMSO, 1987. This volume summarizes evidence in actions before the Court of Sessions, giving details of those involved and of the cases, along with reference numbers. Publications of the List and Index Society are in collections of some reference and university libraries.

Livingstone, Alastair of Bachuie, et al. See under chapter 8.

MacDougall, Ian. See under chapter 8.

MacLean, J.P. *An History of the Settlements of Scotch Highlanders in America Prior to the Peace of 1783*. 1900. Reprint. Baltimore: Genealogical Publishing Co., 1968.

MacQueen, Malcolm A. *Skye Pioneers and the Island*. Stovell Co., 1929. Details, including many genealogies of families who went to Prince Edward Island.

Moody, David. *Scottish Local History*. See under section A.

Nicholls, Sir George. *A History of the Scotch Poor Law*. London: Murray, 1856. Reprint. New York: Augustus M. Kelley, 1967. Includes much interesting information from two early nineteenth-century surveys of the poor.

Patten, Jennie M. *The Argyle Patent and Accompanying Documents*. Published as part of the History of the Somonauk Presbyterian Church, 1928. Reprint. Clearfield Company, 1991. An account of this settlement near Fort Edward, New York, including a map with settlers' names.

Seton, Sir Bruce Gordon, Bt., and Jean Gordon Arnot, eds. *The Prisoners of the '45*. Vols. 13-15, 3rd series. Edinburgh: Scottish Historical Society, 1928-29.

Sinclair, C. *Tracing Your Scottish Ancestors*. See under section A.

Sinclair, Sir John, Bt. *Statistical Accounts*. See under section A.

Taylor, Alistair, and Henrietta Taylor, eds. *The Jacobite Cess Roll for the County of Aberdeen in 1715*. See under chapter 9.

The Digest: Annotated British Commonwealth and European Cases. London: Butterworths, 1994. There is also a user's guide issued by the same publisher, no author given.

Virginia Gazette. Published weekly at Williamsburg, 1736-1780. This was filmed by the Institute of Early American History and Culture in 1950, and is available on microfilm.

Watson, Fiona. *In Sickness and in Health*. Aberdeen and North East Scotland Family History Society, 1988.

Walker, David M. *The Scottish Legal System—An Introduction to the Study of Scots Law*. 5th ed. Green, 1981. Try to get a look at this if you are going to dig into court cases, as it is filled with details of Scots law, the published court cases, and the repositories of legal documents.

Whyte, Donald. *A Dictionary of Scottish Emigrants to Canada Before Confederation.* Toronto: Ontario Genealogical Society, 1986 (Part I) and 1995 (Part II). Part II adds 11,000 entries to this index and a thirty-seven-page appendix of updated information on Part I.

Whyte, Donald. *A Dictionary of Scottish Emigrants to the USA.* 2 vols. Baltimore: Magna Carta Books, 1972.

Whyte, Donald. *The Scots Overseas: A Select Bibliography.* 2nd ed. Aberdeen: Scottish Association of Family History Societies, 1995. Does not include any family histories; greatest emphasis on Canada.

Young, George, H.L. Tennant, P. Fraser, and W.H. Murray. *Cases Decided in the Court of Session, Teind Court, and Court of Exchequer, Nov. 1849 to July 1850.* Edinburgh: T. and T. Clark, 1850.

Chapter 11

Hinchliff, Helen. "William Edward, Part 1, Identifying an Eighteenth-Century Miller." See under chapters 1 and 2.

Mills, Elizabeth Shown. *Evidence! Citation and Analysis for the Family Historian.* Baltimore: Genealogical Publishing Co., 1997.

• Index •

C

G

M

Please remember that this is a library book,
and that it belongs only temporarily to each
person who uses it. Be considerate. Do
not write in this, or any, library book.